On My Swedish Island

On My Swedish Island

Discovering the Secrets
of Scandinavian Well-being

JULIE CATTERSON LINDAHL

Jeremy P. Tarcher/Penguin
a member of Penguin Group (USA) Inc.   New York

JEREMY P. TARCHER/PENGUIN
Published by the Penguin Group
Penguin Group (USA) Inc., 375 Hudson Street, New York, New York 10014, USA • Penguin Group
(Canada), 10 Alcorn Avenue, Toronto, Ontario M4V 3B2, Canada (a division of Pearson Penguin Canada Inc.) •
Penguin Books Ltd, 80 Strand, London WC2R 0RL, England • Penguin Ireland, 25 St Stephen's Green,
Dublin 2, Ireland (a division of Penguin Books Ltd) • Penguin Group (Australia), 250 Camberwell Road,
Camberwell, Victoria 3124, Australia (a division of Pearson Australia Group Pty Ltd) • Penguin Books India
Pvt Ltd, 11 Community Centre, Panchsheel Park, New Delhi–110 017, India • Penguin Group (NZ), Cnr
Airborne and Rosedale Roads, Albany, Auckland 1310, New Zealand (a division of Pearson New Zealand Ltd)
• Penguin Books (South Africa) (Pty) Ltd, 24 Sturdee Avenue, Rosebank, Johannesburg 2196, South Africa

Penguin Books Ltd, Registered Offices:
80 Strand, London, WC2R 0RL, England

Most Tarcher/Penguin books are available at special quantity discounts for bulk purchase for sales promotions,
premiums, fund-raising, and educational needs. Special books or book excerpts also can be created to fit specific
needs. For details, write Penguin Group (USA) Inc. Special Markets, 375 Hudson Street, New York, NY 10014.

Photograph on page 103 Sussi Petersson.
All other photographs Julie Catterson Lindahl and Claes Lindahl.

An application has been submitted to register this book with the Library of Congress.

ISBN 1-58542-414-5

Printed in the United States of America
1   3   5   7   9   10   8   6   4   2

The recipes contained in this book are to be followed exactly as written. The publisher is not responsible for your
specific health or allergy needs that may require medical supervision. The publisher is not responsible for any adverse
reactions to the recipes contained in this book.

Outdoor recreational activities are by their very nature potentially hazardous. All participants in such activities must
assume the responsibility for their own actions and safety. If you have any health problems or medical conditions,
consult with your physician before undertaking any outdoor activities. The information contained in this guidebook
cannot replace sound judgment and good decision making, which can help reduce risk exposure, nor does the scope
of this book allow for disclosure of all the potential hazards and risks involved in such activities. Learn as much as
possible about the outdoor recreational activities in which you participate, prepare for the unexpected, and be cautious.
The reward will be a safer and more enjoyable experience.

While the author has made every effort to provide accurate telephone numbers and Internet addresses at the time
of publication, neither the publisher nor the author assumes any responsibility for errors, or for changes that occur
after publication.

For Claes, Hannes, and Jesine

Before this, I had lived in my own little world; but now I wanted to tell the people of my discovery. I was part of the universe—of the millions of stars and planets, part of the sky and the moon and the sun, part of them, the people of the earth. And I wanted to tell them that although there was violence, ugliness, and cruelty in our world, there also could be harmony, love, and peace.

I ran from the town back to the fields. I drank the water. I kissed the earth, began to run. I picked flowers and imitated the flight of birds, longing to offer a huge flower to the world.

MARCEL MARCEAU,
The Story of Bip[1]

Contents

Acknowledgments

W HEN I LOOK OUT of the window of my study, I often ask myself how I came to live here, to be privileged to experience this
place, and to be given the chance to write about it. While part of my message is that we can determine these things ourselves with the will, I often
have to pinch myself. How did I really get here?

All experienced travelers know that the journey cannot be successful,
indeed, cannot even take place, without the mutual interest, enthusiasm,
patience, kindness, and love of other people. My journey has been in
progress for more than four years, and during that time there are very
many people who have shown me these qualities. To anyone whom I forget below, I say a very big thank-you in advance.

To all of those individuals in the Nordic countries who agreed to meet
and/or share information and ideas—Marina Axelson-Callum, Hans
Axelson, Sally Beardsley, Carina Billetun, Cay Bond, Martine Colliander,
Alan Dilani, Kristian Eriksson, Pär Granlund, Magnea Gudmundsdóttir,

Sigmar Hauksson, Erkki Helamaa, Matti Kivinnen, Gert Klötzke, Lars Krantz, Gunilla Ladberg, Henrik Linusson, Kerstin Llungqvist, Børge Ousland, Camilla Plum, Arja Saijonmaa, Lisen Sundgren, Rolf Åkerlund—thank you for taking the time. I thank also the many Scandinavian-based organizations, commercial and nonprofit, who have agreed to provide me with information. Among these are the Alvar Aalto Foundation, Archtours, Artek Byaliv, the Danish Design Center, the Department of Landscape Planning, Alnarp, at the Swedish University of Agricultural Sciences (SLU), Design Forum Finland, Ergonomi design gruppen, the Finnish Sauna Association, the Natural Step, Ornamo, the Spa Museum at Loka Brunn, Suderhälsan Spa, Svensk Farm, the Swedish Sauna Association, University of Art and Design Helsinki, the Swedish Museum of Architecture, Växbo Lin and Wij Gardens.

To the Scandinavian consulates and tourist boards, I owe a thank-you for providing contacts and ideas. To the Department of Natural Resources (DNR) in Wisconsin, thanks for clarifying issues regarding the consumption of wild meat in America. To Lena Biörck Kaplan, I thank you for your friendship, vision, and invaluable support. To my longtime friend Gabriele Ludwig—many thanks for sharing with me the stories of your outdoor adventures in America.

To my good friends in Scandinavia, I say thank you for your patience and generosity: to Inni-Carine and Gunnar Holm, who shared their beautiful homes and energetic spirits; to Tage and Eva Klingberg, owners of one of Scandinavia's most beautiful apple orchards; to the Wellesley College network in the Nordic region for providing excellent contact points throughout Scandinavia; to Søren Holm Johansen and my friends at Rambøll for their continued kindness long after my departure from the company; to Bo Karlström and Kristina Kuylenstierna for helping me to decipher the meaning of old Norse words; to Åsa Moum and Rachel Stenback for being the best-ever team; to Silke Millan and Rasmus Winther for their persistence in believing in the idea; to Vendela, Willy, and Victor, our shining light on the island across, for helping us to get through the dark months with cheer; to Mats, without whom we would have had frozen pipes for days on many occasions.

Within my Wellesley circle of friends, I would like to take a few lines to remember Margaret Kentta, who was part Icelandic and who devoted a good portion of her life to reconnecting with her Icelandic roots. Margaret and I never met, but had an engaging yearlong communication about Iceland and the importance of promoting preventive and alternative approaches to good health. This was very moving to me, since she was in the closing stages of her battle with cancer and based in Germany where she was being treated. Margaret, your selfless hope and vision beyond your own life are remembered by me.

To Betsy Thorpe, my agent and good friend, I say thank you for your will of steel and your vision. To the team at Tarcher—Joel Fotinos, Terri Hennessy, and the others—thank you for believing in the idea and working with it painstakingly.

To my cherished family in Connecticut, Evelyn and Jonathan Ochsner, and Donald and Ginger Heller, I say thank you for always seeing the positive and never failing to show your delightful enthusiasm and affection.

To my parents, Frank and Uta Catterson, I thank you for providing your example of confidence, courage, and persistence. I send you my love.

To my mother-in-law, Marianne Lindahl: your courage in finding beauty in life despite enduring the most terrible losses that a mother can imagine will always be remembered by me. Your spirit lives on.

To Claes, who always saw the island as a place for rest, play, and thought, I add one more feature: love. I hug you from deep in my heart for doing the best thing that one human being can do for another: putting the one you love before yourself. To Hannes and Jesine, my adorable children, I thank you for waiting patiently for Mother to be done in her study. Although Lucy, my golden retriever, will never understand this, I thank her for dragging me out into the forest each day and proving beyond any reasonable doubt that there is no bad weather, only bad clothes.

At the time of writing, many people all over the world are suffering the pain of loss brought about when nature showed us her hard and unrelenting side in the form of a tsunami. Here I dedicate a thought to my friends in Asia, and to people all around the world, including in Sweden and the other Scandinavian countries, whose lives have been touched by this disaster. I sincerely hope that the beauty of nature, which is equal to its destructive powers, will bring you strength and hope.

Introduction

I AM AN AMERICAN living on a small island in Sweden. Here, I have had the privilege to become immersed in a magnificent source of inspiration that I would like to share with you: the energy-giving power of nature. My island, with its ancient forest and clear waters, is symbolic of Nordic culture, where there are traditions rich in their connection to the outdoors. In this place, I have learned to appreciate my world by bringing my life in tune with it: by changing my patterns to experience the seasons and their beauty. Something happened to me here that I think could benefit other people, even if they do not live on a small Swedish island.

Mine is the story of a person who had seen the world, was fit in body and on a path to "success," but still did not feel well. On my Swedish island I discovered what the indigenous peoples of many cultures have long known: that being able to identify yourself with the stones, the trees, the sand, the water, or the sky in a certain place is essential to feeling whole. It is my goal to show you how you can nurture this sense of well-being and begin a process of personal development that will increase your satisfaction with yourself and your life. Equally, I aim to share with you my discovery that there are many elements of lifestyle in Nordic culture that people elsewhere can pursue in order to bring them in touch with the essence of what it is to live well.

My Story

I had been raised as a veritable globe-trotter, alongside my sister, by parents who were in the international banking community. My parents had both come from difficult, humble beginnings: my father, the first son of Scottish immigrant parents, began his working life early as a soda jerk in a drugstore in post-Depression Brooklyn; my mother, who was raised in war-torn Germany with her brother and three sisters, had left her homeland with her parents in search of a better life elsewhere. Like many parents of their generation, mine vowed to make life better for their children. My parents were as determined and courageous as they were persistent, and it was thus from their very different humble beginnings that they together created a life for their two daughters that was privileged by anyone's standards. My highly energetic mother threw all of her might into creating the nicest of homes for us wherever we were: all ten of them on all three continents. She had a hard job and she did it beautifully. My father worked for a major international bank for more than forty years. He once told me that I might need to be ready for a change in his fortunes, but he would never let it affect me. This change never came, and he continued not only to provide for his own family but also to make efforts to help everyone in his extended family in whatever way possible.

My parent's story is without doubt the realization of success in modern times: hardworking people prepared to stretch themselves in order to achieve a vision of something better. With their example as a precedent I had quite a job trying to figure out what vision it was that I should work toward with equal vigor. This is perhaps the classic dilemma of a rising standard of living: What vision do the inheritors of better standards have to strive for? How can we make life better for our children? What is well-being in our definition?

Partly as a result of this family heritage, I thought that it was my destiny to travel and to live the fast life in the great cosmopolitan hubs of the world. I decided that I would succeed as my parents did, by traveling widely and working harder than everyone else. And so I ended up choosing a profession that had me flying off to all ends of the earth, working as a management consultant on projects to solve global ills such as poverty and environmental degradation. Within a few short years, I had a promising position at a major world-class management consulting firm; a nice, large, centrally located flat in London; and a jet-setting lifestyle, business class and champagne included. In a modern definition of success and the previous generation's definition of well-being, I was on the way.

Yet I was not happy. There were causes specific to my situation, to be sure. But the problem that I had run into reflected a dilemma that many people living in the wealthier parts of the world in our times are running into: the frenetic pace of modern life has many of us moving around faster than the speed of light without our own vision of how we want life to be. As a result, the psychiatrist's waiting list is today a long list to be on. In contrast, the list of simple things that we could do in everyday life to genuinely improve our lot as well as that of future generations remains rather short.

IT IS THE HARDEST THING to realize that there is no blueprint for how to live your life. I wandered around the earth for years, expecting to find happiness through my parents' pattern of life, but found no purposes, although there were many of them all around me. The hard work of finding my success, my well-being, and the home inside myself still lay before me. I would find these things in a journey that took me to a place where I would never have expected to find my vision.

In the spring of 1996, I found myself feeling at home on a small island west of Stockholm. Although the island was close to the city, it had no car access and we had only one year-round neighbor. I had fallen deeply in love with a Swede, whom I had met during my travels. Claes was the inheritor of this summer home, which had been in his family for three generations. We married in July 1997, and in September 1998 our twins, Hannes and

Jesine, were born. For the first three years that I lived in Sweden, we spent only the summer months on the island. Our self-run consulting business allowed us the flexibility of being based wherever we liked. During those years, I think I barely noticed my surroundings, my mind usually totally absorbed in faraway professional matters. Still, as soon as I set foot on the island, I felt very comfortable.

One fine day, I decided to take my destiny into my own hands, and to defy the cosmopolitan-globe-trotter fate that I thought had been dealt out to me. My husband and I were sitting in the beautiful bathroom of our beautiful, large Stockholm home, watching our then one-and-a-half-year-old twins piling bubbles onto each other's heads in our Jacuzzi-style bathtub. Both of us looked ashen with the exhaustion of work. Even if we worked around the clock, there was no way that we could get through all that we had taken on. Since the birth of our twins, I had moved to a more home-based existence within our consulting business, which I was no longer finding rewarding, mainly because I could not visit the people in the faraway lands I was working with.

"Why don't we move out to our summer home for a year?" I suggested. "No, no . . ." Claes muttered, still trying mentally to reason the amount of work we had taken on. Suddenly he switched on to what I had just said. "Are you serious?" he exclaimed, realizing that I just might be. Claes had now and then dreamed about experimenting with living a Hemingway-esque lifestyle, out in his family summer home for one year. In his wildest imagination, he never dreamed of doing this with his new, young family. He had rebuilt his old summer residence himself, and perhaps did not quite trust that his construction was tough enough for our family to dwell in during the harsh Swedish winter. During these months, it seemed a dark and isolated place to be, with no lights in sight and one quiet neighbor who was off-island working during the week. In absolutely his nuttiest moment, Claes would never have been able to imagine that I, cosmopolitan globe-trotter without appreciation for the flowers and the trees, would make such a suggestion in a serious frame of mind.

I don't know what possessed me, but on that evening I made my arguments like the best-trained lawyer making a final summation to the jury. In reality, I was working hard on convincing myself. My instincts were telling me that my life, Claes's, and the future happiness of our family depended on it. Yet it was a tough case to argue. Shouldn't we both responsibly be pursuing our careers and contributing to our pension plans through our consulting business? Strangely, I felt that it was precisely for our future that my arguments were valid. The two of us were both burned-out for our own reasons. Our children would never respect us; neither could we respect ourselves for being burned-out, irritable parents. Finally, we agreed that we would do it. Of course, we would retain our home in Stockholm just in case things became too tough. Naturally, we would return to it after one year.

When Hannes and Jesine turned two, they entered the Swedish day-care system. Their day care was located in a beautiful characteristically Swedish dark red countryside house surrounded by fields of grazing horses. A gigantic body of water called Mälaren lies between our island and the school, which is on another island connected to the mainland. For the first few months, when the water was still open, we took our children to day care by boat. When the water froze up, they went by sled. For four months of the year, to get them home, we needed flashlights—the sort that you wear over your hat so that you can keep your hands free. During that first early winter, the watermark rose to unprecedented levels. Our docks were submerged. So was the small and precariously constructed footbridge, which was the only other way to get off the island. Fortunately, I had filled up our food cellar so that we could manage for a few weeks. We had plenty of water, and a very kind and patient electrician-cum-handyman, Mats, for a neighbor.

There was a lot of what most people living in modern-day society would call hardship living on the island. Even in the nature-loving society that we were living in, many of our friends thought we were more than slightly odd for volunteering to face such inconveniences. Mats had warned us that during the previous winter the electricity, which was conducted through fifty-year-old lines, had gone off for four days. The lines were being replaced, but not until the next spring. I felt a little fazed, but remained committed to our plan.

Claes began to contemplate all sorts of survival and evacuation schemes. We found ourselves having to line the forest path just across the footbridge with pine branches to get our car over the ice that had formed on our winter-exit route. We had to bring in water from the mainland every two days, since our well water had too high an iron content for our young children to drink. We had to haul water into the house in buckets from the lake on the numerous occasions when our water pump decided that enough was enough. We once fired up all of our old nineteenth-century cast-iron stoves, since we knew a planned power cut was taking place midwinter for one day. But we never had a major power cut over several days. And, Claes has, to date, never had the chance to execute any of his wonderfully elaborate schemes.

Strangely to some, I began to see opportunities for expanding my experience everywhere. I saw them particularly in the things that one could call inconveniences. The chance to see the stars in a crisp, cold winter sky illuminate the snow on our solidly frozen lake completely transformed for me what might otherwise have been a cold walk over the ice in the dark, from the car to the house, pulling sleds full of children and groceries. Gradually, a process started to take place whereby my identity started to become bound up with this island home. The air, the water, the plants, the animals, the water reeds, the rocks, and the sand became more than my friends. They became a part of me. This source, with which my life had become bound up, gave rise to many new perspectives and ideas. I felt that I had somehow become for the first time connected with the world around me, although, paradoxically, I was living farther away from other people than ever before. I slowly began to understand why I had argued with all of my might in favor of this life on that night in our Stockholm apartment.

Connection to nature opened up a means for me to begin to understand the part of the world that I had chosen to settle in. This is both because nature holds such a special place in its culture, and also because nature was raising the blinds from my eyes and filling my senses with the sights, smells, sounds, and textures of everything around me. Suddenly, I was speaking Swedish to my mother-in-law after five years of having wandered around like an immigrant woman speaking English to Swedes. I took in all of the culture that I could, and began to see a definite thread in it. I traveled with my family to the surrounding Scandinavian countries, and learned to work my way through Norwegian and Danish text. The thread relating different aspects of life in these countries became thicker and longer: there were an extraordinary number of lifestyle traditions linked to nature. In modern times, we would call this an approach to well-being. I had discovered that I was living in a special place, which had encouraged something special to happen to me.

My mother sometimes reminds me that my interest in well-being started in the womb. While she devotedly exercised in preparation for my birth, I got tumbled and gently massaged. It seems that my mother and I beat the trend, since we were doing all of this before most other mothers and fetuses were. Some years after arriving, I began to display an unusual interest in fitness. As a teenager and young adult I always had a keen eye out for how different cultures saw the idea of well-being, and I made a special effort to try out new things in the very many cultures that I came into contact with. Beyond this, I eventually began to read a great deal of the latest research on different elements of human well-being.

The way that I have come to see the whole business of being a well person has changed vastly over time. Despite all of the different perspectives on well-being that I observed, I saw it for myself as spending twenty minutes on a treadmill, lifting a few weights, and consuming low-fat foods. I do not wish to downgrade the healthfulness of such things, since I recognize that they can be part of a fitness regimen that makes all of the difference to a person's quality of life. Still, I have come to appreciate that the factors that make a human being blossom are factors to do with one's emotional state of health: Are they sensitive to the world and the people around them? Do they notice the beauty? Do they feel free to pursue expressions of their own creativity, or do they only see their own limitations? Do they have a strong and positive sense of self, or do they constantly feel victimized and done unto? The rest tends to follow.

The Scandinavian Inspiration

What I have to tell you about is an approach to well-being, which combines body, mind, emotions, and spirit. Nature is spiritual, but it is also very tangible and something we can appreciate with all of our senses. Thus, the approach that I write about and the heritage that it is based on are both physical and tangible at the same time, and about inner processes. Scandinavians are well known for not being body shy—take the old tradition of unclothed sauna bathing, for example. This is an attitude that goes hand in hand with openness to experiencing the feelings that nature can evoke. Scandinavians are also famous for getting physical outdoors, pursuing all kinds of sports and hobbies. Cross-country skiing, tour skating, and hiking are all popular sports. At the same time, I am always taken when I hear even the most competitive of Scandinavian athletes saying that what originally inspired him or her was not the desire to win or to be first, but a longing for greater closeness to nature, which is physical, spiritual, emotional, and mental all at the same time.

Another American once seated next to me at a dinner wondered how I could write about an idea of well-being inspired by a place with a reputation for darkness and depression. Scandinavia has had this shadow over it since President Dwight D. Eisenhower regarded Scandinavia as dangerously close to red, and claimed unjustly that Sweden had the highest suicide rates in the world (in fact, Sweden just had the best statistics at the time; today it has one of the lower rates in the world). More recently, the international press has highlighted the number of people who are enjoying Sweden's generous sick-leave benefits due to stress-related illness. There are many interesting theories as to why this is so, from high numbers of middle-aged women in the workplace to a natural consequence of economic growth and ever-rising expectations of well-being. My own sense as I have traveled and listened is that people are not more stressed in Sweden than they are anywhere else in the industrialized world. It is just that people discuss it more in Sweden, and in Scandinavia as a whole, due to the fact that generous public health benefits make stress a public issue. On the whole, my feeling is that bringing stress out into the open, not brushing it under the rug, is a good thing. Interestingly, Sweden and its Nordic neighbors have repeatedly placed at the very top of recent surveys ranking the nations of the world for quality of life.[1]

My aim is not to show that Scandinavians are the healthiest people in the world, although the health statistics of the Scandinavian countries are right up there with the best in the world. Sweden is, for instance, at the top of worldwide healthy life expectancy statistics (age to which you can expect to lead a healthy life), preceded only by San Marino and Japan in a list of 192 countries.[2] This is mainly an impressionistic book intended to highlight settings and qualities, which I believe to be unique based on a great deal of travel and observation. Ultimately, I would like to show you that in the Scandinavian countries there are many facets of living that add up to a consistent approach to well-being. When I say to my Nordic friends that I am writing about their common idea of the Good Life, as I see it, everyone seems to understand. The concept that I write about is my own construct, yet deeply inspired by Scandinavian values and ways. While many things that I write about are uniquely Scandinavian, the essential ideas can be pursued for a life of well-being anywhere in the world.

One of the benefits of being a global nomad is that I have had the privilege of being able to experience many cultures. That is the reason why I know that what I have experienced here on the island and in Scandinavia is both unique and possible for others living elsewhere to experience. Sometimes I have wondered why no Scandinavian has written much about their common idea of the Good Life in the English language. The only credible explanation that I can come up with is an extraordinary sense of cultural modesty.

I should clarify here that when I refer to "Scandinavia," I am using it in a broad cultural sense of the term. To me, the idea of Scandinavia includes Denmark, Finland, Iceland, Norway, and Sweden, although I know that technically Finland and Iceland are not part of Scandinavia. I have traveled to all of these countries and am quite aware of their many differences. To me, there is a definite thread that draws them together when it comes to that unique connection to nature and their special joint culture of well-being. They also acknowledge that thread themselves.

The fact that Sweden is my home has many implications for this book. It is the place where I have experienced the most in Scandinavia, which I know well, and where I can speak and comprehend the language best. Fortunately, Scandinavians are extremely capable when it comes to the English language, and, to my great advantage, four out of five of the languages are very similar to one another. That said, I have visited all of the countries and made a serious effort to interview a wide range of individuals in each country.

How You Can Use This Book

Connection to nature was the beginning of a process of personal reevaluation for me, which I believe could be of tremendous value to others. I felt trapped in a box of long-standing problems, which was really one of old perceptions about me and about others. In this situation, I felt sapped of my energies, isolated, and as though the complexity of modern life has just gotten the better of me. I think there are quite a number of people out there who feel this way, if not all of the time, at least often enough that it bothers them. This is the main reason that I felt moved to write this book. Here on this unique island in this special culture, I found a way to reevaluate my life, to distinguish the important from the unimportant, and to live life rather than to watch it pass me by. I began to feel an obligation to share this experience with others who might also be helped by hearing about it.

I sincerely hope and believe that people elsewhere can try to pursue the ideas that I write about in their own natural environments, and that it will lead them toward a renewed attitude in their relationships, their communities, and their world. It is not only the thinking that you can try to apply to your own life, wherever you live, but also the concrete actions and many enjoyable activities that I suggest you might try out.

One of the benefits of this book is that it does not need to be read from cover to cover, although, of course, I hope that readers will be engaged by my every word. Chapter 1 spells out the philosophy of well-being, the "science of life," that I have derived from my experience on the island and through Nordic culture. The next five chapters consider five dimensions of living, including outdoor life, plants and herbs, relaxation ideas, design, and food. These chapters include ways of thinking about different aspects of our lives and concrete ways in which we can pursue these ways of thinking. They also include fun things to do, such as making your own aromatic birch water or cooking a great seafood soup for a stormy night.

Chapter 7 explores how this Nordic-inspired system of living is relevant beyond ourselves and to the greater well-being of our societies. I reflect on my own experience of working in developing countries with the really serious problems of our world, and eventually coming to the conclusion that I had to start in my own backyard. This last chapter shows that, in this way, we can augment something that is essential to our well-being: our sense of meaning.

Throughout this book, you will notice that attention is given to children, whom I regard as most in need of an approach to well-being that is exciting and enjoyable while at the same time it encourages peace and calm. Children are faced by many of the same challenges as adults are today, only they have a much greater part of their lives ahead of them in which they must cope. Within each of the five dimensions of good living that I portray, I provide ideas about how children can be included.

The Resources section of this book provides you with a range of carefully selected information sources, services, and products that can help you to begin enjoying the ideas that I write about. The section includes both Nordic-based and American resources, and provides Web sites wherever possible so that you can explore from wherever you are. There is something for every interest, taste, and pocketbook.

Somewhere deep in the soul of the Nordic countries is a passionate silence. It is nature's silence: simple, pure, and soulfully beautiful. It is the silence of trees, of the sea and lakes, of mountains, and of birds and other wild animals. It is a silence filled with life energy and a seamless, non-affronting power. It is the source that people tap into for inspiration, for love, and for consolation. It is a source with unparalleled potential to heal and renew. I have found all of this where I now live with my husband and our young twins. We are in our fifth year of that one-year "experiment." It is a life far removed from the one I used to live. Sitting here looking through the study window of my island home, I can see a radiant sun coming up from behind the forest across the lake to illuminate the fantastic winter scene. I feel inner peace and inspiration, and would like to extend these emotions to as many people as I can. This book is an effort to share my experience with you, and to let others know more about the extraordinary realm of possibility that exists in nature.

ONE

A Nordic-Inspired
Science of Life

D URING AN EARLY VISIT to Sweden, Claes took me on a little adventure that he was not at all sure I would enjoy. In retrospect, he took
quite a risk, since we did not know each other very well at that time, and I
seemed to be something of an urban jet-setter. It was mid-April and about
seven or eight in the evening when I found myself sitting with this tall,
slim, soft-spoken Nordic man in a white station wagon, which was gingerly
making its way through rough forest terrain. I had just flown in from London that day. There were no lights or houses, it was dark and cold, and the
lake, which ran parallel to the forest, was frozen. He parked the car in a forest glen and, without explanation, loaded my suitcase into a wheelbarrow.
"It is about ten minutes from here," he said without any shadow of a doubt.
With high heels, a navy blue pencil-skirt suit, and a mock alligator-skin
handbag strung elegantly over my wrist, I picked my way over the gnarled
tree roots covering the path, shivering a little. Claes hung his thick, lead
heavy coat, which had weathered many a cold winter, over my shoulders.

My knees buckled a little under the weight. Getting around in this place was a shade different from getting around in the London Underground.

Once we reached the house, a fire was lit in a beautiful hundred-year-old tall, round, white porcelain-tiled stove. I visited the bathroom and noticed the sweet, baked smell of a sauna that had been turned on. I sat down at the dining room table and took a moment to appreciate the house around me. It had a warm, wooden, sparsely furnished, do-it-yourself feeling about it. Some dried flowers hung from the ceiling—probably gathered on a walk in the woods sometime during the summer. I waited while a small meal of poached salmon and boiled potatoes was prepared.

My eyes were drawn to the windows by a deep sound coming from outside. It was the sound of huge, cracking ice sheets. I looked harder, and the striking scene all around us began to reveal itself to me. The forest was a gigantic silhouette surrounding the frozen water. The uncompromising beams of the constellations and the moon lit up the smooth, gleaming sheets of melting ice, which stretched as far as the eye could see. There were no man-made lights in sight. The deep barking sound of a stag seeking a mate echoed in waves across the ice sheets. It was a totally absorbing scene. All of the irrelevant details inhabiting my mind were instantly deleted. Two strong hands had reached in through the window and carried my soul out into the night. My sadness and happiness, and mistakes and achievements, were for a moment no longer only mine; they were a part of something much bigger. I was at once motionless and could accomplish anything.

Some years after I came to live in Scandinavia, I began to realize that the environment that I had come into and the feelings that they evoked on that first night on the island were the result of something more than just a momentary scene of beauty in Claes's family's summer cottage. Yes, they were partly about falling in love. But there was more. They were about a whole Nordic cultural idea of how to live well. Swedes call it *det goda livet,* or the Good Life. Of course, what I saw was the just-outside-of-Stockholm Swedish version, and there are national, regional, and individual variations on the idea. But, in its essence, people in Scandinavia have a very clear vision of the Good Life. This idea is inextricably linked with well-being. In fact, it *is* a life of well-being.

My goal is to give you a picture of this vision of life as seen from my perspective and through my own experiences on the island and elsewhere in Scandinavia, what I call the Ayurveda of the North. Here I doff my hat as a sign of respect to the Ayurveda originating in South Asia, which is a distinct and ancient system of living in itself. I borrow the word only, since it is the best one that I can find that in one word summarizes what I saw when I came to live in Scandinavia: a series of lifestyle aspects that cohered with certain ways of thinking that, in my mind, became a science of life, for being a well, whole person.

I decided to pull together the many threads of what it was that I was learning on this small, Swedish island, in my encounters with people in Scandinavia, in their vision of the Good Life. A philosophy with distinct values began to emerge. It was mine in its construct, but it was inspired by everything that I was taking in around me. I did it mainly as a means to help myself, but then realized that the results could also help others. As a person who had lived in many places, I also realized that what I had decided to do could be useful to people anywhere, wherever they were.

An Exotic Culture with Universally Relevant Ideas

But how can a Nordic idea of living be useful to people elsewhere? You could say that Scandinavians have rarefied conditions for living: vast tracts of wilderness, extreme seasons, and, at least in theory, more free time than most. At the same time, it is worth remembering that each part of the world that is associated with particularly healthful practices has some special preconditions for the emergence of those practices. These are usually to do with a mixture of the natural environment and the way that the society is organized. Scandinavia, too, has its own special preconditions. I would say that there are three.

The Common Law

On my first morning on the island I asked Claes where I was allowed to jog. "Where do you want to jog?" he asked, somewhat perplexed. I was concerned about crossing into other people's private property. Later on, I learned that this concern was unfounded due to a body of unwritten law regarding

Allemansrätt, or the common right of passage across the land and the waterways. This is a rule dating back to the Middle Ages, which has been carried through into modern law. The rule is accompanied by a series of other unwritten rules specifying what this right includes with respect to various outdoor activities. Essentially, however, it means that you or I or anyone else has the right on foot to cross another person's land, observing certain rules and, of course, using our common sense about the privacy that people like to preserve around their own homes. In the lakes and coastal waters it means roughly the same by boat. So, I could jog anywhere. Perhaps not right in front of another person's house and across their flower beds, but just about anywhere. Scandinavians are the inheritors of an extraordinary wilderness at the doorstep of their cities, and they have created a body of rules which makes experiencing it even more extraordinary. This is precondition one.

The Seasons

Precondition two is the tremendous variations in light and temperature that Scandinavians experience each year. On the darkest day of the year the sun as seen from my island (if I can see it through the clouds in December) sets at around 3:00 P.M. On the lightest day of the year I never see it set. I have experienced over +30°C (86°F) and under −25°C (−13°F) in this place. Together with the first precondition that I mentioned, this means that one becomes focused on nature and what is happening in it. In Lapland, in the very north of Scandinavia, where the variations are even more extreme, people explain seasonal variation in the way that one would explain fine art in any other part of the world. There are eight seasons, they say, not four. Living in the way that I do, I see a new season each day. A small change here and there tells me that change is happening in this place that looks so peaceful.

Free Time

Precondition three is that people generally have had more time to think about their well-being than in other places. The rise of social democracy in the Nordic countries has meant a socially conscious system with the belief that people need five weeks off work a year in order to be well. Many people own simple holiday homes where they have the time to develop ideas about the Good Life. However, this precondition is a twentieth-century development, and many of the ideas that this book refers to in subsequent chapters are much older. It is also the case that the pressure of globalization and the creeping of working time into free time have challenged this social institution.

Out of these uncommon conditions have emerged certain practices and associated ideas that I believe can be useful to people anywhere in attaining a life of well-being.

What Is Well-being?

Well-being has become a puzzling word. We all have our own specific ideas, and definition upon definition has been offered by books, public and nonprofit organizations, the corporate world, and the media. Everything down to what type of socks you wear can be well-being. It can be confusing, to say the least.

There are four different dimensions of well-being: physical, mental, spiritual, and emotional. Today, there is an emerging body of science called psychoneuroimmunology that tells us what we have known for a long time: these different dimensions of well-being are closely related. The World Health Organization tells us that "health is a state of complete physical, mental, and social well-being and not merely the absence of disease or infirmity." Well-being is a total situation that is dependent on our way of living. It means promoting positive trends in the way that we live and not just preventing disease. Well-being is best thought of as a process. When we ask ourselves whether we are well, it can be a difficult question to answer, since it is not a static state. It is much easier to ask ourselves whether we are in a process of well-being. Is the way that we lead our lives taking us in the general direction of feeling good and happy?

Learning About a New Well-being

Before coming to the island, I had an astoundingly concrete idea of thinking about this puzzling term: keeping physically fit, being organized, working hard, and keeping problems at bay. It sounded reasonable. Still, I would never have described myself as being in a process of well-being. Why not? I was in a pathogenic approach to life: fight fat, fight chaos, fight exhaustion, and fight problems. What options do we have in lives with such a large number of demands on them? It seemed to me, as it does to many other people, that solving life's little problems and fighting them individually was the best way to keep one's head above water.

When I came to Scandinavia, I discovered a completely different way of being. I must admit that I found it a little irritating at first. I couldn't locate anyone to hold meetings with in town during June and July. People at work responded with blank expressions when I fought to lead the battle for goals and aims rather than lingering in the process of the conversation. Gender, child, and environmental perspectives took us off on long tangents. We had to reach a consensus. On the social side, people had the habit of arriving at my Christmas party with things that had no directions for use on them, like plastic bags of fish eggs, buckets of self-harvested root vegetables, and seasonally harvested moose steak. The gift givers were not country folk—they were certified city dwellers. Still, people told me with tremendous enthusiasm how they were looking forward to spending their Easter holidays out in the countryside building a place to live in during the summer.

Some time after I came to live on the island, I began to experience many of the things that the people I had met valued. Several of those ways that had been irritations became things that I myself began to understand and embrace. Living with my family in this isolated place also sorted out for me the important from the unimportant. Gradually, my ideas about well-being began to shift. Paradoxically, in a place that presented more physical challenges to "fight," I laid down my sword and shield, and began to see and listen.

The Main Ideas

The first thing I learned in Scandinavia was that *well-being is about being in nature.* The great outdoors in my new home was both humbling and empowering. I could stand out in the unforgiving winter and understand why Norse mythology had given rise to tales invoking the gargantuan powers of this earth. At the same time it moved me with its tenderness. I was a part of the intense beauty, of everything that gave life. I was surprised at myself. I had never been religious.

I began to read, to talk to the experts, and to understand that this was not my mind just gone hopelessly romantic about my newfound home. The value of connection to nature can be explained scientifically, says my brain-expert friend, Gunilla. We have different types of nervous signals sent out by the brain to the body, which work in different rhythms called alpha, beta, delta, and theta. Beta (the fastest) is our normal state of being awake and active—our "beta life" is our everyday life. It is also our stress signal. It tells our bodies to react. Alpha is a deeper state of being relaxed yet awake. Meditation can help us to achieve this. Deep meditation can take us into our delta state, which is like dreaming while sleeping. In our delta state, we can access uncensored material that we are not conscious of. Theta is a state of deep unconsciousness.

In our normal, everyday lives, it is becoming increasingly difficult for us to experience our alpha state, which is important to our well-being. Our brains react to increasing stimuli everywhere, and shoot out beta signals in abundance to tell the body to react.

By establishing patterns that tune us in with nature, we can regularly increase the alpha signals sent out by the brain to the body. Alpha signals stimulate our bodies to produce a hormone called oxytocin, which sets in motion a process of relaxation that our bodies need in order to be well. Our blood pressure goes down, our circulation improves, we have lower levels of stress hormone in our systems, we have better digestion and nutrient up-take, and we heal more easily. This whole process has changed very little throughout our evolution.[1]

The question still remains as to why our brains start shooting off alpha signals when we experience a beautiful natural environment. My experience is as follows. In that moment of connecting to nature, when you see the water catching the sunlight and reflecting it back to you, the trees supporting a symphony orchestra of birds and the earth oozing with life and familiar smells, *you matter*. Our friend Kjell teaches his toddler daughter, Lucia, to touch the leaves and the trees when she is outside. In doing so, he is trying to endow her with a special support system that will guide and protect her throughout life. Whenever she returns to the leaves and the trees, she will always know that she is not alone, and that she matters.

The second thing I learned was that *well-being is about the creativity that nature can inspire*. During those first weekends of living on the island, I felt motivated to set up a working table outdoors. At the time, I wasn't quite sure just what I was going to create on that table, but I felt the urge to do something. The first creations were odd and probably best kept in my back pocket. But the ideas came, one after the other. And, as it turns out, I ended up creating something else at a table indoors (my writing). I reflected on how odd this urge to create was. At the time, I had no aspirations to be an author or an artist.

Nature, creativity, and well-being are ideas that stand prominent in Nordic culture. A Swedish prime minister once said about his beloved walks in the forest with his wife that he was never able just to take a walk. He always felt obliged to gather things, and reflected that this had been a part of his childhood—something that his father always did. In a description of a spectacular journey through Europe in his boat, *Liv* (Life), one of Scandinavia's most famous contemporary designers reflects, "Nature is my source."[2] I flipped back through a collection of Icelandic poems and reread the one that I liked best but had not been able to understand. Now it made sense to me.

ON LANDSCAPE

We were given this landscape
and as we become part of it
it no longer exists.

We become free:
Glittering and free thought
outside every landscape.

Landscape is not the land,
But an idea of a land waiting to be settled
By an alien dream.

The land sleeps in a poem about a bird
flying above river and shrubs,
Rejoicing at the wind
that lifts it higher and higher.[3]

The third thing I learned is that *well-being is about the inner sanctum that nature can inspire in each person.* Some people call it personal space. Others call it self-awareness. This sanctum is not an isolated place. It is open to those whom we choose to let into it. It is a space where we can breathe, think, and feel a strong sense of balance. It is a space where we do not feel pressured by events or people around us. Ultimately, the ability of each individual to create personal space is an important contribution to the well-being of the group or whole. When people feel free and unthreatened, they respect one another's personal space, they communicate clearly, and the possibilities for joint human creativity expand. People with a strong sense of self will find it easier to be close to others than people who are not in touch with their right to "be."

The whole notion of personal space is increasingly important for each of us to value and work toward in modern societies where the whole world seems to reach into our homes, our most private places, and through the Internet, the television, the radio, and other media, and the cell phone as well. The siege is made all the more difficult to deal with because it is intangible.

Living in a part of the world known for its efforts to bring about a more egalitarian society highlighted another issue to do with the importance of developing an inner sanctum. According to the experts, social comparison has become a major threat to our well-being. I call it "the comparing ourselves to the Joneses disease." We come to conclusions like: I don't have a high-powered job like Tom, so I must be incompetent; I don't have a BMW like Mary, so I must be very incompetent; I don't have shoes like Peter, so I must be totally incompetent. The most competent of people can feel this way. And, according to recent research, drastically increasing numbers of us are feeling this way with catastrophic results: depression, panic attacks, breakdowns, even suicide. Sadly, one of the more competent people I knew at university went as far as the last of these in her twenties.[4]

The first weeks that I spent on the island were a great leveler. There was no one to compare jobs with, no BMW (in fact, no cars) to be envious about, and no shiny shoes (only soiled garden sandals). Most importantly, standing below the towering spruce, pine, and birch trees and before vast Lake Mälaren, I was just like every other creature alive there, concerned about shelter, food, and warmth. It was like going back to square one and deleting advanced capitalism, at least for a short while. I began to form the theory that the reason for a distinct lack of social hierarchy throughout the history of the Scandinavian countries was a deep cultural closeness to all that grew, grazed, flew, swam, and crept.

Here on the island, I found that the literal space imparted to me by my environment—the seeming endlessness of the water, the sky, and the forest—began to open up that inner sanctum. After the first couple of summers here, someone once asked me what I saw inside of myself. Without thinking, I said, "A rock." One of the distinctive features of this island is the many smooth, round stones to be found here. Now one of them was there inside me, delineating my personal space. At first, I felt silly. Then I opened a beautiful book about the hiking in Storfjorden (Great Fjord), written by none other than H.M. Queen Sonja of Norway in a tone notably forthright for a person of her station in life. In it, she asks herself why she always chooses this area with its steep mountains and fjords, and concludes that the intense experiences and the quickly changing landscape perhaps fit with her nature.[5]

There is a healing that goes on in the identification of ourselves with certain natural environments—certain places. The Sami, the indigenous peoples of northern Scandinavia, believe that healing comes about through striving for bodily health, and connection to our environment and community. In Sami thinking about healing, that connection to the environment is so close that elements in nature mirror the body. A flat rock is likened to an open healing hand. In Sami narratives of healing, people express themselves *through* the bears and the reindeer, not about them.[6] In this culture, a human being's inner sanctum is turned inside out, and the place where they can be well is the natural environment.

The fourth thing I learned was that *well-being is about the intimacy that experiencing nature together and alone offers.* This means not only being able to get close to another person. It also means being able to experience all kinds of feelings and senses. Living on an isolated island with three other people to whom you are closely related will either result in total disaster (and departure from that place), or in experiencing a wide range of powerful feelings and a tremendous closeness. I cannot count the number of times when people looked at Claes and me askew for being able to "stand one another" in this place. I have never encountered any relationship with another human being that is completely smooth. But it is the willingness to go through all manner of emotions together that results in that relationship surviving.

In my early days of recreating in Scandinavia, I noticed that people were intent on getting out into nature with their partners and families and living very close: camping, hiking, skiing, skating, and sailing. Some people I met *even* moved out to remote places with their families. Before having children, I grimaced at the thought of heading off into the wilderness or out to sea for a few days with a gaggle of young ones. Still, I was curious as to why people liked to do this.

Our local doctor remembers with tremendous fondness the days that he spent as a young physician with his family in the Stockholm archipelago. The conditions in this area, with its rocky small islands and an often rough sea, can sometimes be treacherous, particularly if one is trying to save lives. Claes's cousin once recounted to us how much sailing with his family meant to him. The three women in his family often found it somewhat uncomfortable to be crammed into a relatively small space for days. Stroking the hair of one of his daughters, he declared that it was the golden chance to really be together.

For myself, I found that the wind, the water, the earth, the sun, the rain, the rocks, the trees, and everything else around me on the island awakened my senses. It spurred my preparedness to feel more and to reach out to other people. I found that Scandinavian traditions in relaxation, such as sauna bathing, and the best of Scandinavian design and food drew on this natural sensuousness, and communicated feelings of unpretentiousness and openness.

When I reflect today on the idea of well-being that I have arrived at after these years of living on this island and traveling in Scandinavia, I am always surprised at how different it is to the one that I used to pursue. Well-being has become to me foremost a way of thinking and feeling rather than a way of acting. This is not to de-emphasize the importance of what you do to be well, but to underline that the value of what you do flows from how you think and feel about what you do.

Living the Main Ideas

As I lived and recreated in this place, I experienced newly both old personal interests and long-standing Scandinavian traditions. Gradually, I realized that these interests and traditions could be divided into five distinct lifestyle areas with common themes that complemented one another and in their totality formed a vision of the Good Life. Below, I explain these lifestyle areas to you: both why they are vital to a life of well-being and how they are Nordic inspired.

Outdoor Life

One of the qualities that Scandinavians are undoubtedly famous for is being active in the outdoors, in their fantastic and seemingly unending wilderness. When I came here, I found that they were not undeservedly famous for this. I noticed a lot of concern among the older generation about an apparent decline in outdoor traditions among youngsters. Still, in a relative perspective, there seemed to be a lot of old and young people getting out there to hike, ski, skate, sail, and so forth.

Although I thought of myself as quite an active person, I often wondered what drove people to get out with such enthusiasm, with such frequency and in such considerable numbers, whatever the weather. After all, one could get fit in any one of a number of local gyms. So as not to keep myself in suspense, I began to ask people. But it was not until I consistently started stepping out myself that I began to get it. Your physical workout is actually greatly enhanced by the effect of having contact with nature.

The Greenery

In a place where it was hard to think of things growing for a large part of the year, I found a culture that adored the idea of things popping out of the ground. It turns out that this was not just my imagination and new-found enthusiasm about making things grow on the island leading me astray. According to *The Wall Street Journal,* which has surveyed what 22,000 people in twenty-one countries like to do in their free time, Swedes prefer most to work in their gardens. I do not know where the other Scandinavians landed in this survey, but, suffice it to say, they too are enthusiasts. In the cold north, watching the reemergence of our plant friends each year is the witnessing of a miracle.

I looked into history and found that Scandinavia has an amazing past when it comes to efforts to understand the world of plants. There were also old traditions in the uses of local medicinal plants and herbs. I set to work in my own garden, growing vegetables and herbs, and learned the qualities of plants that grew wild all around me. The possibilities for creativity were endless: I made tea from herbs, delicious new foods, and even prepared my own salves and creams. Yet there was something else that knowing my plant world gave me, which was also a long-standing Scandinavian idea: what grows around us can help us. I found that even if I did not use everything that grew around me in practical terms, just the knowledge of its powers imparted to me a positive feeling about my world. There is evidence today that this view is extremely important to our sense of well-being.

RELAXATION

Today it is more important than ever to find ways of winding down. The industrial and technological revolutions have brought us many wonderful things that we would not wish to live without. One of the unfortunate side effects, however, is increased feelings of stress. As people succumb in large numbers, approaches to relaxation, previously regarded either as a social taboo (for instance, as massage was among the finer set in northern Europe in the early twentieth century) or as a luxury, need to be taken more seriously.

Traveling around the world, I had experienced sauna in the health clubs of many hotels. However, none of them quite prepared me for what I was to learn about this great art of relaxation in Scandinavia. I had somewhere heard that sauna, a tradition that Finns are credited with keeping alive, was a pretty tough experience. I was to learn that it was the most nature-connected and sensuous path to cultivating one's inner life that I had experienced.

An enthusiast for massage and all manner of therapies, I began to look into the faint whisperings that I had heard about Scandinavian traditions. I learned about the elusive story behind the famous Swedish massage, which is today regarded in Western culture as a classical, basic form of massage. It was amazing to me that so few Swedes—even those in the business—actually knew the story. I also found that there were old beliefs in the powers of water in this always at least half-pagan culture, making this part of the world receptive to the spa culture, which emerged in Europe during the Renaissance. Today, the remains of Scandinavia's old water-therapy culture form the basis of an interesting new spa industry, which places its emphasis less on luxury than it does on natural sensuousness and unique experiences.

DESIGN

The idea that we can design our living environments to promote our sense of well-being is both very old and very new. There are ancient systems for thinking about design in relation to how we feel. New research and new sciences in the field of design (e.g., ergonomy) are showing us just how important the design of our living environment is to our sense of well-being. This research becomes all the more important to us today, since we spend more time indoors these days than ever in human history.

When I came to Scandinavia, I saw a society that at some point had placed its faith in the powers of design to deliver a better life for all people. During the twentieth century the Scandinavian countries had taken themselves from being rural, peasant societies to highly sophisticated industrialized ones. One of the powerful forces in this transformation was the belief in design and technology. I foraged into this historical legacy, but also looked around me at the very many typically Scandinavian interiors that I experienced and, for reasons that I was not quite sure of, adored. The latest research on design backed up what I was appreciating: the close connection to nature in Scandinavian design, its inclusiveness, and its focus on function. It became clear to me that there were many things that I, and others, could learn from these distinct Scandinavian design principles.

FOOD

Food must be the single most written about subject matter area of well-being. The number of books available today describing various types of diet recommendations is countless. Yet the number of people who suffer eating- and weight-related disorders is increasing all the time. To me, one of the great health questions of our time is: how can we normalize our relationship to food and make it something that is nourishing and enjoyable? Living in Scandinavia, I arrived at some answers.

I can summarize what I knew about Nordic cuisine when I stepped on my first flight to Copenhagen like this: strong-tasting fish, meatballs, and mashed potatoes. Today I am thrilled to tell you that this is not accurate, and can summarize the food world of Scandinavia much more accurately in even fewer words: discovering possibilities in nature. Learning to harvest and gather different types of ingredients on the island, Scandinavian style, I found that relating food to its origins brought both a reality as well as a wonderful excitement to the idea of food. Preparing meals for my family in my kitchen, as I did each day (with no restaurants or take-out places anywhere nearby), I discovered that using fresh ingredients and preparing them in new ways made the world of food a creative process that, in itself, was a tremendous boost to my sense of well-being.

Aside from the discovery of this unique Scandinavian food culture of gathering and preparation, I was also thrilled to find the very large number of healthful, seasonal ingredients that made up the Scandinavian diet: fish, rye and oats, root vegetables, and apples and berries, just to name a few. I learned that there were old healthful regional traditions in preparation, and also began to explore new possibilities for using these dynamite, fresh Scandinavian ingredients using preparation techniques that I had learned from other parts of the world. I began to see an as yet unrecognized healthy food culture with ideas useful to anyone anywhere.

Whose Well-being?

Beyond the resources for learning about food and well-being, there are today many others out there for learning about well-being in general. When I look at my bookshelves, I notice that most of my books are directed at the well-being of adults who are beginning to realize that their lives are finite. Yet we know that today our children are succumbing to some of the same diseases as adults are, and at an alarmingly rapid rate. The difference is that their future looks even more endangered, since they will have to grow up with diseases, such as diabetes and heart disease, that we adults have contracted only later on in life. As we find new means of fighting illnesses and thus keeping ourselves alive for longer, we are also increasingly aware of the sad lot of many elderly people. The types of challenges that people face in the sunset years are often not taken seriously and put down to old age.

Living on this island with young children, and my over-eighty-year-old mother-in-law who visited us during the summers, these issues have come close to my heart. Furthermore, living in a society where the well-being of children and the elderly are hotly debated social issues, and where the public sector has put in an unusually high degree of effort and funds, one begins to think. The problems continue to mount, and public policy just doesn't suffice. How can we deal with these problems?

Well-being is much about personal choices, for instance, whether I as a parent choose to feed my child fast food or something that can be made in a matter of minutes, but is healthy and fresh. Getting people to make good choices for themselves and for their families is not only about education but about inspiration. It is about holding up a vision of life that is beautiful, enjoyable, and possible. This is where I believe the vision of well-being that I offer in this book can help out.

Values and Patterns for Getting into a Process of Well-being

Like all other authentic and well-grounded ideas about well-being, this one just doesn't *happen*. It is a lifetime's work, and well worth every moment. In my own process, I have found it necessary to change some of my patterns and certain values. I was forced to think about certain aspects of my life that I had never thought about before. Below, I describe to you patterns and values that you can essentially regard as the tools for getting into a process that leads to the sort of well-being I have described above. These tools are emphasized throughout the following chapters, where I show you in detailed, concrete ways, how this idea of well-being is manifested in a Scandinavian-inspired way of life.

Activating Your Natural Rhythm

In the past, human life depended on living in tune with the patterns of nature. In modern times, we have created structures and means of living that separate us, sometimes completely, from the natural environment. Particularly in a Scandinavian winter, one is thankful for many of them.

There has, however, been a cost and that is the weakening of our bond to a source of vital energy, which we desperately need in order to function well in a modern world. Our life patterns are increasingly energy-sapping rather than energy-giving. The good news is that we can revive that bond so that it serves our needs. Now and then, I have heard it said that a person needs to be born with natural rhythm in order to have it. In a way, we all are, since that is part of the legacy of our evolution. In some of us it has faded a little, as it had with me until I came to this island outside of Stockholm.

Although I saw a lot during my travels over the years, I often wonder how much I really took in. I can remember sitting on the terrace of a straw hut overlooking a lagoon on a small South Pacific island—a place that very few people actually manage to get to, since it is so far away from any other place—and thinking only about the fact that my portable computer would not work because there were no electrical outlets in my hut. I did my work and saw what I needed to see for those purposes, but did not take any recreational time to get out and connect with this extraordinary environment. The irony of this situation is that my Danish employers would have fully expected me to do so. I remained more or less out of tune with this place for the week that I was there and, once I had survived the long journey back to Europe, was more tired than I really had to be.

Tuning in to the Seasons

Changing your patterns of life to tune in to the seasons is one way of activating your sense of natural rhythm. Stuck in a well-insulated office, it is easy to ignore the change and keep everything in a more or less safe and effortless status quo situation. The trouble with this is that we slowly stagnate. But if you looked into your life and saw the many rich opportunities that each new season has to offer you—new foods, new outdoor activities, new ways of decorating your home—your life suddenly takes on a new sheen.

If there is anyone who needed to be faced with the intensity of the Scandinavian seasons over an extended period of time, it was me. They were a wake-up call to all of my senses, and to that very fragile natural rhythm that was buried somewhere deep inside. Each season struck me with a new range of emotions: spring awakened faith in the miracle of life, which seemed to crack its way out of the thick ice; summer was the time of forgetting and enjoying long days; autumn brought a super energy through its crispness and clarity; winter was the witnessing of a supreme drama and the will to survive.

Tuning in to the beat of our natural rhythm takes us out of time that is managed by clocks, the future of the stock market, and the nervous onward progression of the human race. It takes us out of a linear view of time, which is associated with things we have missed and the finiteness of our lives. It puts us into a cyclical view, in which we somehow always get another chance. Natural rhythm is a tool for coping in times of trouble. It takes us out of our crisis in linear time, and creates the personal space for us to experience both the moment and the totality of our lives. And, in very extreme circumstances, where there is no cure, it makes a form of inner healing possible.

The curious thing about tuning in to the seasons is that you will never tire of it. Intellectually, all Scandinavians know that seasonal change will happen each year. Emotionally, they are always surprised when it takes place. While I was visiting in Helsinki one November, the first snow came. A lot of it. The management office in the basement of the apartment building I was staying in was thrown into chaos. Nothing could be repaired in the building on that day. The smooth and businesslike building manager quipped that although it happened each year, and the weather reports always predicted it, the snow was like the landing of an alien spaceship when it arrived. Each year nature's transformational powers are at least as breathtaking as those of the year gone by.

One of the thoroughgoing principles of Nordic society is that all people should have equal access to similar benefits. This principle is most clearly understood in the laws that create freedom of movement for people in Scandinavia's natural environment. People can pick berries and mushrooms, and sail and hike just about wherever they like. This is a rarified condition and one that gives rise to thinking about how people who want to pursue this approach elsewhere can get a feeling of accessibility and inclusiveness.

Most of the Scandinavian practices that I describe in the following chapters are possible for you to pursue wherever you are. What I want to impress upon you most is that much of the experience that has made such a tremendous change in attitude for me has happened around my home. I have changed my patterns and tuned in, not by looking elsewhere, but by looking locally, and particularly into the local nature that has provided me with endless opportunities. While I do hope that this work inspires you to come and visit Scandinavia and to experience the culture behind the concept that I write about, I also hope that it encourages you to look around your own home or area and see what there is available that could help you to stimulate your natural rhythm and to tune in.

One of the reasons that I encourage you to look locally is that the form of well-being I talk about is not something that you can make of lasting value in your life during a onetime visit to a sauna or a one-week holiday. It is something that you need to integrate into your life: into what you eat, how you recreate, how you design your living space, and how you relax. It is, in its essence, a way of living and not something separate from your daily life. For this reason, the aspects that you pursue have to be reasonably accessible to you.

One of the features of this approach to well-being is that it doesn't have to cost you the earth. If you look locally and for things that you can do that are easily integrated into your life, they will probably also not cost you very much. The Resources section of this book tries to take an inclusive approach by offering possibilities for every bank account.

One of the little things that was a giant wake-up call for me here on the island is a good example of how local, integrated, and affordable tuning in can be. Each year in the late spring on our island, bunches of gigantic yellow irises start to pop out of the ground everywhere. They were planted here during the 1950s by Claes's grandfather. These irises are nature's signal to us who live here to come outside and take a look. For years I paid absolutely no attention to this signal, and continued hammering away at my PC as I had throughout all of the cold months. Then one day, after five years of not experiencing the same thing, I finally did go outside and look at the irises. Some were still firmly closed, some on the verge of opening up, and others already wide open. The drama had started. On each day after that I ran out to see whether the miracle had happened, and whether those on the verge of opening had opened. Those moments with the irises became something wonderful to look forward to each day. I became charged with their energy, and began to see magic and beauty everywhere in my garden. These days I block out time to be in my garden during the growing season. I have given a lot of energy and caring back to it.

The giant yellow irises have become a mental anchor for me, just as other natural aspects of my surroundings here on this Scandinavian island have. Each spring, when I see them coming up, I know that it is time for me to change my pattern. Making this change brings an explosion of new vital forces into my life. My channels of communication feel cleared by the connection that I have made with my natural surroundings. I can see all sorts of new possibilities and my creativity is spurred. I affirm my sense of personal space by making the proactive choice to change my pattern. Affirming that personal space gives me the peace of mind to enjoy my life in that perfect moment with the irises. Each time that I do this, the same thing happens. The effect is never weakened. I had no idea that something so basic and simple as going out to have a look at the irises in my garden in the spring could make such a difference to my life. It did.

To a great extent, accessibility is about taking a simple approach to things. In other words, in order to dine seasonally, you don't need to book a table at a faraway restaurant renowned for making great seasonal food. This could be a nice treat, but not an accessible and simple practice that you can integrate into your daily life. Alternatively, you could just drop by your neighborhood market on the way home and buy some local fruits and vegetables in season. Some of these items you don't even have to cook to enjoy. Presto! You are spurring your natural rhythm, seasonally and simply.

One of the cultural features that struck me when I came to live in Scandinavia was the simplicity that is adored by these modern societies so driven by high technology. I found this to be manifested in almost every area of life, and most famously in the field of design. The dream of a summer home in Scandinavia is one inspired by the ideas of simplicity for closeness to nature. Simplicity also means affordability of such seeming luxuries by a greater number of people. As a foreigner, I sometimes found that this simplicity challenged me (i.e., in the form of outhouses). On the whole, however, I found that it created mental space for creativity.

Getting Involved and Learning

Sometimes I think that today we watch life and don't live it. There is a service available for almost every aspect of our lives these days, with the result that we watch other people doing a lot of the things that we would otherwise find enjoyable and good for our well-being. We don't have to cook. We don't have to build or decorate our own homes. We don't even have to move, since we can watch people doing that for us on TV!

Whatever well-grounded approach to well-being you pursue, including this one, it means being consistently proactive, participating and learning. It doesn't mean that you have to start doing absolutely everything yourself, which would be unrealistic in a busy life, but it does mean that you need to get involved.

The good news about getting involved Scandinavian style is that it is a tremendous amount of fun. When I came to Scandinavia, I came into a do-it-yourself society. I understood that this was due to the high cost of services, but knowing more, I find this to be an insufficient explanation. There is an understanding of do-it-yourself as a part of culture that is somehow associated with well-being. A well-known Scandinavian master gardener whom I have spoken with on occasion says that today culture is often about passively taking part in someone else's creation. Growing something ourselves is an ancient art and an original form of human creativity, which is perhaps the closest that we can come to a real people's culture.[7]

Living and recreating in a place where I am forced to do many things myself, I learned about the way that being proactive and taking the initiative in your own life can be endlessly rewarding and enjoyable. I had to cook each night, and thus a whole new world of food opened up to me. I wanted herbs, vegetables, and fruits from my garden, so I had to create a garden. I wanted a garden of beauty for meditation, so I had to learn to create that as well. I wanted our home to be as practical and beautiful as possible, so I had to get involved in making it so.

Being proactive can awaken your sense of play, which is important to all people, no matter what age. I learned about this through the many irresistible and impossible home projects that Claes often took on. His idea of a great summer holiday was to enjoy a cup of coffee and a sandwich out in the sunshine for breakfast, wander around for a while, and then start work on whichever project he felt like working on, on that particular day. For the Results Oriented Management (R.O.M.) consultant that I was at the time, it was beyond frustration; it was incomprehensible. Today I am a convert, mostly because taking such initiatives is fun and, in our case, necessary. I am also convinced that there must be a link between sense of play and longevity, although I have not seen any scientific evidence. I know several Scandinavians who have or are still living well into their eighties and who get engaged with such projects. Most memorable is an elderly couple, Birger and Birgit, who used to come and stay in their simple house on the facing island. We could hear a lot of what they said, since they usually said things loudly, and the lake carries sound. While they were engaged in one of their many summer projects, Birgit quipped as she did half-jokingly a lot of the time, "Mmmmm, summer house, more like slave camp." She was at that time eighty-three and still busy harvesting the potatoes. For fun.

The term "learning" has cropped up a few times here. All of the dimensions of well-being that I show you in this book require some form of learning. In the Resources section of the book, I provide you with leads on information for increasing your knowledge. They are intended to provide you with a start or a fine addition to what I hope will be a lifelong learning process about well-being.

Taking Beauty Seriously

Beauty is not a frill. Research on some of the oldest people in the world shows that a common factor is that they appreciate the beauty of nature.[8] There is other research showing that good relations to certain places can be wellness-promoting because they stimulate the body's system for relaxation.[9] Should we then be surprised that patients who can look out the window at a beautiful natural scene seem to heal more quickly than those who cannot? Not at all.

Nature and beauty exist together in one breath. In this book, I paint for you many visions of natural beauty in the hope that they will stir your sense of well-being as well as your desire to find natural beauty within your own environment. This can be an inspiration to bringing your vision of what is beautiful more closely into your life.

TWO

Outdoor Life and
Overcoming the Fitness Dilemma

I FELT AS THOUGH I were in a Nordic *Canterbury Tale.* Out on the vast ice not far from our island with our skates on, Claes and I met one traveler after another. They were all heading somewhere, but it was not the end destination that mattered. It was the process of getting there: the unexpected meetings and places; the unfolding story with all of its many unexpected twists and turns; the feeling of freedom that comes from discovering the natural beauty of the world we live in all over again.

While resting on a huge rock on the edge of an island that we usually took great care to sail far around during the summertime, we noticed a single figure gliding toward us from the distance. On his person, he had a small backpack, probably containing some spare dry clothes, a thermos of coffee, and a sandwich or two. He took graceful, long strides, helped along by his skating poles, which he plunged into the ice every second stride. "Hello," he said without showing any signs of being out of breath, "the ice is fine and solid out there." His nymphlike face made it difficult to make out his age. My wild guess was that he was about seventy-five. "Great day to be out," we remarked. "Yes, in fact the last three days have been," he added. "Makes me reluctant to get on the bus and go home tonight." We learned that this senior citizen had been out skating on the vast lake ice for the past three days—ten hours of skating, on and off, on the previous day— and that he would take public transport back to his home that evening. "Good luck," he said, and with that he was off in an instant. We watched him for a short time, looked away for a minute or two, and then looked back to see where he had gone. He had vanished and the silence had returned. Was he real, or was he just a figment of my imagination? The whole incident remains magical in my memory.

That early afternoon out on the ice represents so many things about the way that I have experienced outdoor life in Scandinavia. There is the magic of its incredible, untouched, and varied landscape. The sort of place that these days we can easily forget still exists. A place that reminds us of the extreme beauty and preciousness of life. There are the people out for the journey of being reminded of these things. A journey that could be a few hours, a day, a few days, or a few weeks. A journey through nature that is full of the unexpected. From infants in prams being pushed on the ice by their mothers on skates to senior citizens in their eighties and nineties (not necessarily traveling at a tamer pace than younger people!), all are on a meaningful yet goal-less journey in the outdoors.

There are two myths that this story upholds that I would like to dispel straight away. One is that outdoor life in Scandinavia is purely about snow and ice. Swimming and boating are as much a part of this culture of *Friluftsliv* (Swedish word meaning "free time outdoor life") as are skiing, sledding, and skating.

The second myth, which I was certainly convinced of before I came here, is that outdoor life in Scandinavia is only for those who really want to rough it. Scandinavia's many famous Arctic and other explorers have perhaps contributed to creating a picture of a region of the world where people are prepared to live in adverse conditions in order to be the first or to show that they can actually dwell in that gray zone between life and death. The truth is that these Scandinavian explorers were after something that we all seek and, one way or another, can get a taste of at our own pace.

One Norwegian explorer I talked to, who crossed the North Pole solo on skis in 2001, called it "closeness to nature and human existence."[1]

There is much that we can get out of outdoor experiences that makes us feel truly well. This adds up to much more than a list of physical statistics (e.g., pulse, body mass index, blood pressure). It is about an attitude toward outdoor challenge that can encourage positive processes mental, emotional, and physical. It is about getting in touch with the essence of our existence, something that I learned about recreating outdoors in Scandinavia.

The Fitness Dilemma

These days we know more about what physical exercise can do for our physical statistics than ever before. We hear frequently of how it can prevent disease. We know, for instance, that vigorous exercise can reduce our risk of heart disease and cancer. Of the at least ten thousand steps that we should be taking each day we, on average, only take about three thousand. This is not good news for our hearts. This is important information that *all* of us should be aware of. However, what I have learned recreating outdoors in Scandinavia is that these arguments leave something very important out of the discussion—that is, the impact of physical motion outdoors on our minds and emotions, and the impact of those on our health. These effects are difficult, if not impossible, to quantify and that is perhaps why they are usually left out of the scientific discourse. Still, anyone who has been out for a walk in the park will tell you that somehow that experience has lifted them, changed their thinking, brought new perspectives, and/or just generally invigorated them.

The same thing doesn't usually happen in the gym. There we are focused on how many kilometers or miles per hour we are doing, what incline we are working at, how many kilograms or pounds we are lifting, what our pulse is, and how many calories we are burning. Plenty to think about, and, of course, it has its own value for hurried, sedentary lives. As an ex-devotee of the gym, I know how it can be. I always felt stellar after a visit to the gym and a hot shower. But it wasn't long before that run-down feeling began to creep in again. There was no thinking or emotional process that going to the gym could spark, which could get me on a longer term process of personal development. Nevertheless, I remained a great gym devotee. A day without the gym was a day of feeling crummy.

One of the big issues that crossed my mind at the time I was arguing for moving to the island was how I would get to the gym. I would find a place nearby, I resolved. "Nearby" was forty minutes away, each way, which was just about impossible to fit in, between kids, work, and domestic responsibilities. The next step was to perform the Herculean task of dragging an exercise bike, a step, and some other ridiculously heavy equipment in a boat out to the island. I still use them today, outdoors on one of our docks, which makes a tremendous difference to the experience. The truth is that the weekly sweat in the gym was overtaken by something else, which I found to be a much more total experience of well-being: jogs in the woods, and once I realized how interesting the woods could become, brisk walks in the woods, eventually made even more lively by the accompaniment of my more-than-enthusiastic golden retriever, Lucy.

What do I conclude from this personal transformation from gym nut to forest gnome? It is not that people who enjoy going to the gym should stop going to the gym, or that there is no value in going to the gym. The first innovator of modern weight-training equipment was, by the way, a Swede named Gustaf Zander (1835–1920), who believed in the potential of his machines for the purposes of rehabilitation and general strength based on his own personal experience. He was quite right about this, and preceded by seventy years the takeoff of weight training through Arthur Jones's Nautilus system during the 1960s. Stick with it, if you are a gym devotee or a devotee of any other type of indoor fitness, and that type of training works for you. But throw in some outdoor motion as well. My conclusion is that being active outdoors, in a natural environment (the local park will do), with some regularity, can start you on a long-term process of total well-being that just cannot be paralleled by any regimen of physical fitness indoors only.

During the past few years, the scientific establishment has begun to feel its way around the tip of this iceberg. A 1995 Australian study, for instance, showed that "trained runners felt less anxious, depressed, angry, and hostile, and more invigorated after an outdoor run than they did when they ran the same distance on a treadmill." There is other work suggesting that the visual stimulation that we get from exercising outdoors takes our minds off what we are doing and thus makes time fly by more quickly, as well as invigorates us more.[2] Brain ergonomists (specialists working with an emerging science about what makes our brains, and thus the rest of our bodies, function best) confirm the benefits of outdoor activity: variety in vision (i.e., the need to look far and near), variety on your path (uphill, downhill, or a log in your way that forces you to hop over it), and, if you have the opportunity, the touch of the earth or grass on the soles of your feet, all stimulate your brain in a way that is positive for your well-being.

My own theory is the one that I learned about here on this Scandinavian island. Being in motion in nature, we are in the company of an incalcuable number of cells of living matter, all acting in their own interests and still somehow moving in conjunction with one another. Together, you and they give rise to a place that is an energy source of unfathomable size. Being a part of this, your mind and emotions are empowered to the point of crystal clarity. The blurry film of everyday life washes off your eyes and comes off as tears that you wipe away. The argument that you had with your husband, wife, or partner yesterday is really all about showing more appreciation of one another. You snapped at your child yesterday not because he or she did something unbelievably bad, but because you have taken on too many responsibilities at the same time. The dissatisfaction you feel at work is really not about your boss, but more about your own sense of self-value and your own choices. And actually, you are a person with great worth and talents, which you should pursue. You might not see it all at once, but gradually you begin to see the possibilities and carve out some space for yourself. A whole process of personal change has begun and will continue, if you keep on getting out there.

Some insightful Swedish historians of *Friluftsliv* conclude that its main role is to take us out of our everyday lives, and to give us the space and perspective to develop our identities.[3] They point out that historically in Sweden and elsewhere, *Friluftsliv* has been both an individual- and society-building pastime. At an individual level, sometimes we feel that we are vanishing in our duties and responsibilities. "What I have to do today takes priority over who I am or would like to be. I become my errands." This is a normal outcome of living, but one we can balance out. To take a few hours walking or perhaps working in the garden gives us the room we need to unearth ourselves.

All cultures somehow recognize nature as a unique energy resource, which all living creatures can benefit from. In Norse mythology, where the world is otherwise full of danger, trickery, and scheming, there is one holy place, where gods and men can go in order to confer with one another and be safe. That is the ash tree Yggdrasil. According to Snorre's *Edda,* the main recorded source of Norse mythology, its branches spread out over all the world and extend across the sky. Everyone has the chance to be under it, but they must recognize it first. This means not simply running past it all with your eye mostly on your wrist timer. It is hard to get out of this habit unless there is something more interesting to do.

Solving the Fitness Dilemma

So how does one beat the mental and emotional fitness stress of our time without giving up fitness or even finding it altogether too threatening to start? In our modern, sedentary societies most of us need to watch our weight, and many of us are told that we need to lose it. As we sit at our desks, tapping on keyboards and staring into screens, our bones and muscles deteriorate at a faster rate than they have to. In this situation, it is not very surprising that, in most instances, fitness has become a drive to fight certain types of body tissue and build other types.

How would it be if we were able to take more than good care of our physical statistics without thinking about them, enjoying ourselves, and developing our thoughts? How would it be if we could double the effects on our physical health of working out without consciously working doubly hard? How would it be if our fitness routines included mental, emotional, and cultural stimulation? How would it be if these routines resulted in the feeling that we have quality of life, even if our bank balances look about the same?

It would be a gigantic freeing from a stress that we really don't need. Our world would become a great, new adventure. Fitness would become an ongoing process of personal discovery. It would be about really living.

But how do we get out of the fitness rut? Having got out myself living in Scandinavia, I have six suggestions to make. They have to do with where you get fit, with whom you get fit, why you are engaging in a fitness activity, and what you get fit doing. In summary, my suggestions are: Get outdoors as a life habit; get outdoors as a social activity; notice the beauty; get outdoors with children; get outdoors to be productive and creative; add variety with natural rhythm. These are explained in greater detail below. Ultimately, the goal of all of these is to change the role of fitness as being a pressing objective to being a natural outcome of activities that you enjoy and that help you to connect the dots in your life in more ways than one.

Get Outdoors as a Life Habit

We live in times when it is easy to forget to go outside at all—to forget the beauty. Most of the course of human evolution has not prepared us for this. Given the nature of modern society's health problems, it doesn't seem like we will ever be prepared. If we do manage to get outside, many of us run into crowded pavements, taxis honking us off the pedestrian crossings, and the faint smell of noxious fumes in the air. But somewhere nearby there is a place where people don't have to walk on pavements, where taxis may not enter, and where noxious fumes are at least combated by the oxygen that the trees and other plants are releasing into the air. This place is the park. Most city governments are becoming increasingly aware of the important role that they play for the health of their citizens, the culture and appeal of their cities, and thus for their economies. If your city government hasn't worked this out, find a few like-minded citizens and make your voice heard. There are now research findings showing that (particularly in the case of senior citizens) people who live on tree-lined streets and within walking distance of grassy parks appear to survive longer than those with less exposure to greenery.[4] On the weekends you can hop into the car and get to a place, hopefully not too far away, where you can enjoy more of the outdoors.

Today I live in a part of the world where the overwhelming majority of people perceive going out into nature as an integral part of life. A 1995 study showed that 80 to 90 percent of Swedes and Danes—double as many as in other selected industrialized countries with plenty of outdoor recreational space (the United States and Australia, in the study)—spent recreational time in forested and natural environments or parks.[5] Although Finland, Norway, and Iceland were not included in the study, knowing the character of these populations, I have no doubt that they have similar or even greater statistical enthusiasm for the outdoors. Fortunately, it is widely available to them, both inside their cities as well as just outside of them. Most important of all, old laws of the land give all people wide access to different types of outdoor environments. Still, wherever you are, there are possibilities to get out into the greenery on a regular basis.

For myself, changing my pattern of running from the office to the gym and back (with the cursory glance at the entrance to the park while racing from one destination to another on the street) has made a tremendous difference to my life. Today, I am fortunate to be able to go from my study into the forest for a walk and back, and, on arriving back, feel that I have gained so much more than a trimmer waistline. But I must say that if someday I returned to live in the city, the park would not just be a cursory glance.

Get Outdoors as a Social Activity

Not everyone has the same attitude toward experiencing the outdoors alone, as the Norwegian adventurer who trekked to the North Pole on his

---

MAKING TIME FOR OUTDOOR LIFE

Making outdoor recreation a part of your lifestyle means making time for it. Many people today feel that they just don't have that time, due to many other responsibilities that take precedence. If you feel this way, think through your day carefully. Could you hold a meeting walking in the park rather than sitting in your office? The downside is possibly less privacy, but your mind as well as that of your visitor will be in a much more creative mode. Could you be out having a walk after work rather than watching TV with a bowl of potato chips? Could you combine being outdoors with your children with your own outdoor routine? Think it through carefully. It is a high priority.

own did. In fact, I would venture to say that the majority of people don't, when it comes to getting outdoors. We are, to varying degrees, social creatures and need interaction with others to feel well. Planning to get together with old and potentially new friends in the outdoors can be one way of getting motivated.

Scandinavians have grasped this fact and provide a home for the world's oldest and largest number of organized nonprofit outdoor life organizations. While visiting in Norway, I found myself in a private library where I could glance back at the Norwegian Mountain Touring Association's recorded stories since 1868, its founding year. It is the oldest of its kind in the world. While outdoor life as a movement is one that is international and well over a hundred years old (not least with connections to the American "back to nature" movement of the late nineteenth century), the Nordic countries have preserved it as a social activity in a way that is unparalleled in the world. I have heard it argued that this is because people have had more free time in Scandinavia than elsewhere. This was not so during the earlier part of the twentieth century and is becoming less true today with careers spilling over into free time. My own thoughts of people outdoors here in Sweden is always of groups: people skating in organized groups past my living room window; people hiking in organized groups up onto the hill overlooking the old sand mine, our home, and Lake Mälaren.

Other important benefits of enjoying outdoor life in an organized group are that you can learn and feel safe. In Scandinavia, people are supplied with an unusual degree of "outdoor education" through a formal and parallel informal system from a young age. Hiking is, for instance, an integral part of the Norwegian school curriculum, and parallel to this, kids can participate in organized groups from the age of one or two about exploring in nature. That means, in general, that the average person knows a lot more about living and being active in nature than the average person in many other parts of the industrialized world. People know that being outdoors, whether for a couple of hours, a day, or a week, is a learning process. They take it as a part of the whole enjoyment. They know that being in a group with people who are more and less skilled can facilitate this process for the whole group.

Notice the Beauty

While joining a group can be a motivation for getting outside, it is no guarantee for beating fitness stress. Take the amusing story recently told to me by one of my college friends, a professional working in Washington, D.C., who frequently partakes in organized hiking in the United States.

Last Sunday I twice resisted the group's urge to move on from an overlook after two minutes of looking out. Their goal was to keep moving, mine was to enjoy the moment and the space in which I was. I have appreciated the pace for getting me in shape, but have been perturbed at the blindness. Last Sunday, the trip leader and I were the last ones hiking out (not because of being slow but because of looking). I noticed what seemed to be a burnt stick and then realized it was a snake just off the trail (turned out to be two snakes in the sex act and rattlesnakes at that!!!). All the others walked by without noticing the snakes about three feet off the trail in plain sight.

In making outdoor life integral to your life, make sure that you stop to notice the beauty (or the snakes enjoying themselves) or take things at a pace that allows you to notice it. It is as much a part of your wellness regimen as the exercise is. I learned to love my back problem when I realized that it had forced me to walk briskly rather than to run. Today my back problem is almost nonexistent, partly, I believe, because walking rather than running allowed me to notice the beauty and also to become conscious of my posture (which was creating the problem). The outdoors, like a piece of exquisite art, a great film, or music, is something you shouldn't just walk by, because it can do something very important for you.

Get Outdoors with Children

Young children have a fascinating instinct of being attracted to the outdoors. Their natural rhythm is more intact than that of the grown-ups. My sister and I both have twins under the age of seven, who often bang on the doors together (my sister's do this with their slightly older brother) in order to get out. As an adult with millions of indoor responsibilities, it is easy to react with either a "not now" or a "later," following which your young children (or the ones that you are looking after) will continue to bang on the door. This may seem a somewhat risky proposition, but here it is anyway: If at all possible, follow your children's instincts. Let them take you outdoors.

So that you are not taking off the three pairs of shoes and jackets that you just put on eager little feet and bodies five minutes ago, think about how you can involve yourself to create action and suspense. This will usually result in your moving around at quite a pace, without your really noticing it until you get back inside. Claes and I discovered that weekend sledding outings with our children in the winter had us running up and down hills for hours. The children thought it was a scream. Telling stories about what the Vikings did on this and that part of the island had us following our kids all around the place discovering new "archaeological" finds.

The great thing about getting out with your children is that everyone wins: You get out, your kids get out, and you automatically help to develop good habits that will guard your children's health for a lifetime. A great saying put to me by a very trim and fit Swedish acquaintance with four children is that "children don't do what you say, they do what you do." If you would rather sit inside on a sunny Sunday afternoon watching television, so will your kids. No amount of telling them to go out will get them out, as they get older. I recognize this in my own upbringing. My father has always walked, no matter where or the weather, he always got out for a walk. I remember him once excusing himself from a big family Thanksgiving lunch, which was running into dinnertime, because he had not gotten out on that day and it was getting dark. Outside of our family, people would have thought him somewhat rude, but we all understood him, especially me. As I get older, I return to walking, partly because I remember my father doing it.

Just as we need the skills to enjoy the outdoors, so too do our children. It makes being in the outdoors as a family all the more enjoyable. Today I can pass on more than just the instinct to get outside: I can light a campfire, I know when not to get out on the ice as well as which mushrooms not to pick. Our day care organizes weekly play in the forest as a part of the curriculum. There our children have learned about the many fascinating things that are lying on the forest floor (pinecones, leaves, worms, ants, soil) and how things work in the forest. They have learned that red ants sting, which berries are safe to eat and which they should not touch, and that they should not pull off their shoes in the forest, since pinecones hurt on a bare foot.

I open my seasonal mail from the Swedish *Friluftsfrämjandet,* or Outdoor Life Association, a membership that costs me the equivalent of $28 for the entire family annually. I find the following activities listed: *Skogsknopp 1–2 år* (Forest Bud, 1–2 years), *Skogsknytte 3–4 år* (Forest Bundle, 3–4 years), *Skogsmulle 5–6 år* (Forest Troll, 5–6 years), and so forth. During the 1950s, Sweden invented the idea of a forest creature, Skogsmulle, a troll who was born of the forest and who had been clothed by the animals in an outfit of green leaves and a hat of birch bark with a red berry-colored feather. Children visiting the forest created a pair of shoes for him so that he wouldn't hurt his feet on the forest floor. He was later joined by three equally mystical and adventurous friends, who were born, respectively, of the sea, the mountains, and a wonderfully clean planet called Tella. A whole school of learning about living in nature, enjoying it, and respecting it was created around these creatures. They awakened children's fantasy to such an extent that the idea was exported abroad, including to the United States.

Lucy, the dog, looks utterly dejected if I miss my forest walk with her on any given day. Unlike many other dogs, she has the luxury to be outside whenever she likes. But it is the walk with me that is the real high. For

Lucy there is nothing more wonderful than the sight of me putting on my hiking boots. Lucy is, of course, right. Just as I should heed the urge of my two children to get outside, so I should heed Lucy's need to go walking with me.

Get Outdoors to Be Creative or Productive

For many people, doing fifty lifts, twenty pulls, and fifteen minutes of stepping is just not interesting enough to do with any real commitment. I am not one of those people, but my husband is. He stared at me with great curiosity as I ran, determined to restore my pre-twin body, up and down the stairs of our stone terraces while the twins slept. As I was running up and down, he asked me what the purpose of this activity was. To me it was self-evident, but to him it was a mystery.

Claes's idea of being outdoors includes, to a great degree, doing something fun that results in something useful to the home. He came jogging with me once and started picking mushrooms for dinner halfway, which promptly ended the jog. Harvesting food in the outdoors is a pastime that remains popular in Scandinavia, despite the wide availability of all types of food in the supermarkets. There are extensive health benefits of getting involved in food gathering, including meditation and motion, which you can read more about in Chapter 6. I have learned about this here in our for-

MUSHROOM AND BERRY PICKING IN AMERICA

America's organized nature trails and natural parks offer rich opportunities for mushroom and berry picking. A permit may or may not be required, and there is often no cost for the picking itself. There is a limit on the amount that you can pick, although three to five gallons per day seems plenty for personal use. Remember to check out a book from the library or to order one of the several available from your local or online bookstore on what types of mushrooms and berries are safe to pick—some are poisonous, so you do need to know what you are picking. Participate in a walk guided by an expert, if there is one available. See Resources for relevant Web sites.

est, which is rich with berries, mushrooms, and wild animals, and on our mini-farm, where we harvest vegetables and herbs each year.

If you live in a climate that is cold or even just somewhat cooler for part of the year and you have a fireplace, like we do here on the island, then having ample wood stocks ready for winter fires is a good idea. Of course, you can probably order in chopped wood or buy it from the local store, but if you live in a heavily wooded environment, as we do, why not chop wood from the felled branches of trees for an hour or so? It is a very rewarding way to clear your mind and focus down, to get fit, and to gain the benefits of being in the great outdoors without feeling that you are deliberately out to exercise. You can also save on the heating bills and use a sustainable energy resource. You can throw the ash from the fire into your compost, which is a real asset in creating good soil for spring planting. As you sit in front of the fire, watching it consume the wood when the day is done, you will feel a special satisfaction.

Preparing wood for the cooler season is quite an art, which will have you enjoying the outdoors throughout the year. Here are a few little tips:

THE FIVE SEASONS OF WOOD

1. Chop wood in the winter. Freshly chopped wood contains 45 percent water. Wood appropriate for burning should not con-

tain more than 25 percent. In the winter trees contain the least water. If you chop your wood too late in the spring there is a risk that the wood will never dry.

2. Crosscut and split wood early in the spring. The early spring sun and the low humidity of the late winter dries wood very effectively. Split wood dries much more quickly than unsplit.

3. Sun-dry wood under the open sky in the spring and summer. If possible, lay wood exposed on top of a hill. The warm sun and wind will dry it quickly.

4. Stack wood in a well-ventilated covered area in the late summer. The wood should be stacked so that a mouse can run between the pieces. It can be stacked just under the roof or some other covered area. However, it is best not to cover the wood stack with anything.

5. Store the wood indoors a few weeks or months before burning. Make sure that you don't bring in any moist pieces to avoid mold inside the house.[6]

For those of us who find wood chopping a little too harsh, there are kinder, gentler activities that can spur creativity and promote well-being. Once a week, my children gather things in the woods, go back to their day care, and make strange and wonderful things out of the gathered objects. This means intense activity in the forest for about two hours before returning indoors. Contrary to the expectation that they might be exhausted at the end of this, they have shining red cheeks and are charged with energy on returning. Gathering things outdoors is a fantastic spur to creative energy. One of their creations with day-care buddies was a gigantic "boat" made of a tree log, with all sorts of things pasted and loaded onto it. Children can so easily imagine what to do with the bits and pieces that they collect in the outdoors. If we use our imagination, so can we.

During all of the seasons, we try to have cut flowers or branches inside our home. Putting together a bouquet of delicate wild summer flowers is a lovely motivation for taking a long walk. You will want to walk the extra mile just to check out whether you can find a few more additions to your masterpiece. The bouquet in a vase on your coffee table will carry on the good feeling of having walked and picked them long after your walk is done.

The outdoor productive/creative opportunity offered to me by the autumn is the one that I find most exhilarating. The crisp autumn days reveal all of creation in its most glorious colors. In October our island pathways become covered with beautiful green-golden and orange-golden leaves. I thought that raking was a futile activity, since the ground seems covered once again as soon as you rake it and the leaves fall again each year. Then I noticed my Swedish mother-in-law racing out to rake at the first opportunity that the autumn offered her. Curious about what could be so tremendous about raking, I picked up a rake myself one autumn and began to scratch at the ground. Having raked up a high pile of leaves, I found myself addicted. The vigor of the autumn, which quickly infiltrates every cell of your body, is hard to resist. By the time I was done, there were four big piles, which had to be gathered together and removed. Then I found that leaves are a superb, cost-free cover for the flower beds during the winter. I also found that strung on a wire, they make an attractive seasonal front door decoration. Most importantly, I found that being out in the autumn and raking them was an activity that could, amazingly, inspire and challenge me.

Add Variety with Natural Rhythm

This raking story is one example of how you can add seasonal variety to your outdoor experiences, with very little need for organizing anything ex-

AUTUMN LEAVES FOR THE FRONT DOOR

Pick a dry, sunny autumn day to take a walk in your local park or forest. Take a basket or small bag with you. Fill with the nicest-looking, largest colorful fallen leaves that you can find. At home over a hot warm drink and a snack, string the leaves onto a thin wire and secure both ends of the wire together. Hang on a nail or hook on your front door. Each time that you walk into your house you will be reminded of that wonderful hour or day out in the autumn.

cept a rake, some appropriate clothing, and some time. Chopping and preparing wood is another one that will give you something new to do outdoors each season, if you have the opportunity and some equipment. While it is good to have a basic physical activity that you can do all year round, it might sometimes get a little dull and, as a result, you might stop putting the same sort of effort into it as in the past. In this way, your outdoor routine just won't have the same *umpf*.

Adding this variety is all about activating your very own deep-seated natural rhythm. What could you do that would make the most out of what this season has to offer? Here in the Nordic countries, I have found that people are very good at answering this question. And the answers do not always require complicated organization. Here is one of my favorite little "adding variety" stories:

> "Mamma, I don't want to stay here at day care, I want to be with you today," pleaded my little daughter with sad, basset-hound-like eyes. I gave her a big hug and told her that I would just be doing "boring work" today and that she would have much more fun with her friends at the day care. She was not bending, strong-willed as she is. "But, Jessie," said the day-care mistress, "what about all of those puddles that have just frozen outside in the playground that we can go and crack the surface of with our boots? Oooh! What fun that will be. You wouldn't want to miss that, would you?" The ship was for turning and my daughter voted for this irresistible early winter activity than for a day with me.

As in the case of the day-care mistress, it is all a question of tuning in to what the great outdoors can offer you today. If you have children, they can often help you to tune in, as I have already noted above. My son is good at enjoying the outdoors in all of the seasons, but it is the snow that he dreams of. As it begins to get cooler in the autumn, he is always on me: "When will the snow come, Mamma? Today? Tomorrow?" Like my son, I have found that people in Scandinavia dream of what they will do outdoors in the next season: my dentist dreams of skating; my electrician neighbor, of evenings out in his boat during the summers; my friends who live at the sea in Norway, of the days when they can start to take a morning dip. The variety offered by a completely new seasonal experience makes the outdoors always a place of expectation and adventure.

Recreating Outdoors, Nordic Style

Once you have made getting outdoors an integral part of your life, you will want more. You will long to try new things and open yourself up to new experiences. Whoever you are, whether Norwegian explorer or committed park walker, it is a part of your instinct, reawakened in the outdoors, of wanting to come close to the elements, to see whether you can master them, to see whether you can *become* like them. It is in these moments—sometimes thrilling, sometimes peaceful—that you feel at your best.

Again, young children are completely open to this experience. I remember visiting the southern coast of Norway, and watching my two-year-olds become enthralled by the wind blasting down our pathway to the seashore. They ran with arms in the air, tumbled in the grass, and squealed with laughter. They had *become* the wind, and were not to be controlled. How I would have loved to do the same thing! Inside I was longing to, but I didn't. Why not? I am an adult with years of conditioning: sturdy fences of maturity, there for a good purpose, but which I would like to build a gateway in, sometimes to allow me out into pure experience. This is not frivolous. Rather, it is deeply necessary, in order for life not to lose its shine.

In Scandinavia I found a place where this pure experience, called *Friluftsliv,* is not separate from regular life, but is regarded as a lifestyle. It is based on an appreciation of natural rhythm and the process that living with nature can set off. The whole idea of *Friluftsliv* in the Nordic countries carries with it the connotation of life quality. Sometimes it can lead to seeking an alternative lifestyle, but usually it coexists with the routines of work and domesticity that everyday people need to pursue. This means that at certain times, Anna X, who is otherwise a nurse, becomes a hiker, and that Lars Y, who is otherwise a bank clerk, becomes a fisherman.

Below, I introduce you to some of the different forms of *Friluftsliv* that I have experience of in greater detail: walking and hiking; boating, including sailing, kayaking, and canoeing; cross-country skiing; and cross-country skating. Other forms of *Friluftsliv,* such as swimming, hunting, and fishing, I will discuss later, while others such as biking and horseback riding I haven't quite got to, although my children have now got me on the way to learning more about them. This is a good thing, since Scandinavia is home to the longest organized biking route in the world (known as the Marguerit Route, in Denmark), and many parts of Scandinavia are true horse country, with Norway and Iceland offering the unique experience of riding on the sure-footed Icelandic ponies.

These ways of "being" can make a big difference in your life. If you are already involved in one or more of them, you will enjoy identifying with the experiences of people in Scandinavia recreating as you do in your own environment. If you are not, this is an opportunity for you to get a taste of what these specific ways of enjoying outdoor life can do for you.

As I have already intimated, getting involved in the activities discussed below is very much about learning and developing new skills. Here I would like to issue a caution: please, *please,* do seek information and/or training, where appropriate, before you start. Everything down to getting out with the wrong shoes on can unnecessarily discourage your original enthusiasm.

I was lucky to have a husband who was trained in the Swedish system, which regards learning to recreate outdoors as a necessary part of a child's education. His education has become mine, and he has many times shielded me from getting myself into serious trouble. Having this education makes all of the difference and will ensure that you learn to maximize the benefits of your experience safely. In Scandinavia there are many resources for learning about how to recreate outdoors. There are also very many resources that you can access for free or at low cost in America. I list them in the Resources section of this book. In some cases, where equipment is expensive and you are not ready to make a big investment, you can find secondhand or rental equipment at reasonable prices.

Gå på tur (Going Walkabout)

Norwegians have this deliciously understated way of saying that they are going for a long walk—often for days in the mountains hiking from one hut lodging to another. Indeed, they have very good reasons for making this a national pastime. Their landscape is a masterpiece of creation, with

America's stunning national parks and the information resources surrounding them are the way to go to experience an outdoor lifestyle in America. Visiting the National Park Service's Web site, one finds literally hundreds to choose from. The World Wide Web offers information on where the nearest national park is, whether close to your home or at a place you are visiting, what opportunities for recreating outdoors exist, and what types of programs there are for learning, both for adults and children. A word of warning: Some national parks have experienced increased security concerns, and you should check in with them about what precautions you can take before going on a longer trip. Still, there are parks that are more secure than they ever have been. See Resources for a few good sites.

mountains rising high above the water, and highland plateaus with lakes and low vegetation, where one can see for a long distance.

I learned a lot about the art of walking when I went to Norway. Our twins were only two years old, which meant that it was too early to go on very long hikes with them. Despite this and the challenging late October conditions, we managed to walk with them up on the Hardangervidda, Europe's largest highland plateau, and visited a museum where we found that H.M. Queen Sonja had donated one of her most precious belongings for display: her hiking boots. In this country, hiking is a fine culture, which, like other great culture, people never tire of. What is it that brings about the amazing feeling of happiness that one gets walking in nature?[7] asks the Queen in her 2002 book about her hiking experiences, the many legends and stories of the locations that she had passed or stopped at over the years, and the many associations devoted to upholding the special culture of the fjords.

During our trip to Norway, we walked with our friend Gunnar, who is a mystery unto the medical profession. When indoors, he notices the pain and stiffness in his back, and is thus reminded of his advanced years (in his eighties). Doctors who have looked at his back cannot fathom how he is still standing. As soon as he steps out for a walk, all of the visible stiffness vanishes. He becomes as lithe as a wild animal silently making its way through the forest. Gunnar's footsteps are so light that as you watch him walk on ahead of you, he seems to evaporate into his environment. He rarely returns from a walk empty-handed, usually coming home with a branch for putting in a vase, or mushrooms, berries, and whatever else can be found on the day. Walking and collecting things seems to relax something that is otherwise tensed indoors.

As we drove toward Gunnar and his wife Inni's mountain cabin for several days of walking around a highland plateau, I remember looking out through the sleet-spattered windowpane and being able to distinguish two well-outfitted figures making their way through the trees along the roadside. At that time, I wondered why they had chosen to be out in such rugged conditions.

These days, I walk in my forest on most days, in rain, sleet, snow, or sunshine. I understand now that it is all about having the right clothes, not the right weather. There is beauty in walking whatever the weather, a beauty that is always different, no matter how often I tread the same path.

This time of walking in the forest is my time of uni-tasking. We moth-

---

NO BAD WEATHER, ONLY BAD CLOTHES

This is an old Scandinavian saying, that has more truth to it than you might think. Even if the weather is warm and fine, going for an outdoor activity with the wrong clothes on can put an early stop to the pleasure. The classic "bad clothes" cold weather scenario is parents complaining that their children don't want to be outside in the snow because their last memory of being out in it is feet turning blue in snow-filled boots, and hands freezing in thin, wet gloves. You needn't purchase expensive designer items to have the right clothes, although many brands are coming up with excellent outdoor gear ideas. The key principles in dressing yourself well for the outdoors are flexibility (Can you move?), comfortable support (Do your shoes and other supports feel good?), temperature regulation (Are you too cold or too warm?), sun protection (Are you in danger of getting sun burned?), and visibility (Can you see where you are going?). See Resources for more information.

ers, by our nature, are multitaskers. But no matter how good we are at doing many things at the same time, we need that time of focusing down on doing only one thing for a chunk of time each day. This requires taking us out of our home and work environments. What better place to go than outside of both of those environments? This need for uni-tasking outside of environments craving us to fulfill many responsibilities is something that I believe everyone has. Going out walking is a great way to fulfill this need. It doesn't require special equipment or skill. You can focus on just putting one foot in front of the other and experiencing the beauty. Hiking for a number of days in a challenging environment does, of course, require certain types of equipment and skill, particularly if you camp outdoors, but most of it is still an activity that does not require coordinating a lot of equipment and skill at the same time.

If you are interested in maximizing the effect of your walk on your physical statistics you might try using a Finnish innovation, which has taken Scandinavia by storm during the past years. Nordic walking works

TAKING A LONG WALK IN SCANDINAVIA

In Scandinavia, mountain huts have been established along organized trails. These trails offer you a safe way to experience nature. Some of the trails form the northern portion of Europe-wide trails, where you can cross the borders into other European countries on foot. Historic trails are also being revived. You can now make your own pilgrimage by walking several of the paths that two of the Nordic saints, St. Birgitta and St. Olaf, tread during the Middle Ages. For instance, the cathedral of Nidaros at Trondheim in Norway has been the goal of pilgrims since 1030 when St. Olaf was killed in battle there. Mountain huts offer anyone basic overnight accommodation. These days it is often necessary to book in advance in order to secure a bed, food, and a filled thermos to start the next day's hiking. If you wish to take shorter hikes with your children, there are many opportunities for renting a cabin and taking day trips from there. See Resources on how to find them, to find the path that suits you, and what you need to walk it.

on the principle that using your arms as well as your legs vigorously while you walk results in greater fitness than ordinary brisk walking. According to estimates, you can increase calorie burning by an average of 15 percent. What I like about this form of exercise is that it does not require a lot of learning (although there is some technique you can pick up on when you buy your walking poles), it is quite natural to the body to walk along with the two poles, and thus it does not take your attention away from noticing your surroundings and even sharing thoughts with your friend or partner.

Boating

Ever since the Vikings created their masterful boat design in early medieval times, boating has been a great outdoor art in the Nordic countries. Viking longships were designed to make the most of the power that the elements, the water and the wind, could give them (and to operate well, independent of the elements, if they were unfavorable). These ships were so light that their weight was unprecedented. They were also streamlined and able to take the "punch" of the waves. Trials with reconstructed Viking ships during the twentieth century showed that they moved in a similar manner to powerboats, just skimming the surface of the water. No nonpowered oceangoing vessels built before, and few since, have been able to outclass the Viking ship model in terms of sea worthiness.[8]

Where the elements favored their journey, the Vikings were *one* with them. This close relationship with the forces of nature is something that almost every Scandinavian sailing devotee that I have met values higher than anything else about the experience. It is a relationship, which exercises you through a whole emotional spectrum from humility to mastery. This is what I have learned through my own short sailing experiences in Scandinavia and through the stories of Claes, a passionately devoted sailor.

For quite a number of Scandinavians, sailing is a necessity. According to my husband, to be forced to be ashore on a breezy, sunny summer day is like not really living. As soon as the ice has melted there is an urge to get the boat into the water and out to sea. A sailboat sounds like a luxury, but the vast majority of sailboats skimming the waters of the Nordic countries during the warming months, though decent seafaring vessels, are not at all luxurious. I have sometimes wondered how couples, foursomes, and six-somes have managed to fit into boats that look awfully small. It is a different kind of life—compact, handy, no clutter, only the necessities. Our close friend Benny, with whom we shared our sailboat, was never bothered about order on land, but became a stickler for it at sea.

My own experiences of sailing have been marred by the fact that I usually end up being what is known as the *ruffhäxa* (cabin witch). This means preparing endless sandwiches and other refreshments in the small kitchen below while everyone else is up on deck enjoying the sailing. An added dilemma I have about playing *ruffhäxa* is that I suffer seasickness when below deck. Claes has heroically offered to take on this role, although in the big boat I feel that we are all better off with him at the rudder.

Despite all of the tribulations that sailing with a young family entails, I must say that there are two things that I value about sailing. One is the sailing itself, which I have done myself in our small sailboat. The other is the chance to be together with the family (including our dog), where we are not all running off in different directions. In the Nordic countries sailing is a pastime that runs in families and is a part of family life. Claes recalls being taught to sail in a small boat called *Larella* by his father. Our twins will soon be coming into the age when they can begin to learn in *Larella II*. When we are out in our "big" boat together, we eat, talk, sing, help one another, sometimes work through arguments, and, most of all, feel a part of things that matter: our family and our natural world.

So far, I have mostly portrayed sailing as something that exercises our minds and emotions but not our bodies. It is also true that sailing can involve a lot of sitting, drinking, and eating. On the other hand, sports sailing involves sharpening your coordination, as well as stretching out your body and using muscles that you might not have known about before, in order to balance the sail. Sailing for longer periods of time involves stopping at different locations and swimming or exploring on land. Bringing along sturdy walking shoes is an important part of sailing for longer trips. Finally, out sailing, all of the cells of your body are supplied with plenty of oxygen, which gets all of your organs functioning better, and can be lacking in many of the environments where we spend most of our time.

SAILING IN THE NORDIC COUNTRIES

The Nordic countries offer sailing experiences that are unparalleled in the world. This is mainly due to a combination of geography (lots of water and is-lands), the laws of the land that allow everyone free access, and well-organized sailing facilities. The Resources section highlights guided and unguided sailing opportunities, of which there are a great number in Scandinavia. Sailing schools are also highlighted.

There are simpler and more accessible forms of nonpowered boating that are popular in Scandinavia. We have seen plenty of kayakers, canoeists, and rowers passing by our place. In the warmer season, people are often out for days, with everything they need attached in small watertight bun-dles. They are out for the experience of the elements, discovery, the unex-pected, and always the beauty. "The important thing is not how far we get, but to be able to be on, near and in the water," says one canoeist out for the summer with a young family.[9]

According to Magnus Fischer, who kayaked all the way around Scan-dinavia for seven months, paddling, or the journey that it involves, can change how you see your life. For the entire period, his only mode of trans-port was paddling, except when geography forced him to drag his kayak on wheels behind a bike or on foot. He reflected that nothing during the trip ever felt meaningless. The problems were concrete, with a clear rela-tionship between effort and result. Back home, Magnus found that he be-came frustrated with unclear goals at his place of work and quit after three months to pursue other projects. He concluded that his trip had high-lighted for him what he had been missing in his life at home, and that he would try to reorient his life to make up for it.[10]

While Magnus's story may be a little radical, there are aspects that are valuable to everyone. One of the greatest frustrations of modern life is the lack of connection between effort and gratification. Even people who earn plenty of money for their efforts still feel the frustration. Who has not at some point felt unrecognized, unappreciated, unloved? We all need to learn to make our need for this type of "result" clearly heard, something that we often forget, and that is effort. Being in the great outdoors can perhaps help us to achieve clearer perspectives on how to get this relationship working. Another Swede, Björn Thomasson, who has immersed his life in the art of paddling, says that to develop yourself as a paddler is to get away from constantly being focused on external goals. Herewith his reflections, which are of value to all of us, whether we are paddlers or not.

"ZEN AND THE ART OF PADDLING"

Developing as a paddler is a question of attitude. Those who pursue paddling as an ego trip are heading for a dead end. . . . It is not about physical strength. . . . Neither is it about mental motivation. [The ego paddler's] here and now lacks value. He/she wants to be "there" instead. . . . He/she has not understood that the goal is inside him/herself and that satisfaction is here and now.[11]

And, yes, paddling or rowing does involve quite a lot of physical exercise. My sister, who was visiting from the United States, discovered just what sort of a workout this could be when she came to see me on the island while I was pregnant with the twins. Claes was away and I had decided that I would like to plant a few spring flowers. For some reason unbeknownst to us, the motorboat would not start. Never one to give up the good fight, my sister decided to row. During the course of three hours, she rowed one pregnant woman across no small distance, and then back, *with* bags of soil and potted plants. There was sweat on her brow, despite the brisk spring weather, and she felt the exertion in her legs and arms for some time afterward. What she remembers most is the satisfaction.

Skiing

"Ski" is an ancient Norse word meaning a split piece of wood. Evidence of skiing exists as far back as four thousand years. Figurines on skis are featured in Bronze Age stone inscriptions found in Scandinavia. Olaus Magnus Gothus, a Swedish bishop writing about the ancient north while in exile

GREENLAND PADDLING

The indigenous peoples of the Scandinavian Arctic, the Inuit, have over hundreds of years developed the simplest-looking and yet most sophisticated of paddles and kayaks. One theory is that they were influenced by the Vikings to develop their streamlined, thin paddles. Greenland kayaks glide along extremely quietly in the water, provide minimal resistance to the wind and require relatively low paddling effort. The Aleut of Alaska and Canada have developed similarly elegant and seamless vessels. See Resources for experiences in Greenland kayaks.

in Rome during the sixteenth century, writes very precisely about the skill of the Nordic peoples on skis, different from those we think of today: one ski shorter than the other, to facilitate agility, and both lined on the bottom with reindeer calf fur (which behaved like hedgehog needles) as a brake to avoid sliding backward down steep inclines.[12]

Skiing was a requirement for both hunting and communication in this part of the world for most of human history. Only one hundred years ago, skiing was the most effective means of getting around during the winter. The Samis of Northern Scandinavia were particularly noted for their amazing talent and speed on skis. An 1884 recording of the events around a 220-km (137-mile) race between Jokkmokk and Kvikkjokk in the very north of Sweden highlighted the following: On the day before the competition, several of the participants are said to have skied 180 km (123 miles), each way, to buy new skis. Many skied around 100 km (62 miles) just in order to participate in the competition. A Sami won the race in twenty-one hours.[13] The Samis are today noted, among other things, for many of their healthful traditions. Cross-country skiing is obviously one of them.

In Sweden, this sport holds the historical status of having led to the creation of the state, and is commemorated each year with the Vasaloppet, or Vasa Race, the largest cross-country skiing marathon in the world. Anyone is welcome to participate (see Resources). A snippet of interesting background to the Vasa Race is that it is held in commemoration of the chase on skis in 1520 by the men of Dalarna to bring Gustav Eriksson (later on known as Gustav Vasa) back to Sweden to unify the country. Eriksson had earlier tried to instigate a revolt against the Danish King Christian II, who had murdered his father, among other Swedish nobles, in a great blood-bath at the palace in Stockholm, and imprisoned his mother and sisters. Having failed to rally supporters in Dalarna, he set off for Norway in snowshoes, since he was apparently unable to ski. The men of Dalarna re-considered and quickly caught up with him on their "split pieces of wood." Under Gustav Vasa, Sweden became an imperial power.[14]

I too had lived south of Dalarna all of my life, and had never fastened a pair of cross-country skis onto my feet. I had strapped my ankles and feet into downhill boots before, but never got much past the ungraceful snow-plow. With this in mind, I was not eager to show my husband-to-be, who naturally was a slalom skiing ace, my "style."

Then, one day, a few years on, when the island and our iced-over lake were covered in a thick sheet of snow, I decided that it was time to try out the cross-country skis that he had bought me just after we got married. How soft the boots were. How easy they were to click on and off the nar-row skis. I stuck to the flat lake at first to practice the technique, which was not difficult to learn. At some point, I gathered my courage and got onto one of the many paths arranged for cross-country skiing on the neighbor-ing island. There were steep uphills and downhills. My dog, Lucy, looked at me skeptically each time I stood atop a high hill and told her to get out of the way. And again, each time she watched me sliding backward down a steep hill. Gradually, by watching others and by practicing, I developed the skills. In a northern ski resort, I watched a very old man "jog" up a steep hill with his skis forming V shapes in the snow. Aha! That was how to do it without sliding backward.

Cross-country skiing farther north, I encountered some of the most glorious environments. Spruces blanketed with snow sparkled in the sun-shine along the endless, uncrowded winding paths. Scandinavia undoubt-edly offers the world's most outstanding and extensive cross-country skiing conditions. This is not to downgrade its downhill resorts, which are, in my view, particularly good for young families, learners, and people who like to enjoy stunning alpine environments without having to stand in line for an hour to get up the lifts and see them.

The distinction between downhill and cross-country skiing as sport is little more than 140 years old. Until then, skiing was just a means of getting around. However, despite some resistance, the separation of skiing types and the emergence of the two sports began to take place. Telemark in Norway is regarded as the home of modern downhill skiing due to a poor farmer's son called Sondre Nordheim, who, during the 1860s, perfected some clever skiing techniques and a modern form of binding now known as Telemark binding. Nordheim's binding was made of thin birch root and was the first device to provide proper lateral control of the skis. It comes as no small wonder that these foundations of modern skiing emerged from a place where, according to one contemporary of Nordheim:

> It was a terrible disgrace to take a tumble. . . . Anyone who had too many falls couldn't dance with the girls on Sunday evening, and if he asked them, they just laughed.[15]

When Norwegians immigrated to the United States during the nineteenth century, they took their skis with them and introduced the sport to many parts of America. Today the American Birkebeiner, lovingly known as "the Birkie," is North America's largest cross-country skiing marathon. The Birkie takes its lead from the Norwegian Birkebeiner, which is held each year in commemoration of the Birkebeiner (birch leg) skiiers who, by virtue of swift skiing, saved the two-year-old Prince Håkon from pursuers in 1206.

My husband is a modern downhill enthusiast and not as crazy about cross-country skiing as I am. Too much effort, he says. But for fitness enthusiasts, this is precisely the point. Cross-country skiing is the best "total" sport, exercising the largest number of muscles and expending the most calories. Cross-country skiing is the best workout you can get for good heart condition. Nordic walking (described previously) is developed from the idea of cross-country skiing and has similar physical effects.

Cross-country skiing in environments like those to be found in the

If you are one for a challenge, you can participate in a guided skiing event, which is not a race, across Finland from the Russian border to the Swedish border. The trip is 444 km (275 miles) long and takes place on three occasions during March. See the Resources section of this book.

Nordic countries is the ultimate getaway, even if you only do it for an hour or two. Gliding gently through white takes us far away from lives that are sometimes choppy and gray. I once asked Gunnar from Norway what he did when his family business collapsed. "I skied more," he said.

Skating

If cross-country skiing is a getaway, tour skating is pure fantasy. On our island, places that the water once divided us from become suddenly accessible without a boat. On one day, there might be a thin cover of snow on the ice. The winter sun shines dimly through an even gray cloud cover, so that the snow looks like an infinite number of diamonds strewn across the vast expanse. When the wind blows lightly, the loose top-snow sizzles across the surface, and the diamonds rush ahead of us, with new ones appearing under our feet. There is evidence of a few others who have experienced this diamond mine: a skater who has been out with his dog, someone who has bicycled across with special tires, a fox seeking good hunting ground. We had not seen them, but the tracks in the snow were evidence that they had been there before us. On another day the ice is a mirror. The sky is a deep blue and the sun shines intensely. The ice deep below is cracking here and there, and the sound is like a laser in a *Star Wars* movie. We can still skate safely. The nights have been very cold.

The Romans recorded seeing people on skates in the far north in the second century A.D. Skates made of horse and cow bones have been common finds in excavations of Viking settlements, and it is known that people also used a pole to propel themselves forward, just as people do today.

As far as we know, skating was not a sport in these times. Like skiing, it was a practical means of transport.

My introduction to long-distance, or tour, skating was complicated by the fact that I had a twin pram along with me. I had skated with regular skates at the age of eight in Germany; "long" skates have much longer blades. However, at that time my focus was mostly on the mouthwatering fresh, thick hot fries wrapped in newspaper and served with mayonnaise for sale at the ice-skating rink. My father had been a college ice hockey player, and I remember "flying" rather than skating around the rink as he grabbed my hand and pulled me with him. My eyes were on the fries.

I ran my finger along the long, thin, knifelike skates and wondered how the mothers that I saw out on the thickly frozen waters in central Stockholm managed to skate along in a relaxed fashion pushing prams. I decided that if they could do it, then I could do it. I parked my sleeping children safely at the lake's edge in this central Stockholm park, and slipped on the skates. The first attempt was fitful, my eight-year-old short-skate technique somehow coming to the fore. Then I saw a sleek figure moving in a straight, unbroken trajectory on the other side of the lake: bent forward, with one hand clasping the wrist of the other and relaxed on the small of his back, and legs pushing out right, long glide, and then left with each skate. His upper body barely moved. He took the corners crossing one skate over the other. Slowly, slowly. Nothing frenetic about it. Watching him, I realized that long skating was all in the legs and a great workout for all of those fleshy bits that many women bemoan.

Perhaps fortunately, I never managed to push my twin "limo" around that skating track. Today I could probably manage, but now my own children are out on skates themselves. They learned at the age of four on the thick ice that forms all around our island. I always find it surprising that humans can master balancing themselves on two thin blades so quickly. For myself, I take longer trips around our area and revel in the feeling of beating the clock as I reach places that would otherwise take hours to get to by car. Sitting on a rock amid the ice, eating a sandwich and sipping a hot cup of tea, while resting my legs, which feel like spaghetti after a couple of hours of skating, time evaporates. I take the habitual look at my wrist-watch, but don't register the time.

Long skating is not one of those things you can plan too far in advance. There is the right moment for it, when the ice is thick enough, clear of snow, a cold night has passed, hardening the surface, the wind is mild and the sun shines. Like truffles in a forest, those great skating days are the most difficult to come by, but the most luscious to experience. My skates are always there ready, down in the boat shed at the water's edge, patiently waiting for those days.

If you want to try this, you need to learn about ice or at least go with someone who knows something about ice. I have not yet fallen through— I say, thanking my ice angel—but know a few people who have. You need to learn to test the ice for thickness, to be aware that there can be potholes in the ice, to know where ice is likely to be thin, and to take safety precautions, such as bringing along ice picks, rope, and spare clothes wrapped in a waterproof bag. Long skating demands awareness of the way nature behaves.

Reaching for the Essence of Existence

A Swedish woman, Efva, dances on the ice. She rehearses in a large container on a polar expedition ship carrying mostly scientists to the Arctic. I picture her poised on the tip of one ballet shoe on the blue-white Arctic ice, smoothing and melting briefly in the spots where she dances. There are

TOUR SKATING LIKE NOWHERE ELSE

Arguably the best tour skating in the world is to be found around the Stockholm area, with its extensive lake system and the Baltic archipelago. Not surprisingly, Scandinavia's largest and oldest skating association is the Stockholm Ice Skate Sailing Association, or SSSK (thus named since skating holding a sail was once the most popular way of enjoying this sport). It has an English language Web site and can tell you many important things that you need to know about trying out this sport. See Resources.

polar bears roaming in the distance, and it is minus 25°C (−13°F). There is a striking drama in this scene: a fragile human being in the enormity of this natural environment, finding inspiration, reaching for her essence, and expressing the beauty that she finds there through her dance. When we come into the outdoors, we can all be figurative dancers on the ice, feeling the vigor and reconciling its greatness with the essence of ourselves, and what it is to be alive.

THREE

The Importance of Being Green

In Norse mythology, people emerged from plants. As the gods Oden, Vile, and Ve wandered along the seacoast admiring the world that they had created, they noticed two pieces of driftwood that had been washed up on the shore. Oden noticed how the shadows of his brothers, which had fallen onto the two pieces of driftwood, were independently moving. He followed the piece of wood that had drifted farthest up onto the shore. It was a piece of ancient elm. He put his lips to the wood and exhaled his godly breath onto it. The elm's bark began to split and then roll together until a woman emerged. She was the first woman, called Embla after the tree from whence she came. Oden breathed onto the second piece of wood, the wood of an ash. Out of this piece, in the same manner as for the woman, emerged Ask, the first man.[1]

There is a long-standing tradition in Scandinavia that plants were made to help us. Just as they were our origin in the Beginning, so they can become a source for life once again. This chapter explains this tradition and draws on my experience of watching people live with plants in this part of the world. I tell you why living here has drawn my attention to the extraordinary and fantastic world of plants and gardening. I explain why it is important for our well-being to develop our relationship to plants. I also highlight some traditional Nordic uses of plants, some of which might also be found where you are.

Why Notice Plants?

Carl Linnaeus (1707–1778), a Swede who established the scientific system for naming plants in use all over the world today, once said that "all was made for the good of humankind." He meant that nature, particularly in the form of plants, was made to serve people. This is a bold idea in a part of the world where most plants vanish from sight or become seemingly lifeless for a part of the year. Most people in Linnaeus's time saw nature as a harsh and stunning god. Fortunately for all of us, he saw things differently.

Linnaeus undertook four major journeys in his lifetime to explore the flora and fauna of his native Sweden. Such journeys were dangerous and uncomfortable during the eighteenth century. Still, Linnaeus saw the plant world as a blessing to people from their Creator.

Linnaeus's keen interest was certainly his own, but also came from a tradition of extraordinary commitment to organizing the plant world into a comprehensible system. In 1741, he became professor of medicine at one of the world's oldest universities, Uppsala (founded 1477). Linnaeus's predecessor there, Olof Rudbeck, the Elder (1630–1702), decided one day while enjoying his own garden, which had become one of the most admired in seventeenth-century Europe, that he would create a monumental volume, illustrating and classifying all of the plants of the earth (naturally centered on Sweden, from his point of view). Rudbeck was determined to bring some sort of final order to all of the competing systems of plant classification, which existed in the time before Linnaeus. For more than thirty years, he observed, drew, and classified. No plant was too small or insignificant. The work was to be called *Campus Elysii,* a Greco-Roman name meaning "the heavenly meadows of paradise." In 1702, the entire work was reduced to ash in a terrible fire that ravaged all of Uppsala. A few of the burnt stubs of the plants from Rudbeck's garden have been preserved by the English Linné Society, and people who have seen them close up say that they still smell of smoke. Rudbeck died within a few months of the destruction of his life's work. Six thousand color drawings, which were to be used for luxury copies of the book, have survived. Although Rudbeck may have died feeling that he had failed, ultimately in his inspiration to Linnaeus his work lived on.

A Life-Nurturing Source

On the island, I find myself possessed by the urge to photograph many plants, for no other reason than that I am moved by their beauty and want to record it for myself. I can understand Rudbeck's motivation, but perhaps not his persistence. In this way, I have come to appreciate the point of view inherent in this Nordic tradition. It has been quite a journey. When I first came to this place in the spring years ago, plants were a part of a background blur that I didn't think much about. The shrubs ought to be tamed a little, I thought, but that was the short and the long of my erudite thoughts on the things that grew around me.

Gradually, my outlook began to change. What had previously been background brush began to come into focus. I noticed that even on this wild, mostly uncultivated stony, sandy place there were many colors, shapes, and textures popping out of the soil. I attended courses. I reopened the herb and medicinal plant books that my more than ninety-year-old German grandmother had once given me as a child.

More than anything else, what struck me once I focused in on this fascinating background was that the things that I needed grew around me. One discovery that struck me more than any other was that two of the most prominent plants growing within view of my study window were once used for treating colds and bronchial problems. I had a history of bronchitis and pneumonia. This was an extremely satisfying discovery for me. Why? If ever I got pneumonia again, I would not rely on these plants to save me.

I opened my old herb and medicinal plant books, and discovered that there were plants growing all around that were fever reducing, pain re-

KNOWING YOUR PLANT WORLD

If you don't have one, invest in a plant and herb lexicon that explains the flora of your environment. If you already have one or two, bring them out of the depths of your library and keep them somewhere handy, so that you remember to check out what you have seen. Reading about the history of the plants in your area and learning about what they were once or are now used for will make a noticeable difference to your outlook on your world! Internet sources of this type of information are improving rapidly. See Resources.

lieving, disinfecting, blood stemming, and stress reducing, among other things. A new window on life had opened up! Not because I wanted suddenly to trade in modern medicine for traditional, but because I sensed that the influence of plants on my well-being was more than the chemical analysis of their properties. Plants had the power to draw me into feeling part of an entity which cared. In this state of mind, I was sure that the very sight of these plants boosted my immunity. It turns out that I was right. Research tells us that there is great value in seeing our world as a mainly nurturing rather than as a mainly dangerous place. This does not mean having an unrealistic view of the world; rather, it means venturing to see the glass half full rather than half empty.

I see myself as part of a gigantic cyclical process of giving and receiving on this island. Neither the plants nor I are forced to it. We do it anyway. They choose to grow out in front of my window, and I choose to receive their green gifts when I look at them or prepare some tea from their leaves or flowers. Giving and receiving, learning to appreciate the subtle and the intimate. Important things that we need continuously to relearn in life to be well.

Training Your Consciousness

While he was able to appreciate the overall picture, Linnaeus was fascinated with the detail. His attention to it revealed the similarities and differences

MAKING TEA FROM YOUR OWN HERBS AND
MEDICINAL PLANTS

Making tea is a simple and rewarding way to enjoy the green gifts of your plant world. Your plant and herb lexicon should highlight what is safe and good to use for internal consumption. This is important, since some plants can be toxic and dangerous for you to consume internally. Pick young leaves and flowers in a clean area (not by the roadside, where plants are affected by car fumes). Take a tablespoon full of the leaves and/or flowers in a teacup and pour hot water over. Leave for 5 to 8 minutes. Enjoy. If you want to save the leaves and flowers for future use, lay them out on a sheet of parchment paper in a dark, dry place for a few weeks. Alternatively, you can dry them in the oven at 212°F or 100° C.

between various groups of plants and thus how they could be systematically classified. I found that attention to the detail of my island plant world trained my consciousness in noticing the detail, revealing subtle linkages and bringing unexpected answers. One year, Saint-John's-wort, an attractive and unmistakable herb with branches of small, yellow flowers, decided to spread itself all around our place. I had counted just a few of these plants on our property during the previous year. Now they were spreading around and popping up all over the place. I went back to my reference books to remind myself of exactly what the new member of our island plant team was good for. Many things, it turned out, due to the presence of a handy little substance called hypericin. Among other things, I found that hypericin is useful for the treatment of certain types of chest infections, since it is antiviral, and is also useful for treating mild depression. During the past months I had been badly affected by viral lung infections, as well as by the serious lung illness of a person I knew. One worry about what could happen to me begot several worries, and so the process went on. I am sure that my inability to get rid of this illness had partly to do with an immune system that was rock bottom as a result of constant worry. The little yellow flowers linked the two problems in my mind and made me resolve to chin up and look forward. I had discovered how training our consciousness to attend to the detail could teach us about the linkages in life—why certain things have happened to us and what we can do about them.

Uses of Nordic Plants

Charged by my new plant knowledge, I wanted to learn how to use some of what grew around me in practice. During this process, I discovered a number of interesting things about the uses of plants in this part of the world: that there is a long Nordic tradition of documenting the uses of plants; that there are unique Nordic plants with unique uses; and that trees have played a special role in the mythology and the reality of good health and healing.

Documenting Uses

One of the things that I discovered was that Scandinavians have been exceptionally good at documenting how people have traditionally used plants and animals for food, medicine, and raw materials, as well as how they have played a role in customs, beliefs, and rituals. The oldest, most comprehensive, and well-known work that takes on the ethnobiology of the Nordic region as one of its tasks is Olaus Magnus's (1490–1557) *History of the Nordic Peoples* (1555). Amid all of the romanticizing about his Nordic homeland and its heroic past, many interesting facts can be learned about the way people used their plant and animal resources.

The pioneering botanists of the eighteenth century received support for their work from the State, which hoped to make savings on imports by developing an indigenous industry of healing plants. In Sweden, Linnaeus, the dominant Scandinavian power of that time, played a leading role in establishing this industry. In the process, he also recorded a great deal about the uses of natural resources by the local populations he visited during his journeys. In his diaries of travel in Scandinavia, he particularly admired the Lapps for their economical ways of living from the land and became increasingly critical of complicated city life.

WILD STRAWBERRY LEAF TEA

The national Swedish pride and desire to be a self-sufficient country is evident in this 1896 recipe for wild strawberry leaf tea in a publication called *Hälsovännen,* or Health Friend:

Why import tea from faraway China when our indigenous wild strawberry leaf makes an outstanding drink and a far more healthful tea than the expensive, usually unauthentic, nerve- and vascular-irritating oriental substance of pleasure? If you want to prepare tea of wild strawberry leaves, first collect wild strawberry plants in June and July, preferably those which grow in sunny, mountainous areas, and be sure that the plants are healthy, dry, and not eaten by worms. Air-dry the leaves in the shade, turning them often, so that they do not rot. After drying, the leaves should not be rinsed, since a considerable amount of their strength can be lost. . . . Back to nature![2]

Speaking with Kerstin, a woman who is devoting her life to preserving Nordic herbal traditions, I found that there are separate recorded Danish, Finnish, Icelandic, Norwegian, and Swedish traditions for using local herbs and medicinal plants, which overlap. I went to the library and checked out what I could find and what the librarian could order in. I ended up with a pile of books high as my windowsill in three of the five different languages.

The traditions that lay on my study floor and in the volumes at the Finnish and Icelandic libraries that I could not read are the mixed outcome of different influences. Some of it was local knowledge—the knowledge of old wives and the indigenous population of the North. But a very large part of it came from the work of monks from Middle Europe (present-day Germany), who had developed a science of working with herbs and medicinal plants that they passed on through their monasteries in Scandinavia. Kerstin had herself put a tremendous amount of effort into preserving the legacy of Rector J. Henriksson, who had recorded many of the traditional uses of plants in the north at the end of the nineteenth century (see Resources).

Original Uses of Nordic Medicinal Plants and Herbs

When I asked Scandinavians about their herbal and medicinal plant traditions, I usually drew a blank, aside from the precious few loners like Kerstin. As I persisted, I was surprised to find just how many interesting and unique traditions there were.

The resurgence of northern Scandinavian Sami culture has brought with it interest in the rich traditions of these indigenous peoples for using plants. Over a very long period of time, they have used about forty wild Arctic medicinal plants. Many of these have been shown by modern science to have real medicinal value.

One of the plants used extensively by the Sami and now being farmed and manufactured in the Nordic countries for its health-giving benefits (particularly its strong antibacterial effects for fighting coughs and sore throat) is *Angelica archangelica*. This tall and hardy plant has a charming story. During the fifteenth century, the monks who had come to spread Christianity in Scandinavia discovered a magical plant that had been sung about in the Icelandic and Norse sagas, and which was already being cultivated in groves in Norway. The monks said that it had been brought down to earth by the angels since its root was said to be useful as a treatment for the plague. Hence its name. Angelica is unique to the north, and the monks arranged for it to be exported throughout Europe.

Angelica is one of the active ingredients in the famous Swedish bitters, which relies on the power of a number of bitter herbs to aid digestion. Bit-

REDISCOVERING SAMI WISDOM

Tours to rediscover Arctic herbs and their uses are now becoming available in northern Scandinavia. Byaliv, meaning Village Life, is a village near the Swedish border to Finland in the Torne Valley, which has organized itself to provide such tours as well as an insight into the other healthful traditions of northern Scandinavia. Byaliv offers an unsurpassed sauna experience in which small bowls of älggräs, *or meadowsweet water, are provided for the feet. Meadowsweet is known among the Sami as being useful in combination with "sweat therapy" for bringing out toxins and preventing colds.*

ter flavors stimulate digestion and are needed in our diets, which these days are increasingly devoid of them. Maria Treben, an Austrian, made this recipe famous, topping Germany's best-seller list for years with her book *Health Through God's Pharmacy* (1980). The book is most famous for its Swedish bitters recipe, which Treben found among the writings of a Swedish physician called Dr. Samst, who had died in a riding accident at the age of 104. According to Treben, Samst's parents and grandparents all reached a similarly ancient age, which she attributed to the regular consumption of Swedish bitters. In Sweden the recipe can be purchased in the form of Svenska Droppar, or Swedish Drops (see Resources for where you can purchase this preparation).

Similar to angelica, Rosenrot, sometimes called Arctic Root, has been used in Scandinavia for centuries as a general strengthener. Modern research has shown that this amazing plant can actually help to prevent fatigue, stress, and the damaging effects of oxygen deprivation. Due to its antioxidant effect, it is regarded as a means of boosting the immune system and protecting against certain forms of cancer, although women with a history or family background of breast and uterine cancer should avoid it.

In Iceland, the tradition of *grasalækning,* or "grass medicine," has been preserved by one family that has dominated Icelandic herbal medicine for four hundred years. The unique natural environment around glaciers and the long summer daylight hours give rise to many different types of unusual and, according to Icelanders, exceptionally powerful, healing plants. In contrast to many other traditions of folk medicine, Icelanders have long had a strong sense of practicality rather than supernatural interest about why certain herbs work.

DITCHING THE ALCOHOL HABIT

Angelica is known, among other things, for its ability to dampen our desire for alcohol. So, if you are feeling like you are having trouble taking a break from your regular alcohol consumption, pick up some angelica from your local herbalist and make sure to check on correct doses. It could help you to ditch something that you don't want as habit but as pleasure.

The Power of Trees

In Norse mythology, trees were not only the origin of man and woman, they also saved man and woman from extinction. After the mythological end of the old world of the original gods, called Ragnarök, there are almost no survivors. Almost all living things have been decimated. Those who survive hide in Yggdrasil, the World Tree, and wait until the terror ends. Two humans, Liv and Livtraser (Life and She-Who-Grasps-Life), survive by taking refuge in the Tree, and eventually become the first couple who repopulate the new and kinder world with humans. Trees give life to humans and save those who grasp life from extinction.

It is not difficult to understand why trees were considered to have such extraordinary power in most of the Nordic countries. Forests cover most of the surface area of this part of the world (save Iceland) and occupy a particularly special place in the culture. Wood is the material of people's living structures and spaces; as the main ingredient of fire it saved people from freezing in harsh winters, and it fueled Swedish industry and that country's rise to becoming a great power during the seventeenth century.

Here on our island, we still have an original or ancient forest. These forests have become fewer with the onward progression of the forestry industry, which has planted new forests with an even appearance. In our forest, the trees are gnarled and some have died, often with many arms chaotically projecting out this way and that. The spiderwebs grow in between these arms, sometimes across my path in between one tree and another. I can feel the webs breaking as I walk through them. A dewdrop slides from one tree to another along the thin thread of a half-broken web, as though the trees are sending messages between them. The trees are alive. In the folk mythology of the Nordic countries, wise people can hear these messages, hear the trees breathing.

I reach a clearing on the southern tip of our island, where the foundation of a seventeenth-century seafarer's inn can be traced under the grass. How daunting the forest must have looked from the window of this small inn during the dark night. No wonder that it was thought to be full of trolls, gnomes, and other creatures. Forces of both good and evil. At times when I leave the path, and walk across the moss, which sinks down like a cushion under my feet, I imagine that I must be stepping on countless little gnome homes that feature in the children's stories of Scandinavia.[3] I make an effort to walk lightly.

Scandinavians have always believed trees to be powerful and that people who sensed and respected this power could be protected from illness, heal, and be healed. From the tree cults of the Bronze Age well into the twentieth century, people in Scandinavia believed in the healing magic of trees. In Danish graves from the Bronze Age, small "first aid" bags for the afterlife have been found buried with the dead. These contained, among other things, bits of rowan and ash wood. Into the 1940s and 1950s, children in the Swedish countryside continued to be treated for certain illnesses by being drawn through trees that were shaped so that a child could safely be passed through from one adult to another.

Trees continue to have power in Scandinavian culture. Now it is of a kinder, gentler power than in the past. The forest has become a safer place for people, with the wolves largely gone. Today, many Scandinavians go forest walking when they need to recharge. What is it about connecting to a tree that gives a person new energy? I have asked the question many a time to bewildered Scandinavians, who take this energy-giving source for granted. Still, there are plenty of people in this part of the world who have thought about it. For many people the trees are about the innocence and endless creativity of childhood.

In Finnish mythology, the World Tree was called Mesitammi, or honey oak. This tree had honey on its branches, mead under its bark, salve for wounds, and healing water for pains.[4] Many trees have been and continue to be prized in Scandinavia for their healing and general wellness-promoting properties, which are quite real. Here are five of these trees, which are commonly found throughout the Northern Hemisphere, and some interesting and simple ways to benefit from them.

BIRCH

The birch is a versatile tree. Its leaves are rich in vitamin C, which is the reason that people sometimes ate them in the past. The tea of newly sprouted birch, which has a fresh and nonbitter taste, has a cleansing effect on the bladder, liver, and stomach.

BIRCH LEAF TEA

An old and simple Scandinavian recipe: Pour some boiled water over a tablespoon of newly sprouted birch leaves in a mug. Leave to infuse for ten minutes. Drink and enjoy.

The extract of birch leaves has a delicious, smooth smell. It makes a sublime steam, when mixed in with water and thrown onto the hot stones in a sauna (see Resources for where you can purchase it—also see the section in Chapter 4 on sauna about how to make your own forest leaf infusion).

Since Viking times, the sap of birch has been regarded as a healthful drink. It is an almost-clear, slightly sweet, and mildly flavored liquid that is rich in many minerals and contains eight different types of natural sugars, amino acids, and antioxidants. Ongoing research in Sweden and elsewhere suggests that birch sugar may be valuable in the fight against certain types of serious illness due to the presence of betulinic acid, which may have antitumor and anti-inflammatory properties.[5]

During the few weeks in the spring when the temperature has risen to above 8°C (46°F) and the leaves have not yet emerged, the sap begins to rise. A large and healthy birch can yield fifteen to twenty liters (four to five gallons) of sap per day. Our neighbor reports lopping off a large branch and the sap freezing in a fountainlike mold overnight when the temperatures dropped. Tapped birch were once known in Scandinavia as the "poor man's cow."

Since birch leaves contain high concentrations of saponins, natural substances that function as a mild soap, they are useful for cleaning the body and hair.

PINE

The pine is another versatile and historically important tree in Scandinavia. In eighteenth-century Finland, the inner bark of the pine assumed national importance. *Petu,* or pine bark meal, was regarded as being a finer

BIRCH WATER FOR CLEANSING

Try making a "cleansing water" by shaking some fresh birch leaves in a container or plastic bag with clean water. You need roughly twice the amount of water as birch leaves. You can use the resulting "soapy" water to wash everything from your hair to your stockings! Extract of birch is sold as hair tonic for nourishing the scalp and for treating oily hair. See Resources.

ingredient for baking than regular flour. A *petu* factory continued production in Kajaani, Finland, until 1918. When Sweden, which dominated Finland until the nineteenth century, tried to put an end to the use of *petu,* Finns sharply resisted. One can understand the Finns' anger, since most of the Swedish peasantry (most of the population) regularly used pine bark for baking themselves. In the journal from one of his expeditions in Sweden during the early part of the eighteenth century, Linnaeus notes considerable tracts of land with debarked pine. National symbolism aside, the inner bark of pine has historically been a lifesaver in Scandinavia. Apart from feeding most of the landed peasantry, it was critical to the survival of pioneering settlers of the north.

The pine has had important uses in healing, relaxation, and cleansing. It has been a vital disinfectant and source of vitamin C for the Sami. They drink a decoct of pine needles against urinary tract infections and to combat vitamin C deficiency. The decoct yields a steam useful for the soothing of nonasthma respiratory problems. If you have any pine trees around your house, you can try the recipe.

PINE DECOCT

1 quart (1 liter) water

2½ cups (6 dl) fresh green pine needles (have some gardening gloves handy to remove them from their branches) or essential oil of pine

Bring the water to boil. Add pine needles and simmer in a closed pot for 25 minutes. Pull back your hair. Form a "tent" over your head and the bowl with a towel and inhale the steam at a comfortable distance from the pot. Continue for as long as feels comfortable, but not for more than 10 minutes at a time. When finished, lie down and relax for a few minutes. Allow yourself to cool down. Don't try this if you have very sensitive skin or if you are asthmatic. If for drinking, pour the liquid through a sieve to remove the pine needles and drink when a comfortable temperature. If you don't have any pine trees around, you can add 15–20 drops of essential oil of pine to the water for inhaling. Don't drink in this form.

Pine-needle bath is an old Swedish folk remedy still available at some health resorts in Scandinavia. It is particularly useful for increasing blood circulation in the skin and easing muscular soreness (see Chapter 4 under Water Therapy).

Pine oil has also made it possible for many Scandinavians to clean their homes ecologically. *Såpa,* the Swedish term for liquid soap made from pine oil, is a soft, almondy smelling liquid that is an excellent standard cleaner when mixed with warm water. It is a godsend here to us on our island, where we have to think carefully each time we dispose of anything, including waste water. We clean everything, including our clothes in *såpa* (see Resources for obtaining *såpa* in America).

Elder

In Norwegian folk wisdom, each home should have an elder tree nearby. Its berries, leaves, and flowers were regarded as a first-aid kit for the home. It was also considered holy, since the goddess Freja was said to dwell in the elder tree. The tea of elder flower is useful as a remedy for common colds, helping you to sweat them out and to relax. Norwegian folk wisdom would approve of our house, since we happen to have an elder tree just outside of it. I have experimented with making a cooling summer drink with the flowers. Great for soothing thirst!

ELDERFLOWER COOLER

20–25 heads of elderflower

6½ cups (1.5 liters) boiling water

2.2 pounds (1 kg) sugar

1 lemon

3½ tablespoons (50 g) cream of tartar

Rinse off 20–25 heads of elderflower and place in a pot. Pour boiling water over the flowers and add sugar. Stir until the sugar dissolves. Rinse the lemon, slice it, and add to the pot. Mix cream of tartar with a little warm water and mix into the pot. Cover the pot and allow it to stand in a cool place for 4–5 days. Stir a couple of times each day. Run the contents of the pot through a sieve and pour the remaining liquid into sealable bottles and store in a cool place. Drink within a week of bottling. For longer keeping, you can also freeze the liquid in cubes. To prepare a cooler, dilute some of the frozen or stored elder flower mixture with water. It will quench your thirst on a hot day. While there is a lot of sugar in the total recipe, remember that you only use small quantities of the concentrate and can dilute it so that your drink has just a hint of sweetness in it.

Note: Be careful to identify the right type of elder: *Sambucus nigra*. There are certain types of plants in the same plant family whose berries are poisonous, so be sure of what you are picking.

JUNIPER

Juniper trees love this stony island. During walks I check the "female" trees, which have berries that I use for spicing food and other household uses. Many of the berries are still green, and I will have to wait another year for them to be ripe. Picking them is not a job for the impatient, hidden as they are among small pine needles. I chew on a small, ripe berry, which has a mild, slightly sweet, yet distinct conifer forest taste. Delicious.

In days gone by, people with infectious diseases bathed in juniper water,

An old recipe for benefiting from the strong antiseptic qualities of the juniper tree is to gently boil together bark, berries, and wood chips. This rich liquid kills bacteria and has a pleasant, fresh smell, which can be used for cleaning the body, the hair, and the home all in one go.

and used it to disinfect buckets in which milk would stand until the cream floated to the top and could be separated out for making butter. To simplify things, you could just buy a small bottle of essence of juniper from your natural health store and add a few drops to your soapy bucket before cleaning off surfaces and floors at home. Everything ends up smelling better and cleaner. Juniper is a well-known remedy for dandruff. A few drops of essence of juniper added to warm water can make an effective rinse. Juniper has also traditionally been used in Scandinavia to treat physical strain and tiredness.

JUNIPER SALVE

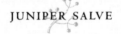

INGREDIENTS:

1 ounce (30 grams) beeswax

⅓ cup (80 ml) extra virgin olive oil or rapeseed oil (olive oil
    yields a richer, creamier salve)

⅓ cup (80 ml) almond oil

2 tsps. (10 ml) essence of juniper oil

EQUIPMENT:

Measuring cup

4 clean plastic or glass jars with tops (1.7 oz. or 50 ml each)

Thick-bottomed nonaluminum pot

Nonelectric handheld beater (i.e., eggbeater)

Non-mercury thermometer

Set out the open jars on a clean counter with a sheet of newspaper underneath if you are worried about getting oil and wax on your kitchen counter. Combine beeswax and olive and almond oils in the pot. Melt together over gentle heat. Place the juniper essence nearby so that it is easy to pick up and use with one hand—but don't add yet. Remove the melted ingredients from the heat and continue to beat; scrape away from the sides any hardening salve until the mixture begins to become thick and look cloudy or the temperature is reduced to about 35°C or 95°F. It is essential to beat continually, since the liquid will otherwise begin to clump up. As you keep beating, add the essence of juniper. Pour into clean jars and seal. The salve will keep for about a year. A note about the equipment you use: It is worthwhile to set aside the equipment that you use specifically for making salves, creams, and other homemade personal-care products, since it is hard to completely get rid of the oil and wax. As soon as you are done making the salves, clean all of your equipment with recycled paper towels.

Rowan

In Finnish mythological tradition, the Earth Mother is called Rauni, which is the Finnish term for the rowan tree. During our island autumns, the rowanberries on our island ripen to a vibrant orange-red color. As all else withers, the rowan, or Earth Mother, fills our landscape with color to remind us that life goes on. A good year for rowanberries means a cold winter, according to the folklore.

Rowanberries are the vitamin C kick that we need as the season of sneezing and coughing arrives. Finns prepare a vitamin C–rich drink from the berries of the rowan. Herewith, an easy-to-make variety.

ROWAN JUICE

2 quarts (2 liters) rowanberries
2.2 pounds (1 kg) tart apples
6½ cups (1.5 liters) water
Sugar or honey to taste

Rinse berries and apples well. Remove apple cores and cut into wedges. Place apples and berries in a pot and pour over water. Cook for 20 minutes. Run through cheesecloth or fine sieve for 30 minutes. Measure the amount of juice and bring to a gentle simmer again. Add sugar or honey to taste and simmer for 5 minutes. Take pot from the stove and skim foam off the top. Pour into warm, clean bottles and cork. Drink within a week of bottling or for longer keeping freeze as ice cubes, as for Elderflower Cooler (page 93).

Here on our island I prepare rowan jelly for eating with wild meats. A few odd berries get stolen by my husband. They reappear a couple of years later looking a light shade of salmon pink in bottles of rowanberry schnapps at special events. Those who partake in it will be reminded of the power of the rowan, which, in Norse mythological tradition (separate from the Finnish) saved the god Thor from drowning.

Gardening

Time and again I have asked people in different parts of Scandinavia why their culture has remained so *jordnära*. This is a Swedish term meaning "close to the earth." Time and again I have been told that, although these countries are now industrialized, their agrarian peasant history remains very close. Many people still feel the need to have their hands in the soil.

I had myself forgotten about my first reactions to getting my hands in the soil here on the island. Perhaps because I now find them so absurd. Claes arrived home one day with some bags of soil, some pots, and some plants. "It's spring," he said. Each year he puts out some large, white, cast-iron garden urns on the top row of our stone terraces. They look interestingly regal for this wild place. The pots and plants were laid out on the ground and a bag of garden soil punctured open. Claes remembers today the uneasy look on my face as I clutched a handful of soil and threw it into a pot. It occurred to him that I might not be particularly enthusiastic about soil, and politely suggested that he could manage the rest if I was tired.

I think I often gave the impression that my place was not here but at my desk, at my computer, or with my pen in hand. This was *just* an impression. The truth is that I was afraid that I would kill the plants. No, in fact, I was *sure* of it. There are countless books out on gardening, I thought, and I had not read even one. More importantly, I almost managed to kill the cactus plant that my mother sent me during her visit to Texas while I was at university in Wellesley, Massachusetts. One of her thoughts must have been that cactus are almost impossible to kill. I put the plant up for adoption, and one of my dorm friends revived it.

In our soil-disconnected modern societies, I am sure that I was just another one among a growing number of people who harbor this type of attitude toward their capacity to make things grow. Umpteen luscious gardens, greenhouses, and potted plants are portrayed in many beautiful books and magazines about creating them. I don't wish to put down these sometimes very useful publications. It is just that there are so many of them out there that the volume of information that you feel you need to digest makes potting a plant feel like rocket science. So, why not just bring out the artificial plants?

Modern research shows that gardening and gardens are good for our well-being and can even help us when we are sick. Above all, it has shown that the act of somehow participating in a garden, even if it is just looking at it repeatedly over a period of time, brings about a feeling of belonging, which increases our resistance to illness.[6] Researchers at the world's most extensive rehabilitation gardens at Alnarp in Sweden are undertaking studies that they believe will provide new scientific evidence showing that mere exposure to and relaxation in the garden is beneficial to health. They have already shown that blood pressure is lowered and concentration increased among elderly people relaxing in the outdoors. In the garden, senses and reflexes that tell us that we can relax are activated. Of course, the physical activity that we get in the garden can also be very beneficial to us, if we don't overdo things and can learn to lift and bend in ways that are good for our backs. The subject of health and gardens is a trend in our times, but I believe an idea that will endure and indeed that people have sensed for a very long time.

The healing effect of gardens is something that I have come very close to. The Swedish family that I married into was, in many ways, "saved" by gardening. Or so my mother-in-law, Marianne, often said. She was a re-markable woman who survived, mentally intact, into her late eighties after the loss of three of her four children. Marianne often told me that plant-ing and maintaining her garden "saved" her. Through my husband, I have experienced the intensity of pain and sorrow brought about by this unimaginable loss. Claes says that his most enduring memory of his mother in earlier days is with her bottom in the air working the flower beds. In later life she used her walking stick to create rock gardens with odd stones and to brush away the fallen petals. I understood her. In the gar-den she would always be a nurturer, belong, give, and receive. She could exercise her maternal instincts. Gardens can give each of us just what we need.

Marianne's father, David, was also saved by gardening. The largest and healthiest of plants in our island garden were planted by him. They were his therapy in dealing with clinical depression. People who are de-pressed have a feeling of worthlessness, of not being needed, not belong-ing. In the garden, David knew for sure that he was needed, that he belonged, and that he had worth. Marianne often commented on the in-tense beauty of the gardens that he was able to create in other homes. My wedding bouquet was a spontaneous collection of flowers that David planted here almost fifty years ago. In some ways I feel that I have some-how been saved by the plants in this place.

I treat my face to a steam bath of lavender, rose, and marigold, gath-ered from my own garden. One of life's divine and simple luxuries. I open my eyes for a moment and notice the gentle colors of the steamed flowers. I close them again, feel the steam caressing my face, and imagine the same shades of beauty in my garden.

HERBAL FACIAL STEAM

For cleansing pores and moisturizing the skin. Bring about 1 quart (1 liter) of water to boiling point. Place a handful of your favorite herb and/or flower in a nonplastic bowl and pour over the water. Make sure that whatever you choose is suitable for your skin and the sort of "mood" experience that you want. For instance, a soothing combination good for most skin types is chamomile, marigold, lavender, and rose. You can read about their properties in any one of a number of excellent books on herbal essences or at the Web sites listed in the Resources section of this book. Clean your face and pull back your hair. Form a "tent" over your head and the bowl with a towel, and steam your face at a comfortable distance from the pot. Continue for as long as it feels comfortable, but not for more than 10 minutes at a time. When finished, lie down and relax for a few minutes. Let your face cool. Don't try this if you have very sensitive skin or if you are asthmatic.

Awake, working in my island study early one glorious and clear summer morning, I heard some stirring in the bushes below my windowsill. Was it a deer looking for the remains of those delicious red tulips that they love to bite off the stem? No, it was my four-year-old son trying to get his nose as deep as possible into a gigantic white peony flower. He looked up at me. "Smells good, Mamma," he said and continued on his way (still in his pajamas) to find other flowers worthy of being nuzzled. One of the great fascinations of our garden for our children is the many butterflies that come to enjoy the flower nectar of high summer. Any adult can see the way that butterflies inspire children. Hans Christian Andersen noticed it when he wrote that, "just living is not enough . . . one must have sunshine, freedom and a little flower."

BUTTERFLY GARDENING

Plant a butterfly garden! You don't need much for this: a balcony or window box is enough! It is beautiful, charming, and helps plant pollination from spring through to the autumn. Our terraces on the island provide perfect conditions, which are easily emulated: stones for the butterflies to warm their wings before flying; water for drinking (a flat pan will do); aromatic herbs and edible flowers (e.g., marigold and nasturtium) with no pesticides (which kill larvae and butterflies).

The classic view of the creation of a garden is that it is all about achieving a pretty result through a favorable combination of plants. Some of the best gardeners in the world have talked about gardening as pruning nature back, weeding, taming a beast. In Scandinavia, I have encountered a view of gardening that is refreshing, and, yes, good for health. The city gardens of Stockholm provide a great example. If you go into central Stockholm on a summer's day and wander into that part of the city gardens called Rosendal, you will find young people with bandannas around their heads, down on their knees working the soil. I find this idea of showing openly the process by which a garden is created unique. In my experience, parts of city gardens that are not "ready" are usually sectioned off.

On one hot summer's day, I stepped up to Rosendal's outdoor bar to buy a bottle of mineral water. Someone ran behind the counter from the nearby herb beds to ring up my purchase on the cash register. Her face was tanned and freckled from long hours of working outside during the long Stockholm summer days. Her arms were soiled up to the elbow. She, nevertheless, managed to ring up my order touching the cash register with the long nail of her index finger. After I left, she rushed back to the herb beds and dug her hands back into the soil. There is a special energy at Rosendal, which reflects a process of joint creativity that goes on between people and plants.

Lars Krantz, a gifted and philosophical Swede who created Rosendal as it is today (the gardens date back to the mid-nineteenth century), explained his philosophy—the ideas behind this place. Gardening was about being part of a macrocosm, a coworker with nature in the garden. Feeling a part of this macrocosm was the inspirational part. The idea that gardening should be about combining form and color in order to get a particular result was misplaced. Gardening was about the health and well-being of people, and about creating room for life. The garden should itself give way to ongoing processes of people connecting with nature and with other people.

Out in the countryside, where I live, there are many home gardens, which reflect this need to be a part of a creative process—a workshop. Under these circumstances, gardens can become a creative chaos, which is incredibly beautiful and moving. There is a lemon-colored house with

DO THINGS GROW IN THE COLD NORTH?

Do things grow in the cold, dark North? Of course! In fact, the long, light hours of the warm season can result in particularly glorious gardens and unusually flavor-filled produce for consumption. Scandinavia is home to some famous historical gardens. The Linnean Gardens in Uppsala provide one example. Olof Rudbeck the Elder made this into one of the most admired of seventeenth-century Europe. A huge fire destroyed parts of it in 1702 and Carl Linnaeus began to use it as his "workshop" forty years later. Today it is open to the public. New garden workshops continue to be created in Scandinavia: If you draw lines from all of the end points of Scandinavia (excepting Iceland), you will find that they meet in a place called Ockelbo, where a spectacular Scandinavian garden is being created. Among very many special features and activities, Wij Gardens will profile flowers, vegetables, and crops that grow naturally in Scandinavia. The Gardens are regarded as a workshop, among other things, for the rehabilitation of sick people. See Resources.

green shutters that have heart-shaped peepholes just across the lake from our place. During the summers, it is occupied by a Danish professor and his wife. The garden on the hill below the house is a stunning creative chaos. All of the flowers that grow there are wild and indigenous to these parts. It was obvious to me that the professor and his wife had roamed around this area for years observing, bringing back one plant or another, and allowing it to spread on their land. The hill itself was never that important. The years of observing, collecting, transplanting, and seeing the plants return after the first long winter are what matters.

I have begun my own hill: a hill of medicinal plants collected from different parts of our sandy island. We have spread a beautiful and long-blooming flower, called Blue Flame, which grows in sand all over our place. I have learned to love the creative chaos of the Blue Flame, which pops up in different parts of our garden from year to year. This plant demands nothing of me—sometimes a little bit of directing but otherwise only appreciation.

Tired of dragging in extra soil, mulch, and everything else that you need to make your garden grow? When you are out on walks in your area try to notice what grows naturally there. What are those pretty plants that most people are busy weeding out around their exotic flower beds or pulling out of their grass lawns? Have a closer look. What sort of soil do they grow in? Do they grow all around? You probably have the same sort of soil naturally present in your backyard. Go home and look into your plant lexicon to find out what it is, how it behaves, including how it spreads itself. If you like the sound of it and the timing is right for that plant (easy to find out from your local library), on one of your future walks see whether you can ask to take one or two of those pretty weeds (carefully, with their roots in water) with you. Before they flower is usually the right time, which may mean that you have to wait another year. Transplant to your soil with plenty of water. Wait until next year and see what happens. Be prepared for the unexpected.

Hands and Minds in the Soil

Getting our hands in the soil was once about survival: plants were our pharmacy and our sustenance. So it is again today, in a somewhat different context. Plants remain our pharmacy and sustenance, only we have disconnected ourselves from their importance since our minds are no longer concerned about the soil. Reconnecting ourselves is important. Vital, it seems. This is the secret that researchers are busy unearthing. It is something that I have sensed in this *jordnära* culture in Scandinavia.

So, what happened to that person who was afraid of potting plants? The plants drew me into the macrocosm of my garden. As I listened and watched I began to understand them, and became a part of their world. They taught me about noticing the fine details, and living in the moment. I am not concerned about "finishing" the garden, since I realize that it will be a life's work and foremost a place for living. When I enter my garden, my defenses go down, I forget other places and things, and am present in my life.

FOUR

Sensitization and the Right to Relax

SCANDINAVIA IS OFTEN thought of as a cold place, where nature can be harsh and unforgiving. On the island, I came in close touch with this side of creation. But there is also another side. There is the place inhabited by the warmth that comes from nature's power to relax, cleanse, and heal. When you feel cared for, you feel warm. The traditions that I explore in this chapter are in some ways literally warm, if you take the example of sauna bathing. They are all warming in the sense that they are about the caring relationship between nature and people, and the way that nature inspires people to care for other people.

For me, these traditions have literally served as a caring "clinic" for working with long-standing physical ailments that are fairly common. Being a tall person, I was bound at some point to succumb to the compromise of human evolution: a bad back. Being a tall person who gave birth to twins who were each over three kilos, or about seven pounds, when they were born, I was just about guaranteed to succumb. When the twins reached the age of one, my back collapsed from carrying them both at the same time, bless them. My heart raced as I lay, confined to my bed in our town apartment, watching them learning to walk near all the sharp corners of the furniture within my view. Of course, all of this had taken place while Claes was off traveling in another hemisphere. A friend did the best she could to help, but, ultimately, I knew that I would have to find a solution to dealing with this long-term problem. It did not help much that my upper back was already troubled by shoulder and neck tension: my way of tucking away stress and the way that millions of people all around the world do as well.

The times in which we live are ones in which many of us have the good fortune to think about our creaking backs and tense necks. While the majority of us in the industrialized world need no longer worry about where the next meal is going to come from, most of us feel with increasing intensity the pressures of competition and keeping up. This has become a very serious threat to our health. Today people feel that their lives are under siege in a world that is faster paced and more complex than ever before. Relationships with family and friends suffer. In this context, it comes perhaps as no surprise that around half of all visits to medical professionals are due to poorly defined symptoms of sociopsychological diseases.[1] In this context, stress reduction therapies should become less of a luxury and more an integral part of living. Whole societies should value, protect, and promote them as a means of creating places that everyone can feel safe and happy living in.

One of the complaints is that the price tags on these therapies often keep them on the bottom of our lists under the new kitchen extension, our children's desire for the latest computer, and a newer model car. Sometimes we need to ask ourselves whether we are prioritizing ourselves and our families, or whether we are just prioritizing *things*. What is more, if you really begin to look into it, you can find low-cost ways of enjoying different types of relaxation therapies, as I will show you. Then the only issue to resolve is time, which is again usually a matter of personal choice and prioritization.

Investigating Nordic traditions of relaxation, I ran into the revolutionary idea that relaxation is not a luxury, but every person's right. I explain it in connection with each of the therapies discussed in this chapter. While the advent of the modern spa industry in Scandinavia has sent prices up in many places, there remains an attitude that people are entitled to relax and to be in peace. The idea goes on: It is not only adults who are entitled to this, but children too! Although child stress and its terrible consequences is taking its toll in Scandinavia, just as it is elsewhere, the best of Nordic relaxation traditions include children, and address the needs of children for intimacy and closeness to the family. This chapter not only introduces you to this idea, but also shows how you and the family can enjoy a number of Scandinavian-inspired therapies at low or no cost.

The murkiness of the health threat that we are experiencing in modern times makes it difficult for even the best-qualified physicians to sort out for us how we can deal with it. That is, unless we are also prepared to take responsibility for our well-being. Modern medicine is a brilliant discovery, but the institution itself tells us that we cannot expect it alone to keep us in good health. The doctor can cure your symptoms, even sometimes your present disease, but your overall process of well-being is your own responsibility. The fact that a pill is available should not be a license to leave your health up to that pill. I have my own story. As a child I was dogged by serious pneumonia several times until one fine day, when I was sixteen years old, an intelligent doctor told me that unless I started to participate in healing myself somehow, I would be a pretty weak person forever. He suggested swimming. I took his suggestion to heart and for the next few years, literally swam for my life. The pneumonia left me, and, so far, has returned only once when I was not conscientious enough about looking after myself.

Like other people who believe in the mind-soul-body connection, I believe that these types of ailments are the result of combined emotional and physical factors, which are connected to each other. I needed to find strategies that could help me with long-term healing for both. They also needed to be approaches where I had to take the initiative, but also feel cared for. In learning about the unique world of relaxation, cleansing, and healing Scandinavian style, I found some of these strategies. Here I show you how relaxation, cleansing, and healing Nordic style—in the sauna, in water, and through massage—address mind, spirit, and body and can become your clinic for health and a shining appearance, as well as a means of personal reflection and growth.

Sauna

"No clinic could more sweetly soothe the jostled mind."
—HELMER SELIN IN "HAIKUS OF THE HAIKU SAUNA"[2]

I have often wondered why sauna feels like such a special form of personal care and why I feel so good during and after sauna. Below, I reflect on the reasons and provide some insights into the magic of the dim, warm room. Sauna provides an environment for us to relate to nature in. It symbolizes a safe haven for each of us. It is traditionally a place for the giving and receiving of care. It provides us with opportunities for getting in touch with ourselves. And, in pure physical terms, it makes us feel and look good.

Nature's Warm Room

Sauna is an experience, deeply intertwined with nature. In it, we feel fire, earth, water, stone, and wood. The word "sauna" derives from the ancient Lapp term *saun,* which means a small hollow in the snow made by a bird called the willow grouse. Sauna today means the act of exposing your body to hot steam followed by cold water, as well as the room, the "hollow," in which you experience the hot steam. It is different to a steam room in the sense that the room itself is dry and a hot stove creates a limited amount of steam. Today, saunas can be experienced in many places in the world. I have even sat in one on the equator.

Here in the cold north, people have created the sauna houses of their dreams in their summer homes: small houses on the water with verandas and long docks. Well-designed saunas in the city maintain that link to nature with smooth pine interiors, dim light, and a place to experience the contrast to the heat of the sauna with cool water.

Before coming to live in Scandinavia, I visited a sauna one early morning in the superb Finnish spa of the Arctia Hotel in Brussels. I had been up late the night before in a Brussels restaurant sharing some memories with old friends from my childhood in the Far East. I had a nine o'clock meeting in the unforgivingly well-lit hallways of the European Commission, and hoped that the sauna would help me to recover in time for my meeting. I don't know whether the Arctia still exists, or what condition it is in now, but at that time it was quite an experience. To be sure, I had been in saunas before, but not in ones where such care had been given to putting across the feelings of nature through good sauna design. As I sat on broad slabs of light-colored pine wood inside the spacious sauna, which was made peaceful by a shadowy dim light, I got the feeling of trees, very tall trees, all around me, filtering the sunlight with their foliage. From the sauna, I looked through a sleek glass door onto a spacious, blue-tiled washing room with smooth, rounded-stainless-steel shower fittings. It was cool and clean, just as the "lake" that I did not yet know about and which, in years to come, I would look upon with similar sensations from the window of my own sauna. I ladled some of the water in the wooden bucket onto the hot stones. Sizzle, sizzle, and then the burst of birch leaf essence, which had been added to the water, all around me. The *löyly* or the steam arising from the stove that I would learn so much about when I came to Scandinavia, exploded over the stones, and sent an invigorating rush of heat over my body. Water, fire, stone, and wood. All were present in the sauna of the Arctia Hotel on that morning when I needed their rejuvenating power so urgently.

Löyly is a Finnish term, which symbolizes connection to the universe in their folklore. A Finnish scholar explains the importance of this connection to healing in old beliefs.

The steam arising from the stove . . . established a symbolic connection between the sacred space of the sauna and its people (microcosmos) and the sphere of the Hereafter and its inhabitants (macrocosmos). An individual healing event occurring within the sauna and concerning the health of an individual is linked to the entire universe. It is easier for an individual to recover when he knows that his ailment is part of that universe.[3]

Whether you believe in the Hereafter or not, the power of sauna as a relaxant and healer is definitely in this quality of making a person feel a part of a magnanimous whole. I believe that this is so, largely because of the strong presence of nature's elements in the ritual of sauna. I like to strengthen this presence in my own sauna, by drawing on and modifying an old Finnish tradition that brings in the familiar smells of the forest leaves. The steam of the forest leaf water that I prepare is like a security blanket that wraps itself around me, sends the shoulders down, and tells every muscle that it is OK to relax.

Every Person's Haven

In Nordic history, sauna is a haven. Not only this, it is my haven as well as yours: a nonexclusive place, available to anyone, where everyone is safe.

One cold November, I found myself enjoying a *smörgåsbord* of saunas, courtesy of the Finnish Sauna Association, which is based on the outskirts of Helsinki. In Finland it is estimated that there is at least one sauna to every three persons. At the Sauna Association there were three types of sauna: an electric sauna, a wood-heated sauna letting the smoke out through a chimney, and, last but never least, the oldest form of sauna, which some believe is a model that cannot be improved upon, a smoke sauna, where the smoke would pass through the sauna and eventually out by a small opening in the wall or ceiling.

While sitting on the dark wooden benches of one of the smoke saunas, I remembered an allusion to sauna as the womb. Everything about the smoke sauna was earthy: it was dark, it had a soft, even warmth, it was filled with naked women of all shapes and sizes quietly sharing their thoughts of the day, and it had a very pleasant smoke aroma all around, although there was no visible smoke. It was a timeless sanctuary: belonging

FOREST LEAF INFUSION FOR THE SAUNA

Collect leaves from aromatic trees in the forest. I use mostly birch. Cut a piece of fine netting. A square with each side about a foot long is fine. Take a piece of thick string and weave it a few times through the netting, so that the string forms a circle within the square. Make sure that there is plenty of slack in the string on either side for eventually pulling the bag together. Put some leaves into the center of the netting and pull together the net bag by drawing on the string. Hang the net bag in a dark, dry place. Make about 10 bags to last throughout the year. To prepare some aromatic water for the sauna, immerse the net bag in water in the bucket that you will take with you into the sauna. Do this about one hour before going into the sauna. Just prior to going into the sauna, take out the net bag and let it dry on the sauna bench. Hang it up again for use the next time. The bag can be used several times. The remaining water makes a wonderful aromatic löyly. *Alternatively, you can buy various types of forest essences for the sauna. See Resources.*

to no time, neither Pagan nor Christian; no clocks that we could see to tell us when we should go in or out. After settling into its darkness, each of us felt safe in this place.

The idea of the sauna as a haven is one reaching back to provincial laws existing in Scandinavia during the thirteenth century. The laws of the provinces often began by stating that the Church and the *bastu* (meaning *badstuga* in Swedish, or bathing hut) were sacrosanct places where the peace should never be broken. Anyone who has been in a sauna senses this right to peace, which belongs to each person sitting in it.

It was a cold November evening on the occasion of my visit to the Finnish Sauna Association's facility. It was Ladies' Night and the first snows had come. With the greatest of ease, women would walk out of the saunas, onto the veranda, and down the dock to the water, where they would take a brief swim in the large water pool, which had been created by hacking away the thick ice that now surrounded the pool. A heated rug warmed the long path leading down to the dock so that none of us had to bother with shoes. I walked down behind two other sirens of the sauna to the water's edge. While watching the other two swimming a peaceful ladies' breaststroke around the edge created by the ice, I dipped my foot into the icy water and then quickly pulled it out again. I retreated to the veranda to cool down instead. How did they manage?

The whole atmosphere was totally unpretentious and unlike the many health clubs that I had visited over time. There were no conspicuous bathing suits or other personal items that could create that familiar and tense air of body consciousness. People came to the sauna in their nakedness, as they were born. There was no pecking order in this place. Each person walked with a strong sense of her right to be there. This spirit of sauna is very old, and unique in past times when European society was highly unequal. Sauna has long been regarded as a basic right in Scandinavia. It is an institution that cuts through social divisions in a way that no other I know has done over the centuries.

Cleansing and Healing

In large parts of Scandinavia, sauna has a long tradition of cleansing and healing. Words referring to sauna are known to have existed as far back as 1500–900 B.C. The folk poetry archives of the Finnish Literary Society attest to a fascinating world of healing in the sauna. Careful attention to the manner of preparing the sauna, massage, "cupping" (bloodletting), slapping with a birch whisk, and other sometimes unnerving-sounding rituals and practices were, and continue to be, a part of the magical world of healing in the sauna. It seems no coincidence that the *Kalevala,* Finland's national epic poem compiled in 1849 from oral folk poetry, contains references to the healing and rejuvenating power of sauna and was written by a physician.[4] In this epic, mothers and sisters prepare the sauna for their sons and brothers, the heroes of the story, before they go out on new adventures. The sauna is that essential source from which the heroes replenish their strength.

In a part of the world that remained essentially rural well into the twentieth century, the sauna was the main place for attending to personal hygiene and for relaxing after heavy work. Sauna was basic to the hygiene system of the Scandinavian countries until running water was brought into the home. Addressing the Architectural Association in London in 1950, the Finnish architect Alvar Aalto described a game he played with his fellow traveler that exemplifies how essential sauna was to living.

> The Finnish bath is a national institution, and in this country of four million people you will find geographically, many hundreds of thousands of bathhouses. I tried an experiment once with the late Madame Mandrot, who some of you may know was a good friend of Le Corbusier. She was on a tour up to Lappland and down to Helsinki, in all the poor districts, and she had the right to point to any place where farmers or industrial workers lived, and we would check whether there was a bathhouse or not. On a journey covering more than a thousand miles there were only two places where there was not a bathhouse.[5]

Norse is the only linguistic tradition in which one of the days of the week, *lördag,* or Saturday, is named after bathing. Often this meant sauna bathing. For centuries, the keepers of what you could call a "system" of sauna hygiene were female attendants who unabashedly cleansed men, women, and children. Charles Ogier, a French diplomat who was stationed in Sweden from 1634 to 1635, writes in his diary about the breathtaking experience of being beaten with birch whisks, massaged, soaped, and scrubbed by women dressed in nothing more than sheer linen.[6]

In Finland, the tradition of *Skrubbtanter,* or scrubbing women, has survived to this day. During my visit to the Finnish Sauna Association, I noticed a room with a scrubbing bed and many different types of natural-fiber brushes for scrubbing down different parts of the body. The *Skrubbtant* was not there, but I could imagine her at the scrubbing bench vigorously exfoliating and massaging grateful bodies.

Today, sauna has lost its role as being essential to personal hygiene in Scandinavia. Still, it continues to offer people an unbeatable experience in deep cleansing, muscular stimulation, and relaxation. By sweating, we bring out toxins that otherwise collect in our bodies and cause disease. By exposing our muscles to heat, we relax them, make them more flexible, and increase our bodies' capacity to prevent injury. By exposing our bodies intermittently to heat and cold, we improve our circulation and exercise our hearts. Most people who take sauna find that it guarantees them a very solid night's sleep afterward, which is itself stress reducing and good for building immunity. Overall, the reduction of stress is a major health benefit of sauna.

Finns like to attribute the successes of their best athletes to the regular use of sauna. The most famous of these is Finnish long-distance running legend Paavo Nurmi, who was a systematic and orthodox sauna bather. Finnish athletes became famous for the importance that they attributed to sauna in their training when they took their saunas with them to the Olympic Games. This was particularly so at the Berlin Olympics in 1936 and the Squaw Valley Olympics in 1960, which awakened interest in sauna elsewhere.

Birch Whisking

Birch whisks were once regarded as an essential part of the cleansing and healing process that goes on in the sauna. In fact, saunas without birch whisks are like food without seasoning, says the Finnish Sauna Society. Exactly when people started using them in the sauna remains a mystery. Suffice it to say, they have been used for a very long time—originally, some experts think, to circulate the heat in saunas when it was difficult to get the temperature high enough.

A birch whisk is not a mere tree branch. It is a traditional art form with techniques regarding the right leaf aroma and texture, length, and thickness passed on from one generation to the next. This was one of the subjects raised in an exhilarating and touching interview I enjoyed with Matti Kivinnen, a Finn in his sixties with an explosive passion for sauna and holding the distinguished title of president of the International Sauna Association. Matti told me during our conversation that he was taught how to make a birch whisk by his grandfather in eastern Finland. According to Matti, eastern Finns have a reputation in Finland for being relatively sloppy with their birch whisks, and so he confessed with a slight hint of embarrassment that he never really learned how to make a birch whisk properly.

My sloppiness in birch whisk preparation aside, I have tried using one in the sauna. There are differences of opinion about which way is the right

MAKING A BIRCH WHISK

Harvest birch branches at around the time of the year when there are most day-light hours. Go for branches on birch trees not smaller than 3 meters, or 10 feet. Cut the branches to about 50 cm, or 20 inches, in length. Hold the birch whisk branches in one hand so that the tops are about 35 cm, or just over 1 foot, from the thumb. Make sure that the branches make a nice, even bouquet. For the binding, select an approximately 1.2-meter-, or 4-foot-long, branch of prefer-ably "hanging birch" (betula pubescens) and with a small, sharp knife, peel off the bark on two sides from the bottom to the top of the branch. Hold the whisk in one hand again and thread the binding through the woody part (not the leafy part) of the whisk, so that about 10 cm, or 4 inches, of the binding sticks out on the other side. Hold the whisk with one hand, and with the free hand take the slack and wind it a couple of times around the whisk. Lay the whisk on the ground, hold it down with your foot, and pull so that the binding is nice and tight.[7] Be careful not to pull so hard that the binding breaks. If you find it hard to get this right, use some thick, natural string with which to bind together the whisk—against the rules, but still effective. Keep the whisks in a dark, dry, and clean place. I keep mine hanging upside down in pairs from a rack in the changing room of my sauna house. In order to prepare a birch whisk for use in the sauna, once it has dried out, soak it in your bucket of water for use in the sauna about an hour before you go into the sauna. Experts recommend mak-ing 10 to 15 pairs for the year, depending on how often you intend to go into the sauna. They can also make a nice invigorating massage on dry skin before you go into the bath or shower.

way to whisk. Some sources say that the correct ritual is to start by whisk-ing the feet and then work upward toward the heart. Other folk sources say that whisking from the back downward dispels cold and soreness from the body. Whisking the other way is said only to bring all of the illnesses back into the body. Contrary to the images I previously had of people "beat-ing" themselves in the sauna, using a birch whisk is a pleasant experience or at least in the words of an old familiar tune, "hurts so good." The birch leaves have a special cleansing and relaxing aroma, which is elicited by use of the whisk. Brushing the body with a whisk raises the blood circulation in the skin so as to speed up perspiration and detoxification. It removes dirt and disinfects. Birch whisks, the leaves of which contain saponins, function as a mild soap on the skin. This "soap" of the past is in many ways much better for maintaining a soft, healthy skin than a bar of soap is.

I now have a row of incorrectly bound and dried birch whisks hanging in my sauna house by the lake. I imagine that an old Finn would cover his or her eyes and grimace at my creations, but still I enjoy using them. About an hour before getting into the sauna, I soak the whisk in the bucket of water that I will use to create *löyly*. This prepares the whisk for use and also has the delightful side effect of turning the water into a birch essence— something like the miracle of water to wine.

OTHER TECHNIQUES

There is a saying that a woman never looks as beautiful as she does an hour or two after taking a sauna. My husband agrees, but, then again, he is always full of compliments.

The sauna is a place to experience purity. It follows that bringing a lot of extra treatments into it is unnecessary. Sometimes self-defeating. In her engaging book about sauna, the Finnish musical artist Arja Saijonmaa tells the story of the overdone treatment at a simple health spa in the Finnish countryside, which imparts a little of this mood to us, and shows up the complex beauty mythology that has developed around sauna.[8] Inside the sauna house there are buckets with mostly simple ingredients that could be found in any kitchen. A whole series of treatments is administered prior to the actual sauna. Salt, honey, seaweed, kefir, and risen rye dough are applied before the sauna, in the fight against time. The humor of this story aside, the truth that resides in it is that your skin behaves like any other organ of your body, taking in the goodness that you feed it as well as the toxins that you expose it to.

Of the treatments described in this humorous account, salt and honey are the most popular. And with good reason. Salt opens pores and cleanses. Honey cleanses, moisturizes, and nurtures.

If you are in a communal sauna where it may be against the rules to bring in anything but yourself and a towel, do not despair. You will still experience the purity.

SALT SCRUB AND HONEY IN THE SAUNA

The simple approach is a cup of plain, fine-ground salt and a jar of honey. Take them with you. Massage your entire body (except your face) with salt before the sauna and wash off. Enjoy a few rounds in the sauna. Just before your last sit in the sauna, massage in the honey. Go in for your last sauna sit, using a towel so as not to make the bench sticky. Rinse off. No skin-leeching soap or expensive moisturizers required! Naturally, you can buy a jar of aromatic salt scrub, if you want to pamper yourself a little more. See page 123 for a salt scrub that you can make at home.

Sauna as Inner Sanctum and Intimacy

The little hot room is a place for getting in touch with yourself and, yes, with others. At this point, please be sure that I have no regard whatsoever for those institutions that degrade the authentic art of sauna. What I have to say about intimacy and inner sanctum in the sauna is meant with greatest sincerity. The elements' appeal to our senses melts down our inhibitions about knowing ourselves and letting others know us too.

SAUNA AND THE SELF

When first I became a regular sauna bather here on our island, the sauna cabin was a mind inferno, where all of those millions of thoughts about work, what I would do after the sauna, and so on swirled around in my mind at an increasingly rapid rate. I watched the clock furiously and would go in and out at more than regular intervals, although this perhaps had nothing to do with what my body was telling me. I endured the sauna in order to be "healthy," but didn't allow it to relax me.

Sauna bathing alone on one cold and utterly clear winter's night changed this. Our lake was frozen and all that one could hear was the echo of freezing ice deep below the surface. Claes had made a small hole in the ice for cooling off in between sauna sessions. During the day a thin layer of ice had closed the hole. I used a thick tree branch to crack it open again. The stars and the waxing moon lit up the sky and the sauna house veranda where I stood. I would interrupt my sauna sessions, not because of the mechanical obligation to go in and out, but because I wanted to cool my body in the quiet, dim, blue night light. I would step back into the sauna because I needed warming up. The changes in temperature and the magnetism of the natural scenery had switched my senses on, and sauna was beginning to teach me about natural rhythm.

Gradually I was becoming so involved with the experience of sauna that I was forgetting about my sauna inhibitions, such as cold-water bathing, sitting in the sauna uncovered, and so on. My mental boundaries seemed to be evaporating with the *löyly*. Rather than a half hour of self-enforced confinement in a hot place, sauna had become a vast frontier of personal discovery. What do I need? How do I feel? What do I like? These are the questions that you begin to ask yourself in the process of sauna. From these questions, the step to "What do I want in life?" isn't very far.

Sauna is a great teacher in creating and maintaining your inner sanctum. It is about learning to be still, alone, at peace with yourself, and, if you share a sauna with others, about learning to be together and choosing either to interact or not to interact. Some sauna experts say that the business of sauna and self is a modern idea. That may be true to some extent, but in the folklore, it has always had spiritual meaning for the individual. I return to the conversation with Matti. In his memories of childhood in rural Finland, the sauna house was a shrine for many of the processes of life: linen drying; sheep shearing; birth, marriage, and death—a place for the group and for practical purposes, but also a place for the spirit and the self. With this background, Matti concluded, "I go to the sauna for myself—it is a private privilege." This did not necessarily mean that he was alone on each occasion that he went to his sauna. Rather, it referred to the way that sauna is a way of affirming his personal space, his right to choose, and his right to exist.

GIVING AND TAKING

Sauna revives and brings out each person's best mainly because it is a place of reciprocal caring. My six-year-old daughter dances her little hands across my back and sprinkles water on it when she is with me in the sauna. Of course this is just plain fun, but it is also a unique opportunity for her to express herself to me. On Friday evenings the women in my community gather at a sauna house to enjoy a good sweat and be good to one another. The whole tradition of sauna is one of people caring for other people, and of any person, no matter how independent, being prepared to accept this caring. The tradition of scrubbing another person's back and receiving that scrubbing in the sauna is an expression of this.[9]

The human warmth that I encountered on my evening at the Finnish Sauna Association was indicative of the caring culture that exists in sauna life. While sitting in the dark smoke sauna feeling somewhat intimidated, a figure I had not seen previously stretched out her legs, which looked fluorescent white in the shady surroundings. She relaxed her head forward for a moment, then looked up and started speaking Finnish. The moment it became clear that I couldn't understand her, she switched to English, and asked me whether I was enjoying the sauna and would like to have more *löyly*. "Yes," I said, "fine." She took the bucket and returned five minutes later with more birch-infused water. "How much would you like?" she asked. "Whatever you think is right," I replied, feeling intensely my lack of knowledge about sauna etiquette. All in all, I found the consideration for others quite startling in this place. In days gone by, we would likely have sat in less sanitized surroundings with drinking, eating, and bloodletting going on all around. In 1885, Sture-badet (still one of Scandinavia's most elegant spas) opened in the center of Stockholm and had a third-class section where literally hundreds of people enjoyed a four-hour sweat bath in the presence of a police constable. The essence of giving and receiving, however, would have been the same.

Sauna has a historical place in the ritual of union between man and woman in Scandinavia. Anyone who is married or in a relationship knows that the key to making it work is the willingness of both parties to give and

---

SAUNA BATHING WITH CHILDREN

With a little experience, your children will come to enjoy sauna bathing as much as you do. To make it pleasant and not too hot for them, bring in a cool foot bath, which they will also find great fun to sprinkle over their heads and the rest of their bodies!

receive. In his detailed *History of the Nordic Peoples* (1555), Olaus Magnus Gothus gives an account of a "wedding sauna," a custom that has endured, with modifications, to the present time. The account in English translation goes something like this:

> It must be admitted that the so-called wedding bath is used by every-one and is undertaken with great solemnity, whenever a newlywed woman is to be given to a man. Maidens and honorable wives, in order of age, slowly walk before her in a long procession. But before them all walk the men, who carry large barrels with good beer or wine, so that when the heat becomes too strong, they can replenish their strength, and then taste a little good cinnamon, sugar, and roasted bread. When they leave, they wear crowns of buttercups on their heads. . . .[10]

Rules and How-to

Finns like to say that sauna is an individual experience and that therefore not too many rules should be laid on. Still, there are a few caveats that you should observe in the decision to take sauna.

Sauna should be avoided in cases of acute inflammation, contagious disease, and poor heart condition. Don't take on more than feels comfortable. That means not challenging your fellow sauna-goers to see who can stay in the longest and who can swim in the hole in the ice the longest. While the Finnish Sauna Society reports that 95 percent of pregnant women in Finland enjoy regular sauna during pregnancy, please check with your doctor before taking one if you are expecting. Sauna bathing after alcohol and a meal is usually not very appealing, so avoid the combination if you should get the urge. With all of these warnings in mind, here are some guidelines for getting the best out of your sauna.

SAUNA GUIDELINES

1. About an hour beforehand, prepare your dried birch whisk and/or forest leaf infusion, if you so wish (and if this is allowed in the sauna you are using).

2. Enter the sauna as you were born: naked. Bathing suits do not belong together with sweating.

3. There are two schools of thought about whether it is better for adults to enter the sauna with wet skin or with dry skin. The wet skin option is perhaps more comfortable for less-experienced sauna-goers, who may find the initial heat of the sauna unpleasant on dry skin. The dry-skin option allows you to see and feel the sweat beads forming on your skin. If the sauna is too hot, you won't see them, since they will evaporate straight away. Kids are better off with the wet option.

4. The sauna bench may be extremely hot on your skin when you first enter, so take a towel to sit on.

5. There are no precise rules of behavior in the sauna, but the ritual is meant to be relaxing. Hurry, noise, and reckless competition about who stands heat best do not belong to the practice of sauna.

6. Wait with the *löyly*. Immediately putting water onto the hot stones creates a sudden heat shock that prevents the normal functioning of the sweat glands. You should begin to sweat in eight to ten minutes. You can use your birch whisk to gently activate your sweat glands.

7. Take a dip or cold shower once you begin to sweat and feel that it is time to cool off. A birch whisk feels invigorating on skin that has just been cooled off. Make sure to rest on a bench or chair before reentering the sauna. Dip and rest in between sauna sessions as many times as you like.

8. Once you really start to get warm and into the swing of the sauna, it is time to create some *löyly*. Three goes is about average.

9. Rub in some honey once your pores are open. Your body will lap up the nutrients, and this is a great form of cleansing.

10. Finish off your sauna with a dip or shower and a rest. Relax; there should be no hurry to go anywhere.

11. Hang up your birch whisk for use the next time.

12. Enjoy a light snack and a refreshing, preferably nonalcoholic beverage.

Water Therapy

Without water, sauna would not be sauna. In Scandinavia there are many other traditions relating to those precious drops, which I would call therapeutic. The Nordic countries have a special love affair with water. It is everywhere: it shoots out of the ground at scalding temperatures in Iceland, large parts of Denmark are surrounded by it, it cuts into the Norwegian highland plateaus to create majestic fjords, it spreads across Finland in the form of over 180,000 lakes, and has created one of the most beautiful archipelagos in the world in Sweden. Little wonder that Scandinavia is home to the world's oldest swimming club (founded in Uppsala, Sweden, in 1774). Each time I fly into Stockholm in daylight, I am first struck by the way that the water shapes the land. Then I remember how it shapes life.

Morning Bath of Clarity

Immersing your body in water as one of the first things you do when you roll out of bed is undoubtedly one of the great pleasures of life. Whether you shower, bathe, or go for a swim, it provides that needed "me" time before the chaos of the day starts. Once you are done, you are focused and clear. In Scandinavia, that morning bath of clarity has, like sauna, been turned into an art form.

One great Scandinavian tradition is that of the summer or, in direct translation from the Swedish term *fritidshus,* "free-time house." Every now and then, particularly in the summer, Scandinavians feel the need to leave the detail of their usual homes and to move out to a place that is uncomplicated and surrounded by nature. I recently learned that of Sweden's approximately 700,000 free-time houses, about 200,000 are located within approximately 100 meters, or 109 yards, of the water.[11] I have no figures for the other Scandinavian countries, but I am sure that the proportions are similarly high in some of the others, if not higher. In these free-time houses on the water, a morning bath from the dock—often a rather worn-looking structure built with dubious expertise—is a great tradition.

Our house makes up one of the 200,000, although we have chosen to live in it all of the time. One of the first things that I learned when I came here was the rigor of morning water therapy. Breakfast is carried down to the dock, and may not be enjoyed before the morning dip is completed. Since summer houses often don't have running water, this morning water therapy really is needed. The rewards are all worth that moment of mental conflict that comes just shortly prior to diving in. In Scandinavia a lucky day is when the water temperature rises above 20°C, or 68°F.

I have since made this morning ritual my own by modifying it. The morning sun comes up from behind me and shines on the water ahead, the visiting sailboats moored in our bay, the forests, and the horizon, dotted with many islands. Everything is in crystal clear focus. I go down the ladder into the shallow water and dive in. The water is smooth as honey on my skin, its coolness waking every limb into action. When it is warm enough in the water, I swim over to the east-facing dock and back. This swim has become much more than just a little morning exercise. It is my morning bath of clarity. It is a time when all of me is sensitized to everything around me. The lines of communication to and from myself become clear and ready. I get out of the water and go into our sauna house, where I have a medicine cabinet. I comb my hair, moisturize my body and face, and slip on a thick robe. I am ready.

When the bathing season ends, I am back to the shower, which can be made as special as that morning dip. It is all about using the water and a few other practical ideas to get you sensitized and ready to tune in to your world. Buy a body brush or get out your birch whisk and, before stepping in the shower, brush away dead skin cells. The new ones want to breathe! Get the circulation going! Dry body brushing is great for boosting your immunity before you get out there among all of those sneezing people. Get under a nice warm shower and sense how invigorating it feels on your live skin. Forget the soap and pull out the salt scrub, which will take care of cleansing, nourishing, and moisturizing all at the same time.

SALT SCRUB

A company producing Scandinavian salt scrub says they got their recipe from an old Finnish woman. It is great stuff (see Resources). Whether salt scrub is actually a Finnish innovation is still up for grabs. Whatever its origins, here is a recipe from Lisen Sundgren, a talented and committed herbalist who works at Rosendal Gardens in Stockholm, among other places. At a time in her life when she was unwell, the herbs gave her what she needed and she has devoted her life to them ever since. This recipe makes one treatment.

You need:

1 tablespoon herb: calendula, lavender, nettle or rose, finely ground
5 tablespoons finely ground unbleached sea salt
4 tablespoons extra-virgin olive oil
1 teaspoon honey
Essential oil of citrus or juniper (optional)

Put the herbs in a blender and process to a fine powder. Place salt and herbs in a bowl. Add the olive oil a spoonful at a time. Add the honey. Add 10 drops of essential oil: lemon or juniper. Stir thoroughly. The scrub should have a thick, smooth texture. If it is not smooth enough, add more oil.

Healing Water

The spa industry in Scandinavia is both new and old. Most of it is seen as being imported from other parts of Europe. But there is a fascinating Scandinavian world of healing waters and the institutions that developed around them. This section gives you a little background and how you can bring some of it into your home.

Since pre-Christian times in Scandinavia, natural springs have been seen as having supernatural powers, both good and bad. In Nordic mythology, Yggdrasil, the tree of life, has its roots in three deep underground water sources: a source of evil; a source of ancient wisdom; and a source where fate is decided. In accordance with this, in olden times people believed that the springs could bring about good or bad luck, depending on how they were treated. If the springs were respected, meaning that gifts were brought and certain rules were observed, the springs could bring about good health and determine that the wishes of its visitors would be fulfilled. Visiting a spring and taking the waters for special purposes was a solemn occasion and only undertaken in serious circumstances. A terrible fate awaited anyone who did not respect the springs. The historian Johannes Messenius (1580–1636) explains the fate of a Protestant clergyman who, on the king's orders, participated in trying to close down the revered spring at Svinnegarn in central Sweden in 1544. The famous crucifix at the spring source was dismantled and loaded onto a wagon that was to be taken to Uppsala and burned in public. During the journey, one of the arms of the Christ figure snagged on to a gatepost on the narrow road and the clergyman cut off the arm with an ax so that the wagon could pass. Shortly afterward his arm became lame and he was unable ever to use it again. In the people's eyes this was a natural outcome of an evil act.[12]

Centuries before, the Catholic Church had welcomed the old custom, and church buildings were often constructed near these wells. The custom of drinking from the wells was transformed into a ritual of Christian renewal, particularly on the first Sunday after Pentecost and during the Midsummer festival. At the larger water sources, these customs of water healing became quite a spectacle, with people gathering in crowds to drink, bathe, and cover themselves in clay, which they believed could heal and prevent illness.

The first drops from the wells in the morning were said to be the most effective in preventing bad health. The elderly, who could not reach the wells themselves, sent for the water. The Reformation saw the old beliefs as a threat and did all that it could to eradicate them. Ordinary people thought that this was dangerous and were not surprised to hear about the fate of those who challenged the powers of the springs. Later on in his story about Svinnegarn, Johannes Messenius reveals that some generations after the first incident with the crucifix, the then owner of Svinnegarn's spring was ordered to refill the spring with stones. According to legend, the source was restored to its previous condition on the same day, and those who tried to stone it up were gripped by madness, from which they never fully recovered.[13]

USING CLAY TO MAKE THE MOST OF
HEALING WATERS

People in days gone by sometimes had the right instincts without having a scientific explanation. Clay, extracted from the areas around the mineral springs, continues to be used as a nutritious organic body wrap, which has the effect of stimulating blood and lymph circulation, removing dead cells, and sucking up dirt and excess grease. These days, it is easy to buy your own clay from a range of suppliers with simple accompanying recipes. Try one, and you will feel how your skin is stimulated almost immediately. Be careful to choose a type that is right for your skin.

Red Clay: Rich in iron content, which means that it is very good for drawing out skin impurities. Useful in the treatment of wounds, skin infections, bites, and acne.

Green Clay: From plant material and volcanic ash. Mild and can be used for most skin types.

White Clay: Alternatively called kaolin and most frequently used in treatments. It is the mildest of all of the clays and can be used in the bath with bath salts.

The Blue Lagoon mineral spring in Iceland sells an excellent and nutritious silica mud with good results in treating serious skin problems. Naantali Spa in the Finnish archipelago today offers a special treatment consisting of a peat bath made from Arctic plants. See Resources.

During the seventeenth century, ancient Nordic beliefs in the healing powers of natural mineral water sources experienced a boost in the form of a European-wide trend in "taking the waters" at health resorts. The curing powers of spring water became a prescribed feature of medicine at the time that was a kind of mixture between religious belief, observation, and scientific experimentation. Medevi Brunn, in southeastern Sweden, was the first of a series of health resorts established to provide "cures" centered on a mineral water source and was established in 1678. It already had a thousand-year-old reputation in healing and was associated with the patron Saint Birgitta, who is said to have taken the waters there.

Urban Hiärne (1641–1734), who had traveled widely in Europe visiting famous health resorts, and who did much to shape the new spa culture that began to develop in Sweden during the seventeenth century, became the first Scandinavian *brunnsläkare,* or spa doctor. From its beginnings in Hiärne's mind, the new spa culture of the time was to preserve the old Scandinavian tradition of access to the spring water for all. The water was made available and bottled so that the poor could get access to it. The unwritten rule was that no person, however poor, would be turned away. Donations for the poor made it possible for food, lodging, medical attention, and spring water to be made available for them. Naturally, there was a hierarchy at the resorts, which Hiärne deplored. He often thought that the upper class missed the point, and that the poor, who kept to a stricter regimen and whose main focus was on curing disease, got the most out of the new services.[14]

While the hype about the medical benefits of spring water itself and of bathing went out with modern medicine, their benefits for our health and well-being are widely recognized today. One very old form of Swedish balneotherapy, which can be enjoyed at various spas around the country, is a bath enhanced with the oil extract of pine needles.

Iceland takes my world prize for the culture most convinced by the health-giving powers of water. When first I visited Iceland with my twins

NEW "OLD" NORDIC SPA CULTURE

After Medevi, a mushrooming of mineral spring spas began to occur in the Nordic region. Today, these spas are reopening their doors with new ideas and treatments yet still an interesting smattering of the old culture. Loka Brunn (or spring), among others, offers a historical journey back into traditions of healing water at its historical museum and through guided tours. Naantali Spa, in the southwestern Finnish archipelago, is a five-star modern spa with a history going back to the early eighteenth century of providing the Russian aristocracy with mineral water treatments. See Resources.

during one surprisingly mild November, we spent most of our time enjoying Arbaejarlaug, one of Reykjavik's seven thermal baths and pools. The English language has adopted the Icelandic term *geysir*, since Icelanders have more of them than any other country in the world. Official sources calculate that there are about eight hundred of them spouting geothermal water at an average temperature of about 67°C, or 167°F.

As I sat outside on a cold November day, submerged in the blissfully warm water of Arbaejarlaug, my children splashing around in the background and slowly realizing that it was better to be in than out, I remembered what a specialist on the spring waters of Iceland had once told me. I was sitting in "thousand-year-old water" rushing up from the center of the earth. The water had wisdom. This turns out not only to be romanticizing and folklore. This "wise" water reduces stress levels, soothes stiff joints and muscles, and has a positive effect on the heart and lungs.

As with the whole history of water as a healing source in the Scandinavian countries, the use of warm springs for cleansing and healing in Iceland is very old. The sagas document it, and there are various recordings going back in time. Eggert Ólafsson and Bjarni Pálsson, the Icelandic pioneers of geothermal energy exploitation, recorded the many uses of the geothermal water, among others, medical, in their travel book during the early 1750s:

As for the medical use of the springs, a whole thesis might be written . . . these baths are considered particularly beneficial after a hard day of heavy work, before sleep. Then you will be spared the sore and stiff limbs from which you would otherwise suffer the day after. This is what they did, in days of yore, after battles, long journeys and other trials.[15]

If the geothermal spring baths of Iceland seem just too far away to get to for now, try your own bathtub. Baths of different temperatures are a gentle stimulant for the release of muscle-relaxing endorphins in the body. A warm bath (over 36°C, or 97°F) reduces blood pressure, improves blood circulation in the skin, and soothes muscular strain. A lukewarm bath (around 33°C, or 91°F) encourages deep sleep.

In modern day, some fascinating discoveries have been made about the effects of warm mineral baths. At some point in the late 1970s, a worker in the nearby power plant started bathing in the lagoon that had been recently formed as a result of the works. He was a psoriasis sufferer and noticed that his condition was improving considerably with bathing. The news spread rapidly and today the spa that has been created there runs a professional clinic for treating psoriasis. Today you can soak in the warm waters of the Blue Lagoon while a therapist administers any one of a range of massages using its products. Visiting the Blue Lagoon with four-year-old twins, I had no such luck.

Seawater

Seawater has also played a role in Scandinavian-style water therapy. Our Norwegian friends Inni and Gunnar are totally convinced by the rejuvenating powers of the sea, and swim in the waters near their home in Norway for as many days of the year as the weather allows. When they came to visit our home, which is on a freshwater lake, they claimed that the water did not have the same effect. Many people would agree with them.

Seawater "cures" took Scandinavia by storm during the nineteenth century, and began to take over the role that the mineral spas had played a hundred years before. By the mid- to late nineteenth century there were either cold-water bathing houses or bathing docks in almost all cities and other populated areas on the water. The first Scandinavian seawater spa, Refsnäs on the West Coast of Sweden, admitted its first patients in 1875.

As the popularity of the treatments spread, so the number of places offering such cures grew. As with the mineral water spas, it was not only bathing that was the healing element of the seawater cures. The sea air was particularly prized, its oxygen content, wind velocity, humidity, and temperature measured daily.

Seaweed baths in warm seawater, well known on the west coast of Sweden, are rich in iodine and other nutritious substances that our bodies lose when we are under stress or as we age.

The Scandinavian Art of Touch

When my little daughter dances her hand across my back in the sauna she tells me in her lovely Swenglish accent that she is giving me a "maaaaassage." I become like a sponge, soaking up the gorgeous feeling of her doing this. In Scandinavia, massage is a form of relaxation that has often gone hand in hand with sauna. It also stands alone as the most "connecting" form of relaxation that I can think of. At the same time as the touch of another human sensitizes us to the people and place around us, it also helps us to go deep into ourselves to find the inner sanctum that is there within.

This idea was well understood by Per Henrik Ling (1776–1839), the originator of "classical," or "Swedish," massage. Strangely, Ling is better

SEAWATER AND SEAWEED THERAPY

At Varberg, on the west coast of Sweden, you can sit in a bath filled with warm seawater and be massaged with large bunches of seaweed that have had their slippery outer surface removed. If you are lucky enough to live near a place where you can harvest some clean seaweed, you can try massaging with it in a regular warm bath yourself and follow this with a short rest lying down under a warm blanket. If you don't have this natural luxury available to you, you can always buy a range of prepared and concentrated seawater or thalassotherapy products (sea salt, plankton, algae, sea sediment, clay, and mud) and use them in the bath at home. If you are worried about costs, go for the sea salt, cheaply available in any supermarket. Add a cup to your warm bath and enjoy.

known inside Scandinavia for the system of gymnastics that he developed, and not for his related ideas about massage, which are, by now, much more famous worldwide. His approach to gymnastics differentiated itself from other main approaches influencing the development of modern gymnastics, in the sense that his was a system of gymnastics for everyone. Today his motivations are treated somewhat suspiciously, since there are imperialist tinges to his work. The Swedish empire was waning in Ling's day. He believed the answer to rediscovering Norse might was to strengthen people's bodies. Still, the system that Ling developed was neither elitist nor competitive, in contrast to others originating elsewhere. His underlying philosophies were rather to do with the creation of inner balance within each individual. The eventual goal of this individual balance was to create a spiritual harmony between people and their universe. These thoughts are strikingly relevant to the rising modern perception that to encourage positive developments in the world around us, we have to "get it right" within ourselves first.

The path to creating this inner as well as outer balance was, according to Ling, to observe nature. The design and functioning of the human body, as it had been created, was the most important starting point for considering any system useful to its development. Close observation of anatomy and how the body worked was the key to physical and spiritual betterment, which were intertwined. In this way, Ling's system of gymnastics became the foundation for medical gymnastics or physical therapy in the Western world. He also believed that through massage one could "treat" the inner organs of the body. Modern research is proving him to be right. Studies show that massage affects the autonomous nervous system, encourages the release of calming hormones, increases blood and lymph circulation, and decreases muscle tension. The overall effect is to strengthen your immune system.

"Ling gymnastics" became a social movement in Sweden during the twentieth century. Children learned it at school, and there were opportunities for everyone in society somehow to participate. *Husmodersgymnastik*, or housewives' gymnastics, became popular. There were mass exhibitions at home and abroad in which Swedish housewives demonstrated their physical prowess. Organized troops of men and women participated in

"Lingiads," where they could show coordinated skills in movement. My husband, who went to school during the 1950s, recalls the standard and un-forgettable Ling gymnastics drill, which began with throwing one arm out to one side and then the other arm to the other side. They were *that* well known.

Ling's ideas about massage traveled across the Atlantic to the United States during the 1850s with Charles and George Taylor, brothers who were also doctors and eager to introduce the practice of massage that they had learned while studying in Sweden. American interest in this practice expanded with the establishment of the first Swedish clinics after the Civil War in Boston and Washington. Among the soldiers who attended these clinics to ease pain and aid recovery was the eighteenth president of the United States, Ulysses S. Grant.

While interest in learning, teaching, and developing new forms of mas-sage expanded throughout the twentieth century in the United States, lay-ing the foundation for its rising popularity today, its morality in Sweden became questioned by the finer set who did not believe that this was the sort of thing that they should be engaging in.

During the 1960s, Hans Axelson working in Sweden decided to revive interest in the forgotten Swedish art of massage. He founded Axelson's Gymnastic Institute in 1962 and worked patiently for more than thirty years to gain greater social acceptance of massage as an important tool for

SWEDISH MASSAGE THERAPY IN THE
UNITED STATES

The Swedish Institute of Medical Gymnastics and Massage (today known as the Swedish Institute of Physiotherapy) was founded in 1916 and remains today the oldest school of massage therapy in the United States (see Resources). Since then the industry of massage has expanded dramatically and there are many places where one can learn about classical, or Swedish, massage in America. The Swedish Institute of Physiotherapy has a newsletter and an interesting bookstore containing information about the benefits and application of differ-ent forms of massage and other therapies well-being. Axelson was extremely progressive for his time; he was a vegetarian who was convinced by massage and yoga, among other health-promoting practices. When I spoke with Axelson, he laid out his startling vision of massage as a tool for achieving a good society. In the tradition of Ling, he spelled out his vision of massage as a necessity for everyone. The whole setting around us, and Axelson's personal appearance, matched this goal: It was normal, everyday. There was nothing luxurious or pretentious about it.

The idea that gymnastics and massage could somehow forge a harmony between people, nations, and the universe is also one of those Lingian legacies that appears to have trickled down, and is strengthened by backing in new scientific knowledge about the peace-creating effects of the hormone oxytocin, which is released through massage. New research shows that adults who are massaged have a lower blood pressure and a lower level of stress hormone, and that children who receive massage become calmer, socially more mature, and less aggressive.[16]

Swedish massage is a thorough run-through of your body's muscles. It is based on Western ideas about anatomy and physiology, in contrast to Eastern approaches, which are based on different ideas about how we function, why we get sick, and how we can heal. That said, in its originator's mind, it had not only a physical but also a mental and spiritual dimension. This form of massage is aimed at reducing muscle tension, improving circulation, and flushing out metabolic wastes. Executed by the right practitioner, this form of massage can provide you with an unbeatable release

PEACEFUL TOUCH

Since 1996, Hans Axelson has been expressing his visions through the inspirational motto Peaceful Touch. *Through his institute, he has been pioneering a movement for massage against violence, which focuses on reducing aggression and improving communication through massage among children and youths. Day-care staff have been trained in massage, and visits have been made to prisons. According to Axelson, the Red Cross and other peace organizations have shown interest in his ideas. See Axelson's Institute in Resources.*

from tension and stress. If you are feeling shy about being massaged by a stranger, make it a part of your family life instead. It is a wonderful way to connect to your nearest and dearest.

I sense that massage is an emotional protection for me, a way of remaining grounded in myself as well as keeping a calm openness to the people around me. Like most other people who enjoy massage, I don't usually talk much about it, since the values often associated with it in the West are to do with excess. Since coming to Scandinavia, and learning a little more about the development of massage here, I see a different range of values associated with it. In the thoughts of the Scandinavians that I have mentioned, these values have to do with creating the good society, where all people matter and where peace is a common goal. These are ideas to which anyone who appreciates massage can relate. They bring massage "out of the closet" and give it its due credit, as an outstanding tool for us to connect with our world and to know ourselves better.

The Importance of Getting Sensitized

Many of the health problems that we encounter today—stress and overweight, for example—are facilitated by a disconnect of ourselves from how we actually feel. Coming between us and those feelings are the pile of things that we were supposed to have done yesterday, and/or what the many media influences that we encounter suggest we should be doing. You might get to the end of a harried day at the office and suddenly realize that all of the time you have been doing this with your shoulders up at

---

BRINGING MASSAGE HOME

Enjoying massage doesn't have to be an expensive affair requiring a lot of organization. To start with, all you need is a little oil from the kitchen (a few drops of essence of lavender oil is my favorite) and a willing pair of hands. Ten minutes on the shoulders can work miracles. If you and/or your partner or friend want to learn more, there are several books available on Classical/Swedish and other forms of massage, as well as how to use essential oils for aromatherapy.

your ears. You might consume a hamburger and a pile of fries once a day because an advertisement shows a flat-abdomened teenager made up to be an adult, chomping his or her way through the same sort of fare. You don't necessarily end up feeling so good after having consumed it. Finding simple ways and making the time to get in touch with our feelings by bringing intimacy into our lives and reaching for that inner sanctum can begin to sensitize us to how we actually feel. Sensitization is not something fuzzy and blurred. It is about clarity, and the tremendous satisfaction of knowing yourself as an individual.

FIVE

Essential Design
and the Creation of Home

L ONG BEFORE I CAME to live in Scandinavia, I used to shuttle between London and Copenhagen on business. Most of the time when I visited Copenhagen, I stayed in small suburban hotels. These could have been, more or less, anywhere in a northern European suburb, save the great Danish food and notes consistently displayed in the bathroom about choosing the ecological option and not having one's towels changed every day. During one of my longer stays in Copenhagen, I rented an apartment in the center of town. It had been leased at an inexpensive rate by a Danish family with five children who were off for the summer.

In all of the time that I had traveled, in the many homes and countless hotels that I had occupied, I never bothered much about whether the design of a place suited me or not. If it was clean and had a desk where I could work, it was fine. In fact, I think I became more or less design immune in order to carry on this transient life. When I walked into the apartment in Copenhagen, my design immunity began to break down. I felt immediately at home and wondered why. I had no personal connections to this place.

I can still smell it. The smell of warm, unvarnished wood emanating up from the wide floor planks. The long, uncurtained windows attracting in the evening light. The connected rooms offering its inhabitants the possibility of togetherness or privacy. The calm playfulness of painted wood in the younger children's room. The understatedness of the decor. The little kitchen breakfast table positioned to catch the morning sunlight at a window overlooking a modest common garden courtyard. The way that everything made sense. I walked into the kitchen, put away my groceries, and made dinner without having to look high and low for pots and utensils. I knew where things were and how they worked. It was as though I had bought and arranged them myself.

This Danish apartment stands for what I now call *essential design*. Its design technology attended directly to the needs of its inhabitants for warmth and light. The extreme Nordic climate has this effect of making design focus on the essentials, even highlighting them, and not just treating them secondary to the decor. As a result of this focus, the character of the materials and objects stood revealed. There was an unpretentiousness, an honesty, about it all, and a thrilling beauty in being able to experience the purity of natural elements, in this case wood and light. In my virtual, stressed, hurried, and transient life, I discovered there that I actually needed in my living environment qualities that felt grounding, steadying, uncomplicated, and in some way connected to those basic elements in nature—the origin of myself, perhaps. Essential design attends to this ever-growing psychological need that all of us have.

Scandinavian design is a much-explored subject. There have been many books and exhibitions all around the world trying to pick out its special edge. I introduce you to it from an angle that I have not seen explored before: the way that Scandinavian design has, over time, through its very distinct characteristics and close connection to nature, evolved into a design approach, a sort of Nordic feng shui, in creating living environments and things for personal use that are good for people and their surroundings. While I do make references to all sorts of design in this chapter, the focus is on design for the home.

As I take you through this short odyssey in the world of Scandinavian design, I provide you with ideas about how you can apply this Nordic-inspired design approach to your own living and working environments to make a significant difference in the way you feel about yourself and your environment. This discussion is mostly not about *things,* but an attitude and ways of doing things that I learned about in my process of finding and creating a home in Scandinavia.

Our cultural heritage and the culture in which we live—these days frequently two different things—affect what design for well-being is for each of us. There are obviously many Nordic design manifestations that just wouldn't make sense or be appropriate in Texas or Florida, for example. There are others that are, more or less, universally appealing because they touch on positive feelings: instincts that are deeply ingrained in all of us. Since I don't have one cultural heritage—one place that I can identify with that shaped my ideas of beauty—I get the feeling that I am uniquely equipped to comment on this matter. There are many elements of Nordic design that transcend borders in terms of their relevance for our well-being. And while the specifics of many Nordic design ideas will appeal directly to those readers living in colder climates, I will show you that there is a Nordic way about seeing the relationship between humans, the environment, and the objects and structures that we place there that is relevant to readers in any climatic conditions.

The first part of this chapter discusses why the design of our living environments and the things that we use on a daily basis is vital to our well-being. It is also about why becoming more conscious of our design choices and getting involved in the creation of our homes is important. The second and largest part of the chapter introduces you to the elements of essential design—the features that can turn our homes into places of creativity, sensuousness, and inner sanctum. It explains why these features are essential to good living and opens up to you their Scandinavian inspiration.

Design Is Survival

When first I visited Finland to begin work on this particular chapter, I heard it said at least three times that design is survival. This sounded at first to me to be rather extreme. Was the shape of my teapot that critical to my life? Certainly, I was not the most receptive person to this type of comment. I was always the one who was the first to start yawning in home interior stores.

This design-is-survival attitude also sounded somewhat banal to me. Of course, good design has been critical to our survival ever since the cavemen created the first cutting instrument out of stone. However, as time went on, I realized that the art of crafting things, why they were crafted, and how we respond to them are issues that inhabit their own very big room in Nordic culture. It is one of those things that strikes you when you come here as an outsider. I wondered why and began to ask around. One common explanation was that in Scandinavia good design really is essential. Living in a cold climate requires innovative thinking about clothing, shelter, transport, communication, food, and all of those things that most of us take for granted these days. People spend a lot of time inside and thus think more about the arrangement of things there, I heard. It is a plausible explanation until you remember that a cold climate is not unique to the Nordic countries. The revered place that design occupies in their cultural soul, on the other hand, is.

An Idea for Our Times

Whatever the reason, in Scandinavia I encountered the general idea that design is there to nurture life. That idea is very appropriate to the new challenges that all of us face to our well-being. Today, people sometimes, if not always, feel that their lives are under siege in a world that is faster paced and more complex than ever before. Relationships with family and friends suffer. Many of us feel stressed and tired, and our poor doctors often cannot give us a clear medical explanation as to why. There is no doubt that our living and working environments play an essential role in determining how we deal with these challenges that modern society is throwing at us. The International Academy for Design and Health, which is based in Sweden, gives scientific reinforcement to what most of us have always sensed.

Scientific research during the last decade has proved the link between poor physical environments, or psychologically inappropriate physical

THE INTERNATIONAL ACADEMY
FOR DESIGN AND HEALTH

Based in Sweden, this academy represents an international network of experts whose work originated in the importance of design to healing processes in hospitals. The activities of this network are constantly expanding, with their ideas gradually being translated into nonhospital and working environments. With a number of interesting publications, seminars, and conferences, and now a degreed course on design and health offered through the academy, its Web site is worth a visit. See Resources.

environments, and symptoms of poor health such as anxiety, depression, high blood pressure, sleeplessness, and an increased need for analgesic drugs.[1]

Today, people in the developed world spend 80 to 90 percent of their time indoors.[2] Since most people cannot easily change this situation due to work responsibilities, the answer definitely lies partly in creating or finding, and installing structures, fittings, and objects that nurture our minds, emotions, and bodies.

Sound easy? Actually it is more challenging than ever in an era when most people don't get much time to spend at home and are not engaged in the main design decisions of their working environment. To add to this dilemma, in our lifetimes we are now more likely than ever to live in several homes rather than just one. Including my current home in Sweden, I count fifteen in my own lifetime (excluding communal student living) so far. In this situation, we need to reinforce the importance of involving ourselves and finding design ideas that we find steadying and can take with us wherever we go.

*The Importance of Making Choices
and Getting Involved*

Since I had the feeling that there were special features of Nordic-style designs that were literally good for our survival, I began to ask the design establishment about what these features might be. Several people understood and responded with clear ideas, which confirmed some of the things that I sensed. Others looked at me with furled eyebrows and responded that, of course, all designers set out to create environments and things that are good for people and their well-being. In Scandinavia, I believe there is some truth in this statement. On the other hand, as a representative of the average consumer, I can also say that the word "design" has, in general, come to represent something associated with social pressure and the resulting stress, which is negative for our health. Design has come to mean the same as identity—i.e., I am as good as my couch, my flooring, and my wallpaper.

Although I would be the last person to say that it is not fun to choose and own nice things (and thus good to have variety and competition), I also believe that the significance of these things has overtaken us because they have become about our self-worth. Ten-year-olds can become deeply depressed these days because they got the wrong brand name for Christmas. Adults skirt the design stores viewing home furnishing objects that they are afraid they haven't quite understood (and cannot afford), and feel deeply inadequate. The modern disease of social comparison gnaws away at our personal space. In this incarnation, design is not wellness promoting. Quite the reverse. How it will look to others rather than whether it will serve our needs has become the thing. As a result, much of design has come to represent anxiety rather than ease. Of course, these feelings have somewhat less to do with what is sold, meaning what designers produce, than the way that it is sold, meaning companies and advertising choices. In this situation, the best thing that we can do is to reevaluate our own attitudes toward design and what it should be there to do for us.

Design and the creation of home is not something that you should allow to control you. You control it. If you don't, you relinquish something that is absolutely essential to your well-being. Something as old as we are as a race: the fulfillment of your urge to create a place of dwelling where you feel safe and comforted.

You would have thought that being pregnant with twins would automatically switch on my nesting instincts. It didn't. Not because I wasn't thrilled to be having twins, but because my feelings of control over where

THE IMPORTANCE OF A *KOJA*

During the first weeks that I took my children to day care in Sweden, I learned that they were building a koja. *A* koja *is a children's hideout in Swedish language. However, the difference between a hideout and a* koja *is that the* koja *is always made by the children themselves. Another essential point about it is that it should be simple, with everything on hand needed to play in it, but also cozy. By now I have watched my young twins squealing with excitement and happiness while creating their* koja *on many occasions. I have discovered that it is great training for taking charge of the design and creation of a living environment. My children have already graduated to rearranging the furniture in their playroom, on their own initiative!*

I lived were so very weak after the many years of itinerancy. Before my very eyes, I watched Claes bearing out my nesting instincts for me in reconstructing our town dwelling instead. In all of the meetings with architects and builders that we had, my attention was on him and the way that his enthusiasm and creativity were spurred by the idea of creating a place of comfort and safety for our family. He sneaked in quick sketches on paper during breaks at work, and his mind whirled around the materials, forms, and colors that would express our home. I stood, and as my tummy bulged, sat and watched as though all of this was happening at a great distance, as though I just could not get there, much as I would have liked to.

At the time, I did not fully realize that I had come into a family whose lifeblood was the creation of homes, and into a society with a deep belief in the possibilities for design to deliver a better life. I was surrounded in a family and a society, which would eventually elicit those instincts that were an essential element of my well-being. They would eventually help me to understand the magnitude of the job that my own mother had undertaken so many times.

The symbolism of my wedding present from Claes runs deep. It was a small house on the water's edge. Part of the force with which I persuaded Claes to move out to the island two years later came from a longing to begin taking control of my dwelling, in a place away from the gaze of others, where I would have the space to nurture my tender, very fragile feelings about the creation of home.

Finding a Sense of Balance

As I embarked on this brave new adventure in this design-convinced society, I began to think about what made me feel good in my living environment and what didn't. I began to wonder about some of the distinctive features of Scandinavian design. Why did they appeal to so many people all over the world? After some years of thinking and talking, I come to the conclusion that there are several characteristics of Scandinavian design that can help to free us from "the siege" that I mentioned earlier. Above all, its inherent sense of balance provides us an equilibrium we are seeking all of the time in lives that constantly tug us this way and that.

There are others who feel the same way. Take my world-traveled friend Martine, who began to restore traditional Swedish designs as therapy midlife because they were "pieces that created a calm, steadying environment" that were "good for the soul." Take Kristian, who got snowed in with his family in their cottage on the Baltic island of Gotland one Christmas, and decided to swap his job of ten years in a major, multinational IT corporation for carpentry. "Everything seemed to be about surface," he said. Learning carpentry (from scratch) and working with real materials would bring some depth into living. Today he runs one of Sweden's successful furniture design businesses. "Design is a way of being well," he concluded. For myself, I sensed it in the Danish apartment, and today I have a better idea of what it is all about.

The Elements of Essential Design

Below I focus on three groups of elements that support and encourage our healthy processes by creating the good life in our living and working environments. These are elements in Scandinavian design that increase our connection to nature at home and stir creativity, impart an intimate, welcoming feeling, and use technology in ways that support our well-being.

DESIGN AS PERSONAL WELL-BEING

The next time that you realize your wallpaper needs replacing or you need an-
other chair, ask yourself about what you could replace it with that would make
you feel good—not just today or tomorrow, but for quite some time. You might
want to flip through some magazines to get some inspiration, but remember to
keep in mind that question of what makes you feel inspired and balanced at
the same time. It often helps to reflect back on the interiors that you have been
in, that made you feel good. What were their characteristics? Then go for the
wallpaper and/or the chair.

Connection to Nature

"The greenery is dense with memories," writes one Swedish poet.[3] He is right. We have a primitive memory. Modern psychoanalysis and research into environmental psychology confirm it. There are certain aspects of our behavior—certain fears, needs, and preferences—that just cannot be explained by modern conditioning. Why do we prefer natural light to the many types of man-made lights that we can purchase today? Because we cannot survive without it. Why are we attracted to glitter and sheen? Probably because it resembles water, which we also cannot live without.[4]

Living on my Swedish island, I think I must be the ultimate proof of this theory. I was not raised to live in this way: far from the city lights, with an ancient forest attempting each day to recapture the ground on which my home stands, without parking anywhere near my house, and without garbage collectors. Yet, given the chance to live it, I am irrevocably drawn to this life surrounded by the elements. Why? Because, like you, I have a memory that goes back up to two million years, which reminds me of the source that fulfills my most fundamental needs.

This memory is a good part of the explanation for why, when I walked into the Danish apartment and into my eventual home on the island, I felt safe, secure, steadied, and comforted. There were several elements of the design in these places that appealed to my primitive memory, in other words, to my need for a connection to nature in design. They appealed to my desire for safety and security, and to my senses of touch, smell, sight, and sound.

Why was this? I was experiencing something very fundamental and dominant in Nordic design: its deep roots in our collective primitive memory. Many design traditions around the world draw their inspiration from nature. In Scandinavia, that relationship runs very deep to the extent that design often seems to be a manifestation of nature. Even the most devoted of modernist Scandinavian designers have acknowledged this.

Finnish mythology talks about the design of an object as something that you are able to do if you observe closely the origins of an object. Nature is the ultimate enabler of design. Perhaps this is the explanation for why Nordic cities are so pleasant to be in. "Nordic architects don't really know how to create urban environments," one successful Finnish architect said to me. Urbanity is not their inspiration.

As I have already mentioned, today people in the developed world spend about 80 to 90 percent of their time indoors, which is quite the opposite of what our genes, the bearers of our primitive memory, prepared us for. I found in the Danish apartment, and eventually helped to create on my Swedish island, a place that was "food" for those genes. Here are some of the key elements explaining how and why.

CONTRAST AND COHERENCE

Research shows us that the best view from your brain's perspective is the one that you have into the natural environment. In the words of some well-known researchers on the subject of nature and well-being, nature switches on our "spontaneous consciousness," which is a much easier state to be in than a state of "directed concentration," which we are usually in, in nonnatural environments.[5] Why is this? Likely because no human construction can beat nature in the combination of contrast balanced by coherence. Our brains can appreciate the difference between each tree, and can at the same time delight in the fact that these different trees all form a part of a masterfully constructed forest. It is the equilibrium between interesting and pleasing detail and a feeling of wholeness that counts.

Basically, we need to take this principle, derived from our response to natural environments, and find ways to apply it indoors. This does not mean turning the inside of your house into a forest or a jungle. It means finding techniques to create places that interest us at the same time as making us feel relaxed and safe.

Our desire for coherence in our surroundings has, on an emotional level, to do with the human race's endless search for meaning— i.e., Why are we here? When we sense connections, patterns between events, we feel that we have got an enlightened glimpse of the Grand Plan. Our environments can go a long way toward helping us to feel that we have meaning in our lives—that we belong to a place that is beautiful. The structures that we live in are supportive if they cohere with features of the natural environment and the culture that surrounds us. No matter where we go— even places that we have never been in before—our senses lap up the beauty of dwellings that are made from natural materials coming from the environment in which they are built. One philosopher of architecture says that "a building that ignores its context is crazy, because it lacks a crucial ingredient—meaning."[6] The same goes for the content of that structure.

The best of Scandinavian design has mastered this delicate balance. Take the Sydney Opera House, which I spent hours staring at when I was a teenager living in Sydney. Of all of the modern public buildings that I have ever seen, this is the one that to me most dramatically and skillfully gains and gives meaning to its physical environment: giant shells on the shores of Sydney harbor. A Dane named Jørn Utzon (1918–), heavily influenced by some of the greatest Nordic design personalities of his time, designed it. The opera house is a masterpiece of visual stimulation at the same time as it "belongs." When you stand inside it and look out, your whole being is filled with its beauty, even if you are not Australian.

Getting your space to "cohere" does not mean making it monotone or monocultural. This can mean sacrificing visual stimulation. Both the Danish apartment and our house on the island contain things picked up in other parts of the world and things that come from home. When I first walked into the main house on the island, I was taken by the visual power of the large African masks and other wall hangings that Claes had picked up during his travels. Today we have replaced them with some items that we bought in Sri Lanka and Bangladesh when we worked in these countries together. The achievement of coherence in these places has to do with a number of factors. One is that everything in them is an expression of whole lives with all of their diverse experiences. But there is more. The elements of essential design that I explain as this section progresses can help you to build up this balance between contrast and coherence.

THE LONG VIEW ACHIEVED HUMANELY

Sitting at my desk in my island study, I look away from my PC screen, over my left shoulder, and can see very far through the large, unadorned window. My eyes, in fact my whole head, feel immediately relaxed as my line of vision runs down across our dock onto the endless lake water and then across to the facing island. All at once I feel safe as well as lifted. Why? My primitive memory tells me that there is no approaching danger from the water. My brain actually begins to work better, since the long view outside gives it the stimulation that it needs. It switches on my "spontaneous consciousness," relieving me from my state of "directed concentration." Visual variety in nature stimulates our brains by strengthening the links between different cells, networks, and systems in the brain.[7]

In Scandinavia I have found that people are obsessed with the long view. And they are prepared to work very hard to get it. Our island home has several terraces and spots arranged for enjoying the view. The focal point of discussion between neighbors is which trees we should take down in order to increase our view of the water and the sunset. Our electrician

---

PLEASING YOUR BRAIN

You can make your brain feel "happy" about your home by asking yourself the following questions and then taking some simple steps to make changes based on the answers. For coherence, ask yourself (a) whether your home fits in with the local environment—e.g., light, materials; (b) whether it is a reflection of your life—e.g., whether it contains items that reflect the totality of your life. For contrast, ask yourself whether your home allows your eye to focus on single items or structures that you find interesting or pleasing to look at—e.g., Are there so many things around that you cannot make out the contrasts?

neighbor went so far as to build a small swimming pool, which he has protected with a greenhouse top, so that at any time of the year he can look out across the water, ice, or snow and enjoy the view from his pool after a long, hard day's work. He "imported" all of the materials for building this pool in a small motorboat himself, and had no previous experience of building pools. He is not alone in this seeming lunacy about the long view. I have come to understand on this island that to be able to see far into nature is to live well.

The human desire for a long view into the outdoors carries over into indoor environments. Being able to see across the space inside our homes— to be visually stimulated by the details at the same time as we see the whole—can also be a visually satisfying experience. A mass of closed doors is never very appealing. Historically, homes in Scandinavia placed an emphasis on being able to see from one room into another. Connecting doors were left open. This was the precursor of modern open-plan living.[8] In the Danish apartment, you could open up the largest part of the apartment space into one room, or divide it up by closing the double doors.

How you achieve the long view into the outdoors and inside your living space is also important to your sense of well-being. One of the most interesting responses to my question about what it is about Scandinavian design that is so appealing, is that it works with "human" proportions. A modernist Scandinavian architect, Niels Thorp, with a reputation for creating public buildings that are good for people's well-being, says that his initial starting point is always "the human scale."[9] What does this mean, I wondered? I started to think about it and look around.

ACHIEVING THE LONG VIEW

How long a view do your windows give you to the outdoors? Is there a wall where you could potentially see farthest in your garden or across the skyline? How far can you see inside your home? Is it possible for you to open it up and have a long view across the space? If not, can you create the long view into the sky by opening up a roof window? Our primitive memory and the way our brains work make these important questions in thinking about what makes us feel well in our homes and workplaces.

To a great extent, it has partly to do with *how* you achieve the long view. In some parts of the world, this is achieved by great height and size, such as by building very high or very large. This can be thrilling for a while, but our primitive memory—actually remembering our origins in savanna habitats with long horizontal rather than vertical perspectives—keeps us on high alert in these environments. It tells us that they are dangerous. So we cannot come to a state of calm in them. Today, this fact is increasingly recognized by leading designers of homes and workplaces all around the world who have come to understand the virtues, from the point of view of our well-being, of "the not-so-big house."[10] Think about this if you are in the enviable position of building a new home. It will make all the difference to your sense of well-being.

In Scandinavia, there is delight in achieving the long view humanely. This has nothing to do with lack of space. This may be partly due to practicalities, such as the fact that there is a strong do-it-yourself culture in building homes outside of the cities. So, people will tend to build lower and smaller. But it is more than this. Even major new public constructions are concerned with the long view achieved in humane proportions. The design for the new Swedish embassy in Washington, D.C. (to be completed in 2006) is one example. From this low-rise "glass box" it will be possible to get a spectacular long view of the Potomac from the first floor. The *Washington Post* called it "a glass box that holds real promise."[11]

Here on our island, our *lusthus,* or pleasure house, which is an enclosed gazebo, is a good example of how we achieve the long view in humane proportions. It fits about eight people, cozily seated. It is a simple wooden structure placed at the water's edge with windows all around it. A team of builders from northern Sweden arrived at ten o'clock in the morning and built it in less than a day. The small space inside our *lusthus* suddenly becomes very big when we look out onto the vast lake. Our brains feel happy in this small indoor space, which feels safe, interesting, and very humane.

ORGANIC FORM AND TIMELESS SYMMETRY

Another important element in achieving that delicate balance between visual stimulation and coherence as well as calm in your environment has to do with the nature of the *lines* that you surround yourself in. We can learn a lot from how to achieve it from nature. If you have ever taken a good look at a leaf, you will remember that it is divided up the middle, and therefore has two neat sides, which are not identical. Similar, but not the same. The leaf has straight lines running through it but is itself rounded in shape. It doesn't appear itself to change before your eyes. Yet it is changing all of the time, because it is living matter. This supreme balance of changing, organic form, and timeless symmetry is nature's mastery. Our brains depend on these kinds of harmonious contrasts for good function. It is the reason that nature positively stimulates our brains like no other source.

Scandinavian design is often admired for its clean lines. Gustavian design from the eighteenth century, still the most popular form of Scandinavian historical design worldwide, is admired for its classical symmetry. Still, it is not just the clean lines in themselves that create the interest. It is the interplay between organic lines, another suggestion of change, and symmetrical clean lines that catches your eye. Painted and wooden carved wall relief patterns look constantly like they are about to break away from the frames that contain them. The most beautiful of Gustavian tables and couches have curved legs, symmetrically arranged, and look like they could break out of this symmetry and change shape or walk away at any minute.

On a more modern note, the SAS Royal Hotel in Copenhagen—the lobby and particularly the famous Room 606—contains great examples of the designer Arne Jacobsen's (1902–1971) skill for understanding the human brain's need for organic form next to timeless symmetry. Jacobsen took his inspiration from nature. His chairs the Egg, the Swan, and the Drop all give the suggestion of change by their curved shape amid other linear forms. His chair the Ant, the best-selling chair of all time, brought life into every lifeless room it entered. The chair looks constantly like it is about to crawl away. Danes descended from long traditions of furniture making are masterful at this art of graceful, live furniture.

Some of the most adventurous modern Scandinavian architecture, with a deep consciousness for the well-being of people, has drawn on this harmonious contrast. On the spectacular side, the Danish architect Erik Asmussen (1913–1998) created an entire complex, a place deliberately designed to encourage healing processes that essentially showed buildings

If you feel that your living environment is looking a little lifeless, it may be be-cause you have got too much straight symmetry going on around you. If you could place in that living space just one prominent object that gave the sug-gestion of change—a curved object—it will make all the difference. If your place feels confusing, it may be because you need a few more straight lines and a little symmetry to make your environment coherent. Try reducing the curves. Put two similar objects together in a prominent place. There are a lot of ideas that you could try in order to achieve this harmonious juxtaposition that your brain eats up.

metamorphosing into one another. A smaller building looks like it could gradually become the next. Different, but the same, straight lines and curved lines, and all part of a consistent whole. Asmussen himself believed deeply in the healing power of nature—turning compost heaps eight hours a day on a Sunday, just to relax—and thought a great deal about how this healing power could innovatively be translated into architecture.

SIMPLY SPACE

One critical prerequisite for achieving this harmonious juxtaposition—organic form and timeless symmetry—is that you are able to see it. What I mean by this is making sure that too many juxtaposed lines do not crowd out your interior: The sort of thing that makes many of us easily tire of rococo style. Your brain needs the *space* to appreciate the harmony of forms around you. This is something that we can learn from our re-actions to natural environments. Space gives us the chance to appreciate beauty.

The art of space creation for the appreciation of clean lines is a great Scandinavian art—even if the space available is not very big. To a great ex-tent, this art emerges out of a peasant culture, where people did not own much and then only what was necessary.

A few single pieces of painted or plain handmade wooden furnishings with finely crafted lines and then only the wide-planked wooden floors—

simply space. This feature has carried over into the best of modern Scandinavian interiors, which shouldn't be confused with the global trend toward minimalism: an interesting design experiment, but a rather inhumane way to live. We tire of it as easily as we do of rococo.

Getting a satisfying interior effect is often about removing things rather than adding them. This is perhaps the most difficult task in bringing and keeping a feeling of well-being in your home. "Clear your clutter" is the common message of today's many spiritual and interior design experts. My problem with this advice is that it is often difficult to draw the line between what is clutter and what is not. For instance, are all of the paper and books in my study clutter? To me, being able to see a harmonious contrast of lines is an easier way to think about it.

I return to the dining room of the Danish apartment. There were books and personal items in the bookshelves around the room. It wasn't bare. Still, most of the space was left free so that one could appreciate the large, oblong-shaped smooth wooden table with matching, straight-lined chairs. Spotlights and large uncurtained windows provided plenty of light. The wide, light-colored wooden floor was left free of carpeting. The space drew my attention to the two organically shaped metallic candelabras in the middle of the table. There was life in this room. There was calm. And enough space for me to experience both.

Looking at any corner of a room, you will realize what to put away or throw out if you focus on trying to see the "clean" harmony of the lines. It may take a while to see, particularly if your place has been the way it is for a very long time. But once your consciousness about this feature is switched on, you will eventually work out what to do.

In Love with Nature's Light

The impact on your well-being of space and the harmony of lines in different parts of your home can only be felt if there is enough natural light. Things cohere with one another because the light falls on them. The love of bright, sunlit interiors in our time is a result of Scandinavian influence.[12] This is no coincidence. If you love something as much as Scandinavians love the light, then you will also learn a great deal about its nature and become a master at working with it. It is appropriate that the aforementioned Swedish embassy building in Washington, D.C., will be a "wicker lamp" for that city during the evenings—a reminder of what people from this part of the world love most and do best.

We need to learn to make best use of natural light in our homes and workplaces from a health point of view. Our primitive memory, our sense of natural rhythm, requires it. It knows that we and all living things around us need it in order to survive. Repeated studies have shown, among other things, that natural-day-lit classrooms—compared to classrooms with conventional lighting—promote faster growth, less tooth decay, higher attendance, more quiet through increased concentration levels, and more positive moods resulting in better scholastic achievement.[13] Lack of daylight leaves us depressed and in some extreme cases can lead to seasonal affective disorder (SAD), which needs to be treated with proper medical care.

The extent to which the sun hides and reveals itself at different times of year is extreme in this part of the world. During the darkest part of the winter, it rises above the horizon for a few brief hours and then sets. During the lightest part of the summer it soars into the sky and seems never to want to set at all. People from this part of the world watch the sun. Claes recounts the story of how he sat marveling at the setting Spanish sun through the small bathroom window of a rental apartment that was facing all the wrong way. Cocktail hour from the bathroom. Anything to watch this daily wonder.

Due to the sun's schizophrenic behavior in Scandinavia, people have become very good at playing with whatever light the sun is prepared to give them. Balconies and windows are places for making magic with the light. One doesn't destroy them with stodgy, lined curtains, as I did when I first set up home with Claes in Stockholm. People who visited looked at the heavy, mock-brocaded curtains I had installed in the living room with concern. I was obsessed by the idea of hiding the view of the apartment building next door. With this obsession, I missed the fact that the morning sunlight, the trees to the left of this view, and the rock garden below could make all the difference to my living room. There were ways of taking attention away from that apartment building next door, without sucking all the life out of the room by installing thick, heavy curtains. Muslin cloth draped gently over the edges or top of the window, unlined light-colored linen drapes, or a delicate unlined cloth blind[14] might have worked. Or, as in Karin Blixen's house in northern Zealand, Denmark, long, laced white cloth trailed onto the floor, like brides gone to marry the sun.

The use of color in many parts of Scandinavia has to do with reflecting natural light. Many interior design books will tell you that white is the color of calm and peacefulness. Why? They don't usually explain. White best reflects natural light, which we remember we need. Knowing that it is there brings us into a deep state of calm. Danish and Swedish designs play with hues of white revealed in faded pastel shades. White can be a cold color if it is not handled properly, and in this part of the world it is handled with true mastery. Sweden's main anthroposophic center is a world-famous "healing" building, in terms of architecture, for many reasons. One of them is that its Danish architect painted the entire wall, ceiling, and outer surfaces in a series of complementary hues with a white foundation, giving the whole place the look of light-filled color.

Using natural light well is important not only in cold, dark climates but also in warm climates. One new Scandinavian invention—conducting natural light through fiber-optic cables—is being tried in the Mediterranean countries, where people have traditionally kept inside spaces dark for the purpose of keeping them cool. Having grown up in several hot countries I understand this need for shade and coolness. Now and again, it would have been nice to have a little more natural light indoors and still keep cool.

FIRE OF LIFE

I didn't get the chance to experience the fantastic impact of sunlight in the rooms of my present home when I first came here. It was night and pitch dark. Instead, I experienced it through another kind of natural light. Within ten minutes of walking in the door, Claes had lit most of his candles. Some were in simple candleholders, others were inside lanterns and wall-attached lamps. Two electric lights were lit. Otherwise the many candles provided our evening light. Within half an hour fires crackled in the small low hearths of the one-hundred-year-old *kakelugnar,* two tall, white-tiled stoves that had been the saving grace of the workers who had inhabited this place during the nineteenth century when there was no other form of heating. We turned off a few of the heaters. The *kakelugnar* are one of the most efficient forms of heating available.

Fire has remained a distinct part of our life on the island. It is a friend

PLAYING WITH LIGHT

Stand where you are in your home. Do you get enough sunlight from your windows at different times of day? Could you minimize or lighten your curtains to let in more? Watch the sun from the windows inside your home or workplace at different times of day. Or, if your house is not yet built, remember to stand in the spot where you will build it and watch the sun morning, noon, and evening. Where should you put your windows to capture the light throughout the day? When during the day are you most likely to have time to spend on your terrace? Do you want to watch the sun rise or set—or a little of both? If you live in a warm and sunny climate, how can you get enough natural light into where you live, still leaving the interior a cool and airy place to be in? Check the color of your walls. Does it make best use of the light coming in from the outdoors? Natural light is your home's most important decor.

and not merely a romantic embellishment. Somewhere deep in our memories, we remember that to be able to make fire and to keep it going is to survive. It is a part of our identity: the ability to make it is one of those things that distinguish us as human. Claes asked me whether we should remove the heavy, cast-iron, wood-fired stoves, once the only means of cooking in this place. "No," I said. "Keep them—if the electricity fails I can make a warm meal." With our kitchen temperature just a tad under 14°C, or 57°F, on the coldest of winter mornings, I decided to try lighting one of these. It was thus that I learned that making a fire was about attention to a friend—not something done hastily on the side.

The darkness is usually discussed in the context of the absence of light. Here in the cold north, the darkness calls on people to evoke their creativity, to make their own light. The Scandinavian festival of Santa Lucia, celebrated on December 13, is in many ways a celebration of human inventiveness, of our capacity to create light and warmth where there is none. Why otherwise would Scandinavians celebrate so widely the death of an Italian woman with a doleful life story? They have fashioned their own Lucia, creating a Scandinavian saint of light, warmth, and hope.

Praising the Water

Light falling on water attracts every human eye. Water, seen in vast lakes, seas, rivers, waterfalls, and fjords, is power, and that always attracts our attention. Why is this? Perhaps it is because we have great difficulties to create it or control it, and we cannot live without it. Water was once the main source of our food, one of the main reasons that early populations settled along the coasts and rivers. Water is about the familiar: When we are born, we are automatically able to swim underwater.

Scandinavians have long been seafaring people who understand instinctively the power of water. Water is a cultural phenomenon in the Nordic countries and manifests itself in their design traditions.

Each time I walk down the steps leading down to the water from our home I feel that I am in some way praising the water. Our entire home is built in adoration of the water. At the age of seventy, Claes's grandfather built three large stone terraces with an aisle down the center leading to the water. He carried and placed each stone with his bare hands. The stones on the top layer of each terrace are all a similar shape: flat and oblong. Each stone on that layer had been carefully chosen out of piles of oddly shaped pieces. Seen from the water, the terraces are the most striking part of this place. They are its mark of respect to the life-giving source all around us.

There are other traditions of building in praise of the water that are more common: gazebos on the water's edge, small bathing or sauna houses, wooden docks with decorative railing, many places to sit in admiration of the water.

Materials from the Earth

Today there is a growing consciousness of the linkage between using natural materials in our homes and our well-being. What is this really all about? Much of the discussion is vague. These materials that have come from the earth in their natural state appeal to our senses, which are as old as the human race. They encourage positive health processes, because they have meaning for our survival. They also relax us because they don't conduct electrical wavelengths, which tire us.

Below I consider four natural materials that have been used widely in Nordic design to make things cozy: wood, stone, linen, and wool. The intention is to inspire you to seek out natural materials from your own local environment and to bring them into your home.

WOOD Since the time that I lived in Asia as a child, I had got out of the habit of taking my shoes off before entering a home unless they were very

---

BRINGING IN THE POWER OF WATER

What do you do if you don't have a body of water nearby? Our friend Peter bought a place near Stockholm without a body of water anywhere close by, and missed the water so much that he started digging. Today he has a lake on his farm. If you don't have the sort of space that Peter has, you could try to start with a pond or a small waterfall. If you need to think real simple, go for an attractive bowl filled with water and perhaps a floating candle on your sitting-room table.

dirty. I was surprised to find that there was a place in the so-called West where people also left their shoes at the front door. There are a lot of good reasons for this in Scandinavia, one of the more positive being that the nerve endings on the soles of your feet frequently get the chance to luxuriate in the feel of soft, warm wood. So it was, each time that I entered the Danish apartment—which had typical wide floorboards, polished and scrubbed with *såpa* (pine oil soap) to create an evenness, but unvarnished so as to preserve the original feel of the wood—I received a gentle foot massage, for free.

Scandinavians have consistently remained loyal to wood as a material, since it is available (aside from in Iceland, which has few trees) and they have managed their forests masterfully.

Even during the advent of modernism in the early part of the twentieth century, Scandinavians continued to prefer wood to steel, a favorite material of the industrial age. Alvar Aalto and Bruno Mathsson, two internationally renowned names in Scandinavian design during the twentieth century, invented clever techniques of bending wood, creating timeless chairs and other furnishings.

Perhaps the most important thing about having wood around you is that it makes your living environment feel alive.

STONE We surround our open outdoor fires with a circle of stones. Stones stop the fire from spreading. In nineteenth-century Scandinavia, stones in the form of pebbled pathways were used to create an even look and stop water pools from creating a muddy path after the rain. Stones stop water from being wherever it likes. Yet while they can stop fire and water, they do have one very curious Achilles' heel. Fire and water together can break even the hardest of stones. This takes time and skill. We have broken down large boulders to prepare the ground for building using this technique. Still, it is something of a miracle. Humans have known all of these things about stones for a very long time. They are our ancient knowledge.

The small stony islands of Scandinavia have resulted in some masterful design with stone. I live on one of them. Walk down the forest path leading to the small footbridge across to the next island, and to the left are the remains of a nineteenth-century stone-and-sand-mining operation

On my desk, holding down the piles of paper from flying off when I open the window, I have two flat, smooth gray-white stones. They come from the small island of Fårö (Sheep Island), which can be reached from the stony and charmed island of Gotland. Here one is struck by the beauty of design with indigenous limestone. The flat, wind-blown landscape dotted with homes built of stone is crossed everywhere by low, stone walls, with slim, flat stones fit perfectly together to create a straight and even look. With some luck, you can find a fossil on the stony beaches of Fårö or Gotland. Just as the stones stop time in this way, they also slow time by preserving the heat of the summer, and, less fortunately, the cold of the spring.

where there remain mountains of stone. Unsurprisingly, we have learned to design with this material, mainly outdoors. On our old stone terraces, we have created small herb enclosures, using stones to keep the herbs in neat formations. Other low stone walls section off various areas of the garden. We do this because we remember the stones' fabulous ability to make us feel as if we have some control over the wilder side of life, represented by fire and water. We also use stones to link different parts of our garden to one another, in the sense that they are the steps leading from one area of our property to another. They shape our outdoor environment and they are an integral part of the dream of a country cottage in Scandinavia.

LINEN When I interviewed the president of the International Sauna Association, he described to me that he remembered from his childhood in Finland the process of linen-making taking place in the cooling-off area of the sauna house. This process had been a part of life for two thousand years in the Nordic region. It is the reason that country homes in Scandinavia have linen cabinets.

I have often wondered how this tall, upright stalk with a small, blue flower that opens for a few hours one morning and then wilts can become the shiny, smooth cloth that I use on our dining room table. I visited the only remaining producer of linen in Rexbö, in north central Sweden, in

Hälsingland, where linen was once a currency. An older man who could remember his parents working flax told me that he had once nearly lost a finger working some of the original water-powered machines. I thought he was on the verge of losing it once again as he slung the flax in and out of a huge spinning wheel. People who worked the linen hammer, to crush the flax stalks, usually became deaf. I covered my ears as I watched it slamming down to reveal the fibers in the stalks. There was always the risk of disaster in the linen drying house, where a fire was lit in a stone kiln and the door of the house shut. Nevertheless, the linen was produced, since it was a critical part of the livelihood of a village. It is perhaps for this reason that, when people in Scandinavia sit down to a table set with linen, it is regarded as so special. The production of linen was an art measured not in ticking digital minutes but in the course of human lives, says one Swedish author, Lena Catarina Swanberg, in appreciation of the preciousness that linen symbolizes here.[15]

I saw the "new" machines, now seventy or so years old. They offer faster, safer, yet still a long and laborious process with nine phases—eleven, if you count sewing the seed in the soil at the beginning and sewing up the linen fabric in the end. Despite the new production techniques, traditions in pattern design are kept. In the past, to weave the same pattern row after row, without any variety, was to tempt bad luck. The women, who sat weaving day in and day out, saw their lives reflected in the cloth. To make a few small changes from one row to the next was to make life a little more interesting, a little more worth living.

Linen has made a comeback after years of being ostracized by hurried lives and inexpensive synthetic materials. Although it is no longer economical to produce on a large scale in Scandinavia, design with linen is still an art well done in the Nordic region because there is an ingrained passion and respect for it. Despite all of the other choices available on the market today, people return to cherish linen. Why? Is it all to do with culture and tradition? Perhaps. Perhaps not.

WOOL At the first chill of each autumn, I pull my favorite woolen sweater out of the closet. I nudge it up against my nose. It is thick and soft, still permeated by the smell of last year's fires, and reminds me of everything that

Linen (along with cotton) lets your skin breathe when you wear it. Used in interior design, linen communicates this feeling of airiness into our homes. Your place breathes. Linen is practical in the sense that it is a cooling fabric in the summer and a warming fabric in the winter. Like other natural materials, it gives your skin a soft massage, when you come into contact with it. You do need to iron it and it wrinkles easily if worn. However, used in interior design, it won't have to be ironed unless you wash it, which you don't need to do as often as you do other fabrics, since it doesn't soil as easily. In combination with new synthetics, linen has become more user friendly.

I have to look forward to in the colder season. There is nothing else that I own that can keep me as warm as this.

In various parts of the Nordic countries, sheep, wool, and the food that sheep can provide have been a livelihood for hundreds of years. Particularly in Iceland, they have been food, clothing, and currency. The novel *Independent People* (1946) by Iceland's Nobel Prize–winning novelist Halldór Laxness describes to what extent men and sheep were bound together in this land. In the story, an infant who is on the verge of dying having lost its mother is nursed back to health with a simple glass bottle that has a few tufts of wool wrapped around the bottle neck. Sheep are damned and praised in this novel, but in this moment their shaggy coat is security and calm.

The Swedish version of "Baa-Baa Black Sheep," which my children sing, focuses more on the fine clothes that the sheep provide than the English version does. Like linen, wool is today being rediscovered for the fantastic material that it is.

Design for Everyone

If the close connection to nature of Nordic design gives it a special appeal to our senses, its content communicates certain ideas that are relevant to our well-being today.

THE VIRTUES OF WOOL

Wool's many virtues include that it is ecological, nonallergenic, warming (keeps you warmer than any other material), a poor substance for burning (and thus good in interiors), soft, and friendly to animals (the best wool comes from the most healthy and alive sheep). Hang it up to air overnight and any unwanted smells that it has absorbed will likely go away—wool is good at "taking care of" bad smells in this way. As if this wasn't enough, I found that the sheep I saw standing out in the rain on the stony island of Fårö would remain warm in the cold rain, since wool protects against damp and preserves warmth even when it is wet. Some people find that wool scratches their skin. If you are one of those people, you might like to know that there is experimentation with wool for clothing that is highly appealing for everyday use in cold climates, both indoors and outdoors, and that doesn't scratch. The combination of wool with modern synthetics, is providing some great new warm alternatives. See Resources.

When I walked into the apartment in Copenhagen, I remember a distinct feeling of being at home straight away. It was elegant yet there was no part of this place that I felt I should not touch or be in. I had this feeling, despite the fact that other people, whom I had never met, inhabited it for the other ten months of the year. The apartment certainly had plenty of personal things in it, which is unusual in a rental place and creates a feeling of don't-touch for an outsider. These things didn't. Why not? I have been thinking about it ever since.

Design has become an exclusive idea in our modern world. This has negative effects on our well-being. In reality, design is an essential part of our everyday lives and definitely part of an approach to personal well-being. This is an idea that Scandinavian design has, over time, attached great importance to. Design that is inclusive without losing its elegance—making the senses feel privileged for whoever walks in—has been one of the main fascinations of Scandinavian design for outsiders. Today, one of the main debates in Scandinavian design is how it can retain this inclusiveness, this talent of designing for everybody, and not collapse into a superficial design party[16] that is purely about commissions and bank accounts.

THE RIGHT TO DESIGN

The idea that everyone has the right to design has been around in Scandinavia for a long time. Even in times when the standard of life inside the court and outside of it were as far apart as they have ever been, there was a belief that everyone should have access to appealing designs. A driving motive was to reduce imports into Scandinavia and boost local industry. One of the features that made Gustavian style so distinctive was that, from its beginnings, it was intended for ordinary homes outside of the court as well as inside it. This practical Nordic adaptation of French court style—with paint instead of gilding and linen instead of exotic fabrics—included furniture and other interior designs made entirely from materials widely available at home. The result is unpretentiousness, even in some court designs.

I visited Design Forum Finland, an organization that keeps the pulse on contemporary Finnish design. There I was told that Rococo would never have worked in Finland. It could never have fit into the practical mind-set created by a historically very close peasant legacy. Design should focus on things that all people need, and not on the frills. Further, not having democ-

THE IKEA STORY

For many people in the world, modern Scandinavian design equals IKEA. Whatever the complaints about the challenges of assembling ready-made IKEA furnishings, this company has managed to furnish countless homes in Scandinavia and elsewhere with well-designed and affordable items. Concerned about a future without its founder, Ingvar Kamprad, IKEA personnel requested his best advice for the future. Out of this came "A Furniture Salesman's Testament," which laid out a strikingly modest and inclusive philosophy, including making a wide variety of furniture so as many people as possible can afford them.[17] Outside of Scandinavia, IKEA has outlets in the United States and elsewhere. See Resources.

racy in design is "like selling your soul," I was told. There is a lot that has become undemocratic when you look at the price tags, I thought, but the intention is still strong and the effect still unpretentious. At the equivalent organization in Sweden, Svensk Form, I was told that another term has to be found for "good design." In Swedish the term is too exclusive. I happened to visit Denmark's Design Center on a day when the entrance exhibit was of everyday objects, items used by people at home on a daily basis.

The Finnish architect Alvar Aalto once said that the "ulterior motive" of architecture has always been "the idea of creating paradise" for ordinary people.[18] This sense of mission partly belongs to Aalto's generation, but it also persists among Nordic architects today. Aalto himself thought a great deal about how his craft could serve people, particularly people at their weakest.

This idea of the right to design has another important dimension in Scandinavia: that ordinary people have the right to choose and create the designs that they like. Before I came to my island I had the sneaking feeling that design was for other people. It just wasn't something that I could manage to do well in my own place. I have learned that, like all rights, the right to good design has to be exercised in order to become a realty.

During the mid-1990s, I had bought an apartment in the London Docklands before it was built. It was in a fantastic location, on the banks of the Thames, and I had the option to make certain choices about the basic interior design as it was being built. The builders kept on asking whether I would rather have this or that option, but I always relinquished my right to choose. Instead, I let them choose. Why? I was worried about making the wrong choice, and was sure that everyone else, the neighbors included, could make a better choice than I in my own apartment. The word "design" frightened me. Wasn't that just for people who go around wearing black and thinking colorful ideas?

During the first summer I lived on this island, I watched Claes exercising his right to design all over the place. The hammer and paintbrushes were never far away from him. Despite constant encouragement, it took me three summers before I could work up the courage to pick up those items and do something with them. By now, I have painted, wallpapered, hammered—the works. I still don't build houses, but I do more than I ever dreamed I would. All of this was not just about my education in do-it-yourself. There are many improvements that we have made with assistance from the professionals. It was really all about unearthing my right to good design, an important part of my sense of well-being.

With this experience behind me, I feel that every house that gets built and interior designed by the professionals should have left in it some creative design space for its owner. It is one of those things that makes everyone feel included in a place—particularly the person who, firsthand, exercised his or her right to design it.

INTIMACY AND THE HOME

Home should be a place promoting the well-being of each person who lives in it. This may seem obvious, but all too often I have been in homes that seem to be designed for people other than those living in it, or for some of its members but not for others. Living in Scandinavia, where we spend a lot of time indoors during the colder months, has got me thinking about this subject.

When I first came to Scandinavia, people were concerned to emphasize how important the home was. "People don't go to restaurants as much as they do in other places," they told me. "We invite our guests and friends home." And then, "Our homes are places that we spend more time in than in other places." I wondered why people were so keen on emphasizing this point.

Scholars on the idea of home use the example of a seventeenth-century Norwegian home inhabited at that time by the Brun family, to show the way that the idea of the home as a place for intimacy and family life began to emerge after the Middle Ages, when even a couple's wedding night was a public event. In this home, the parents began to have a place for themselves to chat in the evenings after the day was done, and older children had their own sleeping place.[19] Homes were starting to be designed for the well-being of every person who lived in them.

In the Scandinavian languages there are many commonly used words for feeling at home, which do not translate directly into English: *Hemtrevnad* in Swedish and *Koselig* in Norwegian are two examples. These terms stand for an approach to design that results in spaces where family members, old friends and new, can feel both relaxed and inspired. This means creating places for being together and apart, all in an intimate setting. The creation of such places does not require a lot of space, but it does require thoughtful design that takes into account the personal needs of its inhabitants.

Scandinavians like to play with the creation of the feeling of home in small spaces, particularly in their holiday homes. My husband and I once visited a couple in the Stockholm archipelago who spent the summer with their *three teenage*rs in two rooms, which became four, when each was divided by a curtain. The bunk beds had small curtains that could be drawn to provide privacy for each sleeper. Storage was provided not by bulky cabinets but by clever small spaces inside the walls, over which small curtains could also be drawn. Space was created by simplicity and by having the possibility to hide small things. This cottage had huge windows facing out to the sea, which crashed up against the rocks below, creating a terrific sense of space inside. Sitting at the dining table looking out, I felt momentarily as though in a very large space.

The Larsson home in Sundborn, Sweden, provided the scenery for Carl Larsson's famous paintings, which became for some people images of a quintessentially Swedish home feel. The house represents a tremendous amount of effort to create home and intimacy for all of the family members. This is the only way to make sense of the place, which is otherwise rather eclectic-looking, inside and out. The things about this house that stick in my memory are the ones that were homemade solutions. Carl crafted a long cabinet high up in a column, which stood in one of the rooms that he painted in. Here he could keep his paint materials safe for when the children wanted to play in that room and he wasn't working. Karin, unsung genius of the home that she was, created a beautiful string fabric divider with the pattern of a gigantic flower between the room that she shared with her infant children and Carl's. This divider would maintain a feeling of togetherness and let in the light through both rooms. Sundborn symbolizes one family's effort to create a happy situation for everyone living in the house.

This home was full of handcrafting, which was partly a sign of the

Small wonder that during WWI, German soldiers took with them into the trenches copies of Das Haus in der Sonne, *or* The House in the Sun *(1909), which momentarily removed them from the horror of their situation with scenes from the Larssons' home. Today this home in Sundborn, Sweden, is open to the public, with tours available in English language and a bookstore where you can buy your copy of* The House in the Sun. *See Resources.*

times. The Larssons were part of a whole movement in Europe called the Arts and Crafts movement, which was about preserving the art of fine handcrafting in the age of machines. In general, though, handcrafting in fabrics, glass, ceramic, and wood is a wide variety of arts highly valued throughout Scandinavia.

What is it about handcrafting that we love so much? Standing in a rosmaled (painted in bright floral patterns) Norwegian interior gets you thinking about it. Handwork is exactly what a machine cannot do.[20] It is a part of the puzzle of creating intimacy in the home.

We literally need to design for intimacy in our homes in order to keep our brains well. Most of us love the possibilities created by our information age. Yet we also realize that it can make life rather impersonal sometimes. We chat daily with people whom we have never met. A person can remain an e-mail address. We deal with a tremendous number of information bytes. Our brains, which require the stimulation of all of our senses and have a good but not unlimited capacity for receiving information, are not equipped for this. In our homes we need intimacy together and alone, for each person who lives there.

HANDICRAFTS FOR WELL-BEING

Capellagården, founded by the furniture designer Carl Malmsten, on the island of Öland in Sweden, is one place worthy of a visit (even of taking a course or two) in different arts of handcrafting. This is one of many handcrafting communities throughout the Nordic countries. See Resources.

DESIGNING FOR A LIFE WITH CHILDREN

In 1951, the architectural firm Eckholm & White from Göteborg came
up with the idea of the *Allrum* (a room for everyone). Then, in 1955, a designer with the same namesake as Carl Larsson shocked the interior design
establishment by putting on display her *Allrum* at an interior design exhibition in Helsingborg. Lena Larsson's design roughly translated the inclusiveness of children in Carl Larsson's paintings into the modern home by
making this *Allrum* the dominating room of the house. The shocking element was that it did away with stodgy living and dining rooms that were
not to be entered by children. At the center of this room was a column with
a ladder for children to climb on. Spaces for toys and storytelling were integrated into the room design. Honesty, unpretentiousness, and an inclusive feeling characterized the whole layout. The adults had their own
private space, but the central area of the house was for family.

During the 1960s and 1970s, Scandinavian design turned itself increasingly to the needs of children. In 1965, IKEA established its first major
outlet in Sweden and wowed young families with affordable and creative

A ROOM FOR EVERYONE

*Ideas about how to give priority to mother's and children's needs in the home
resulted in some very interesting and often amusing proposals in Scandinavia.
Some of the ideas have endured. They can be seen today at the Museum of Architecture, in Stockholm, and in a special book about Swedish architecture
during the twentieth century they have produced, which is available for purchase in an English-language edition. See Resources.*

design solutions. Clever bunk beds that could be lengthened as children grew and other children's furnishings had been created by Muurame of Finland and were becoming popular in the United States. LEGO, meaning *leg godt,* or "play well" in Danish, established their product principles, including: unlimited play potential; for girls and for boys; fun for every age; year-round play; healthy, quiet play; long hours of play; development, imagination, creativity. In all, the best designs for children were characterized by an advanced simplicity that would allow for calm, comfort, and fun all at the same time.

Advanced Simplicity

> Then Loki gave . . . *Skidbladnir* (the foremost of ships) to Freyr, and announced the features of all the precious things . . . *Skidbladnir* had a fair wind as soon as its sail was hoisted, wherever it was intended to go, and could be folded up like a cloth and put in one's pocket, if desired.[21]

If there was ever a well-designed thing that could be folded up and tucked into your pocket, that thing would have been created by Scandinavians. Love of boats and boating aside, clever design giving rise to an advanced simplicity is one of the hallmarks of Nordic design. What makes for this advanced simplicity is not only intriguing, but also useful to understand from the point of view of our well-being.

Technology is a double-edged sword. It can help us and it can harm us in our day-to-day lives, depending on how it is used. Here in the Nordic countries, I have encountered many uses of technology in design for the promotion of healthful living. It is one of the characteristics that define that special brand of Nordic humane functionalism. Below I discuss two ways that technology is used in this part of the world to create an everyday life that feels freer and more comfortable. There is a third aspect of the way that technology is well used for design in Scandinavia, which has to do with good ecology. Discussion of this is taken up in Chapter 7.

High Tech versus Low Tech

Easy manageability in our homes and workplaces is becoming increasingly important to our well-being as the information age presses on. This characteristic is created by choosing appropriate (not necessarily always high) technology. Despite all of its triumphs in the high-tech world, one of the secret strengths of Scandinavian design is its mastery of low tech. I thought of the butter spreader that I first encountered in the Danish apartment. It was a flat, wooden paddle that allowed the butter or margarine to be smoothed onto the bread slice without breaking it. In Scandinavia, it has been sold in countless numbers; a low-tech, old idea that cannot be beaten.

I visited the office of a well-known Scandinavian designer, Bjorn Dahlström, who believes in the value of low tech. Visiting the bathroom, I ran into a few of his designs for children that were distributed around the floor: a rounded, glossy painted wooden car in fantastically large eye-catching size, another in lacquered chipboard on roller bearings so that it could be driven smoothly in any direction.

Scandinavians have learned about the benefits of choosing appropriate technology through trial and error. The best example that I can think of isn't in the field of home design but in shipbuilding. The Vikings created boat designs that continue to be admired around the world among sailboat designers today. The *Oseberg* ship in Norway, the best-preserved excavated Viking sailing vessel, is long, sleek, and extremely simple-looking. Aside from the single wood carvings on the bow and stern of this long, wooden boat there are no embellishments. About seven centuries later, Sweden launched the *Vasa,* its largest and most elaborate vessel until then. It sunk on launching. While this raised white elephant is hauntingly impressive to look at in the Vasa Museum in Stockholm, just one look at it speaks of technology gone mad. Crazy as it may sound, when I shop for new items

LOW TECH, KIDS, AND WELL-BEING

Low tech can be the realization of your dreams, if you have young children. The noisier and more complicated a toy is, the more batteries it guzzles and the more sound bites it blurts out, the less likely it is to promote happiness in your home. Everyone gets overstimulated and tired very quickly. I remember locking one particularly noisy toy into a closet, in the hope that it would stop bothering us. I learned that in our house of young twins, one should choose technology for maximizing peace and conserving energy.

for my home and place of work, my mind sometimes goes to the *Oseberg* ship and the *Vasa*.

ERGONOMY

Sometimes we choose things for our homes and places of work that might look nice, but don't feel so good to use. Take those chairs that leave you feeling twenty years older each time you are done sitting in them. Ever since I had to wear ugly orthopedic shoes as a child, I thought the reverse was also true: comfort came at the expense of beauty. This is no longer true. Ergonomics, the science of making things comfortable for the human body to use, has come a long way.

Scandinavians have been thinking about ergonomics for a long time, even before the word existed. This partly comes from traditions of furniture-making handed down in families and developed into a master craft. During the 1920s and 1930s, the Danish designer Kaare Klint undertook anatomical studies (using real cadavers) in order to humanize design and to create furniture that would suit the human body. This was perhaps a little extreme, and Klint became more famous for his lighting than his furniture.

"His furniture is a poem of the sitting person,"[22] said one commentator of Bruno Mathsson's creations. Mathsson was himself extremely health conscious. He ate his strawberries with squeezed lemon rather than cream. He slept outdoors between May and November—and always after lunch between covers—on the world's first thermal bed, which he had designed himself. The connection between relaxation, creativity, and good design was constantly in his mind. His chairs are famous for the way that they

CHOOSING ADVANCED SIMPLICITY

When next you venture out into the jungle of items that you can buy for your home, ask yourself whether you really need the all-singing, all-dancing version, which will guzzle energy, brain power, and probably collapse within five minutes of using it. Is there anything basic and reliable performing the same function that would leave you time and extra energy to do other things?

curve with the shape of the body. Mathsson objected to conventional, uncomfortable office furniture and shocked his workplace by taking away the big, stodgy director's desk—a little brain ergonomics at work here too. During the 1970s and 1980s, before anyone else, he designed workstations for computers that provided elbow rests for people who had to work long hours at the keyboard. He liked to say that computers were nice slaves, which should serve people and not the reverse. This was reflected in his design, which started with the physiological and psychological needs of people first.

The Importance of
the "Design of My Teapot"

In Scandinavia I discovered that the proverbial "design of my teapot" is actually important to my well-being. This may seem trivial, but it isn't in a time where we have the possibility to surround ourselves with piles of things that just don't do anything for us—in fact, they make us feel worse. If there is anything that I learned from the Danish apartment and through the ongoing and never-ending process of creating my home here on the island, it is that design for well-being—at least at home—is about simple, instinctive, and often ancient knowledge, and exercising your right to choose based on that knowledge. In our time, this is survival.

DESIGNING FOR HUMAN ANATOMY

Performing the same motion repeatedly with poorly designed instruments or in a poorly designed environment can result in repetitive strain injury (RSI). Scandinavians have been thinking about how to solve this problem longer than most. The interesting-looking coffeepots and teapots from which passengers get served their caffeine on Scandinavian Airlines (SAS) are designed so as not to overstress the stewardesses' wrists. They are designed by Ergonomi design group, a company that produces an expanding range of ergonomically designed items (see Resources). IKEA has managed to integrate ergonomic considerations into some of its products (e.g., knife sets) at prices that many people can manage.

Pure Energy and a
Nordic Taste of Well-being

THERE IS A BIG PITCHER of wild strawberries on my kitchen counter. I know that Claes has been out picking them during the very early morning when his mind has been so full of thoughts that he cannot sleep. He picks them as the sun casts its precious early rays onto the birch branches. The sound of a few waterbirds taking off or landing in the lake below is the only background noise. This work is a form of meditation. Thoughts stuck somewhere in the crevice of the mind loosen and float past with each berry that is picked and dropped into the pitcher. The mind is eventually cleared of all of those thoughts blocking sleep. The eyelids begin to feel heavy. The full pitcher is placed on the counter, and Claes is back in bed, fast asleep.

Those wild strawberries are one of the finest quality foods that I can think of. They are appealing to the eye: evenly round and pinkish-red with the characteristic speckled appearance of a strawberry. They are nutritious and low in fat. They are clean, growing in good soil and having been washed sufficiently by occasional rain. We should do as little as possible to prepare them for eating. Perhaps nothing at all. Our children have the right instincts. They eat them straight away, just as they are. We, the adults, wait until the evening, and allow ourselves a dollop of cream and half a teaspoon of sugar on top for dessert. We chew slowly, savoring the flavor explosion. Wild strawberries allow you to appreciate the fact that nature is ingenious.

The whole art of good food and cooking in Scandinavia is about realizing the possibilities inherent in nature. It is a process of falling in love with your ingredients outdoors, meditating through them by focusing your mind on them completely, and finding tasty ways of using them that change their composition the least. This process fills us with a health-giving force that I call pure energy: uncluttered, not minimized and stripped away by overhandling, overprocessing, and overpackaging. When you work hard to gather precious food, it is empowering that you have somehow participated in bringing in the treasure that is on your plate from the outdoors. You are a little tired and very hungry as a result, and the food that you have brought in, prepared in an uncomplicated way, meets exactly the need that you have at that moment. You have been longing to eat this all day, all season, perhaps even all year. You prepare just the right amount, leaving a little for tomorrow, or store the ingredients for another fine meal in the future. Bon appétit.

These days, it can be exceedingly difficult for those with busy schedules in urban environments to get this pure energy from food. You know that you should eat a healthy diet in order to live a healthy life. You can go to a bookstore and pick up many suggestions as to what you should eat and what you should not. Each book conflicts with the next in one way or another. Having read such books, you go to that food jungle called the supermarket and try desperately to find things that are possible to eat. You read the labels, which are half incomprehensible. Is there anything left that is safe to eat? You return with your shopping bags, into which certain unhealthful products have crept, feeling exhausted and somewhat disappointed. You go out to dinner or order in on that evening, feeling too confused and tired to even think of starting to cook a healthy meal. The food arrives and gets consumed. You have no idea how fresh the ingredients are, or for that matter what the ingredients actually are. You fall asleep on the couch feeling lethargic and full, yet not quite satisfied. You know that there is very little that is revitalizing about this pattern, which is totally disconnected from the origin or preparation of the food.

Having been a city dweller who followed this pattern for years, I have a suggestion to make: If every city dweller spent at least two days of their year out in the countryside gathering and preparing their own food, either in cultivated or noncultivated environments where there is something to be harvested, they would get a taste for this pure energy that I am talking about. Their expectations of what information and products supermarkets and other food suppliers, including restaurant and food delivery companies, should provide would become quite different. They would increasingly demand fresh ingredients, many grown locally, using farming and preparation techniques they could understand. They would demand to have comprehensible information about content on the label. Restaurants that overcook, overfeed, overseason, and do not ensure the freshness of their ingredients would go out of business. All food suppliers would have to use their creativity to bring some of that food clarity to the table.

To some extent, this change is already taking place: in restaurants that provide more information on the menu and take more care about the quality of their ingredients, among specialist food suppliers, and in supermarkets that concentrate on improving the fresh food selection on their shelves. Still, the change is very slow, and there is too little of the right information that we lack, such as information on the source of our food. This is at least in part because people's expectations, in general, are still too low, because they have not experienced what getting an uncluttered feeling of fulfillment from food is all about.

Our modern societies have given rise to a very complicated and often unstable relationship between people and food. There is much more food than we need available to us everywhere, all of the time. While we can be thankful that we do not have to worry about famine in the industrialized world, we now have other problems that we need to work out as a result of our lavish surpluses. Food has become something that many use to avoid dealing with certain problems in their lives. Often these are about relationships between men and women, parents and children, and children and their peers. The results, with increasing frequency, are serious illnesses such as bulimia, anorexia, and obesity. In many instances, food has unfortunately become an energy-sapping weapon. Much needs to be done by all of the suppliers of food and image creators to reinstate food as something nurturing, and not something that is related to how we look or whether we have control over our lives. In order to achieve this, food needs to be connected to its origins in the energy-giving environment of nature, where people can find the personal space and the inspiration they need in order to work through those things that trouble them. Even if we do not have the time or the possibility to be out there harvesting our own carrots and potatoes on a regular basis, at least in our minds food will be connected to feelings of possibility and personal space. We will choose better, we will feel better, and we will not misuse it.

I have a dream of a city center, where pollution is low, and where, on their days off, people can visit their local parks and find greenhouses cultivated with fruits and berries, vegetables and herbs. People would have the option to watch or to get involved hands-on. They would learn about good ways of using these fruits, vegetables, and herbs to make nutritious and tasty food. There would be simple kitchens designated for food demonstrations, for showing people how to make delicious herbed breads, wonderful, aromatic vegetable dishes, simple and tangy fruit desserts, and many other things. There would be fishing lakes kept clean and supplied with fish for people quietly to enjoy that experience as well. There would be small areas for cooking all around these lakes where people could take their catch and grill it for lunch or for dinner. The harbor waters would be kept clean, and areas for fishing and cooking the fish provided there as well. The city government of this place would be eager to constantly improve and expand these services, realizing that to give their population even a small taste of the pure energy that food can provide is to improve the health of that population immeasurably.

These ideas are not entirely my own. I have taken some of them from places that I have seen, both in and around Stockholm. Here too there is still more progress to be made in terms of making it possible for people to participate in the creation of food in the city. A lot needs to be done so that city-dwelling children do not lose that love of fresh food, which is still present in this culture and elsewhere in Scandinavia. I think back to my first years of living here, and my amazement at the types of gifts that people brought when they visited: A friend arrived with a simple plastic bag filled with frozen, golden-colored caviar he had harvested from *vendace*, a herringlike fish common in the north; a relative once brought a fine, lean cut of deer meat from autumn hunting; another friend came with a bucket full of big, beautiful soil-covered root vegetables, which her mother had harvested from her small garden patch in a suburb. At first I was amused at these gifts in their simple, plastic bag or bucket packaging with no directions for use and no fancy gift wrapping. Eventually, I began to give similar gifts myself: self-harvested, fresh, without additives, and ready to use. They are the gift of nature's vibrant energy from one person to another. There is no better present.

Scandinavian Diet and Health

During most of my years of growing up all over the world, we had Wasa hard bread on our breakfast table. It came in a rectangular shape and was hard, dry, and crisp. You may have seen it in the grocery stores in America. It was our absolutely-no-frills breakfast bread, and it was my favorite. I can remember sitting in the small breakfast room of the apartment that my father had rented for us in Tokyo in 1977, looking at the Wasa hard bread package with the royal crowns printed on it originating in a symbol used by the "Rye King" Gustav Vasa (likely because Gustav collected his taxes in the form of rye). I remember thinking that all people who came from Scandinavia must be very lean and healthy, since, according to the existing wisdom, absolutely everyone ate Wasa there. I imagined tall, muscular men with horned helmets and applecheeked women in full-length linen dresses sitting at long, wooden tables breaking the Wasa bread.

However lean and healthy Scandinavians were in 1977 or earlier, they are less so today. Scandinavians, like many other people in the industrialized world, are sadly succumbing to poor energy food patterns. More of them are eating too much for the amount that they move, and too little of the right stuff. The good news for them is that by world standards they have outstanding traditions of healthfulness in their diet, which are still very much alive today. There are many common elements of any Scandinavian supermarket cart or basket that I would put in the fresh and uncluttered category. What is more, people are still out there, in considerable numbers, harvesting parts of their own food. I have by now quite often faced furled eyebrows when I talk to Scandinavians, who are critical of their own nation's deteriorating eating habits, and about the healthfulness of a typical Scandinavian diet. The truth is that they have a great advantage as far as their traditions go.

When I used to commute between offices in Copenhagen and London, I noticed the difference. On one day, I would be sitting with a British work colleague in a pub watching hoards of people digging into steak or sausage and chips. On another day, I would be with my Danish colleagues choosing between four different types of pickled herring, or *sill,* and the same number of different types of hard or nutty, dark brown breads. Danes, as a nation, are guilty of other bad food excesses, but this fish and hard bread element in their diet is one shared by all Scandinavians. It is ingrained in their food culture and it is also full of the right stuff. (I should also not be too harsh on Brits and their food. They have come a long way in creating healthy and tasty options as well as talent.)

Developing a Healthy
Relationship with Food

As I have suggested above, I believe that having a positive relationship with food means at some point being keenly involved in bringing it to the table. That means getting involved with harvesting and/or preparation in the kitchen—perhaps not for every meal, perhaps not every day—just every now and then. Just enough for keeping clear those channels for receiving the goodness of the food.

This belief comes from the personal experience of healing my own relationship to food, which went badly wrong during my late teens and twenties, as it does for many young women today. At some point in my teenage years I virtually stopped eating, and it took well over a decade to begin to overcome the fear of food that developed over that time. Of course, this development was linked to deeper problems, which manifested themselves by clogging up my relationship to food. Ultimately, I had to disentangle food from these deeper problems, to begin to treat it with respect and love. The deeper issues had to be solved on their own terms.

My healing process in relation to food started with a pitcher of wild strawberries here on our island. On that occasion, I had watched Claes working hard outside to pick the best ones for a romantic dessert for two. I watched with longing the behavior of a person whose relationship to food was completely clear. Food began to lose its threat. It became more connected to where it came from than to my emotional problems. The gathering of those strawberries was an act of love, pure, beautiful, and simple. I began to learn about other foods that I could gather around the area where we were living—at that time only during the summers. Slowly, yet shakily, I began to toss those foods into pots and make things out of them, sometimes with good results, sometimes not.

Today I find tremendous joy in food that I have harvested myself. That joy has permeated my whole relationship to food. This extreme experience that I have had with food has led me to reflect a great deal on what it is about the culture of food that I have encountered in Scandinavia that I find valuable for well-being. My conclusion is that there are three positive mental/emotional effects that the gathering and preparation of food, which is still so popular in this part of the world, can have on a person. They are described below.

Food as Food

Getting involved with food brings a realistic perspective to what food is. A potato is a potato, a root that has been pulled out of the soil, rinsed, perhaps peeled, and then boiled, baked, or sautéed. A potato is not a carbohydrate-drenched threat to one's image. It is not the source of all problems. Neither will potatoes magically make these problems disappear if we just keep on eating more.

When I talk about pure energy food, I am, of course, contradicting the idea that food is food. I began this chapter by suggesting that this type of food can bring us many other positive feelings than just the consumption of the food itself. Still, I believe that in order to be able to receive those positive feelings, we need to clear our channels first. We can do that by coming to grips with what the food really is and where it came from; in other words, by connecting it with nature.

Food as Meditation

To meditate means to empty the mind of thoughts and to think of nothing, or to focus the mind on one thing. Meditation can help us to develop and maintain our sense of personal space, since it means that we take control of what we focus on, and do not allow all of the other stimuli around us to clutter that space. Those who have tried it will appreciate that this is not an easy state of mind to achieve. I have found that the leisurely gathering of food is one way of learning about how to meditate. Of course, I am not a farmer and I do not have the pressure of harvesting in order to make a living. I am sure that most farmers would not say that harvesting food is like meditation. I am like most other harvesters of food in Scandinavia, who do it for leisure.

People who fish know that it can be a particularly good form of meditation. I have noticed how happy people can look after a few hours of fishing, even if they have not caught anything. Why would that be? Isn't the whole point of fishing to catch fish? One Swede described it something like this:

> There are a number of things that the boy in me longs to do more often. Rest is one of them. Sleep under an open sky. Climb trees. And fish. But it is not the fish that I long for. It is the state of being. The long hours of nothing. The lure's dance in the movement of the waves calms the soul.[1]

My Danish ex-boss, who bought a cabin in Norway next to a salmon fishing river, had the following to say to me in an e-mail, when he heard of my new vocation in writing about well-being:

You must include salmon fishing in your plans, as there is absolutely nothing—apart from mountain hiking—which can take your mind as much away from business as fishing!

If food can come to symbolize meditation and personal space through our involvement in gathering it every now and then, we will have a more healthy and respectful relationship to it.

Food as a Creative Process

A Norwegian friend of mine, Inni-Carine, has written about food as a creative process. The title translates as: "Impulses from My Kitchen: Food for Happy People."[2] She talks about the important role that harvesting our own food and making things with these fresh ingredients play in relation to our well-being. Her emphasis is on the importance of not being pre-programmed when it comes to food and using it as a means to develop our sense of initiative, which all of us have, particularly in the kitchen.

In her chapter about the joy of finding food in nature, Inni relates the story of three children from overseas who came to Norway to stay with her and the family for the summer. These children had friendly and intellectual/artistic parents who were determined to give their children what they thought might be a good balance of sport, culture, and schooling. The downside of their efforts was that the children had not had the chance to develop their own sense of initiative due to everything being more or less preprogrammed. Inni had been preinformed by the parents that these children had all manner of allergies and needed certain types of medications, which had been sent along in a bag. They could apparently only eat a limited range of foods and were afraid of eating most things that didn't look processed. For instance, fish that looked like fish was out. For any parents reading this, does this sound familiar? A Norwegian summer of outdoor food harvesting seems to have "deprogrammed" these kids, according to Inni. The bag of medications remained unopened. The children returned home healthy, but probably somewhat unruly and wanting to pursue their own ideas.

I have myself seen the dietary impact of learning to be creative in the kitchen with fresh ingredients. A friend who lived with us on our island for an extended period of time had precisely the same problems as these children. Couldn't eat this, couldn't eat that, and in the process ate an extremely unbalanced diet. We began to cook together—with ingredients that were recognizable and unprocessed. She became amazed at the things that she actually could eat, once she became involved in handling and preparing the food, and seeing just how many options there were. The urge to be creative with food became irresistible. At one point she began preparing very tasty meals for us all by herself. They had become an expression of her initiative. Three years later, she returned to visit us and offered to make dinner. I was very grateful, since I don't get to many restaurants, living as we do. On the table I found several pots of food, each one filled with wonderful, fresh ingredients that previously she would not have considered touching. I asked whether she had prepared this just for us, since several of the pots contained things that she would not have eaten in the past. "Of course not," she said, spooning some steamed carrots onto her plate and grinning at me with newfound satisfaction.

Elements of Scandinavian Taste

During the 1960s, Time-Life published a series of international cookbooks. One of them, produced by Dale Brown, featured Scandinavian food. Brown was on the editorial board of Time-Life Books, had been a student in Denmark, and visited Scandinavia many times thereafter. In this book, he encapsulates what is special and healthful about Scandinavian cuisine in a way that few others have.

> In Scandinavia the food maintains its own taste. It tastes of the sea, of a fresh water lake, and even of the soil. . . . I have never stopped being surprised that so much freshness and naturalness still can exist in the world. During my last visit, I once again felt mentally and physically freshened, the same way I had felt during earlier visits.[3]

The subject of taste, which Dale Brown highlights, is one that Scandinavian chefs are emphasizing as their driving inspiration today. They contrast their approach to a more technically driven approach to food preparation. Their ingredients are very fresh and have that taste of nature in them, and Scandinavian food preparation traditions offer unique and memorable tastes. However, Brown made a linkage that seems to have gone amiss in modern Scandinavian cooking. That is the connection between the taste of certain foods in Scandinavia and well-being. My own view is that this unique wellness-promoting taste relies on a number of criteria. These include freshness, cleanliness, simplicity, nonpretentiousness, and traditions in the form of strong linkages to the past combined with a welcoming attitude toward combining these with traditions from other cultures, the rhythm of the seasons, and sensuality. These qualities are all characteristics that provide elements of Scandinavian food, which I would call pure energy foods, with their distinctive flavor, and which make them a unique wellness-promoting experience. A note about the recipes that follow: They are mostly for four to five people, unless otherwise indicated, since that is the number that I cook for here on the island and the quantities work out pretty well.

Freshness

Inni-Carine and Gunnar have a home in a place called Tjøme at the sea in southern Norway. Every now and then, Gunnar can be found wading amid the rocks at the shore gathering mussels and seaweed. On one evening while we were visiting, the seaweed was served sautéed with just a little simple seasoning. It was terrific.

This seaweed was so fresh that it brought about the feeling of merging with the natural environment that it came from. The division between myself and the origin of that seaweed began to dissipate, and all of the wildly beautiful energy and inspiration of the Norwegian seashore became a part of me. If your ingredients are fresh, they are usually local. If they are local, you can identify with the environment that they came from. That makes a big difference to how much "oomph" your food can provide.

SAUTEED SEAWEED

Shiny brown strips of clean seaweed, 1½–2 inches (4–5 cm)
Olive oil
Salt and pepper

Cut the seaweed in julienne strips. Lightly brush a frying pan with olive oil. Sauté the seaweed, being careful not to brown it. Season to taste with salt and pepper.

Cleanliness

Over time, Scandinavians have demonstrated their love of nature by keeping it clean. In instances where they have dirtied it, as in the case of the waters in and around Stockholm, they have made strenuous efforts to tidy it up and created strict rules to keep it clean. One issue that faced the Scandinavian countries that sought entry into the European Union during the 1990s was that they would have to lower their environmental and food-safety standards in order to join. In any event, they have not, in practice, lowered their standards. It is no coincidence that the Scandinavian countries have been leading champions of environmental sustainability, including protection and maintenance, worldwide. The first UN conference on the environment, which took place in 1972, came about as a result of a Swedish initiative. The Nordic countries are also world renowned for developing tools for keeping their environment clean and for exporting these tools.

Scandinavians claim that they have the safest ingredients in the world. There is evidence to support them. Homegrown salmonella has been a virtually nonexistent problem in these parts since the 1950s, due to strict monitoring of animal and food hygiene. During 2002 it was found that large amounts of imported meat in Sweden were salmonella infected. During the debates that emerged during this crisis we heard that other European countries normally live with up to 30 percent of their meat infected with salmonella. In Sweden the .01 percent that is said to be infected is still regarded as unacceptable. Since the early 1980s a ban has been placed on the use of antibiotics in animal feed, which means that resistant strains of bacteria are significantly less frequent here than in countries where antibiotics use in animal feed is tolerated.

All of the public concern for the environment and for the associated quality of food in these countries comes less from knowledge of fact than it does from the deep connection to nature that people sense and need preserved intact in their lives. There is a feeling that food products should stand for the people's right to the resources of nature. In relation to this point, there is a beautiful story about the eightieth-birthday present of the famous Swedish author of children's stories, Astrid Lindgren. One thread running through Lindgren's stories is respect for animals, and thus it comes as no surprise that she was a passionate campaigner for animal rights. From 1985 to 1988 she published a series of animal stories in the Stockholm evening paper. They were disarmingly charming, told in the voices of the animals as they were, at the same time as they spoke out eloquently about the plight of domesticated animals raised for food. One poignant episode recalls the story of Lovisa, the white leghorn hen, who struggles to maintain a sort of dignity as her scrawny, featherless body and disfigured claws are questioned by Augusta, the pig. The other three hens she has shared a cage with have just been sent for slaughter.[4]

In 1988, in return for her eloquence and persistence, the then Swedish prime minister, Ingvar Carlsson, gave Astrid Lindgren her own law as a birthday gift. It was based on the principle that all livestock management must consider the animals' natural behavior. Like others in the Swedish public, Lindgren was passionate about showing kindness and respect to nature, which had given her so much inspiration in life.

I have so far tried to keep away from the word "ecology" or "ecological," since I think they are drastically misused in politics and commerce. The word "ecology" has meaningful roots. *Eco* comes from the Greek word *oikos,* meaning house. The rest of the term stems from the Greek word *logos,* meaning to learn. The idea that we all live in the same house and need to continually learn how to coexist in it happily are basic to the culture of the Scandinavian countries.

Finland, Denmark, and Sweden rank in the top ten countries worldwide for organic farming. Their targets for increasing the percentage of farming that is organic over time are very high by the standards of the industrialized world. At the beginning of the new century, Denmark's then government stated that it wanted 50 percent of all farming to be organic

ENJOYING A DAY OF ECOLOGY IN DENMARK

Camilla and her husband Per's farm, Fuglebjerggaard, in northern Zealand, Denmark, is at first sight a pleasant-looking small Danish farm. But it is also a place electric with the belief in the power of "clean" food. Through her food programs and cookbooks, Camilla has done much to convince Danes to eat well ecologically. Many Danes I know told me that Camilla had inadvertently caused large numbers of people to be up late at night after work baking bread from her bread cookbook. At Fuglebjerggaard you can, by making prior arrangements with Camilla and Per, learn just about everything there is to learn about ecology and questions about genetically modified foods. Preparing food ecologically and tasting beer from the interesting ecological collection that Per has amassed are other pleasures that can be enjoyed by booking in advance. The north-facing Danish coast, with its stunning and restrained colors and many beautifully designed coastal restaurants and inns, is just a few minutes away. See www.fuglebjerggaard.dk.

within ten years. Some Scandinavians would say that this is just common sense, just as one of Denmark's most popular food "activitists," Camilla Plum, said to me when I visited her at her 100 percent ecological farm near the northern coast of Zealand. She had previously run an organic food company whose work it was, among other things, to convert public sector institutions, mostly kindergartens, to organic food.

There are others who argue that the ecological movement is an unnecessary and even harmful creation of Western urban consumer-oriented society, since it creates impossible standards for poorer countries in warmer climates to compete with, and, they claim, so-called ecological farming is also not necessarily environmentally better than the alternative. One can argue back and forth endlessly. For myself, I am instinctively glad that I can harvest vegetables and herbs from the clean, nonpesticide-affected, and naturally fertilized soil of my small farm on the island and that I have the option to choose ecological products.

I heard on the radio that most Swedes have a compost. I cannot imagine this is so usual in the industrialized world. There aren't any global statistics for waste managed by compost. Yet what is really so appealing about creating mounds of quietly rotting material near your home? Composts are a brilliant way of getting rid of organic matter from your kitchen in an efficient, nonoffensive way and making your garden grow at the same time, if you have one. You participate in bringing nature full circle, in bringing life where something has died. Among the initiated, the secrets of good composting have passed into legend. Here are some basic points demystifying this great art.

SIX STEPS TO HAPPY COMPOSTING

1. If you are composting household waste only (mostly discarded food materials from your kitchen), you need to set up a warm compost, meaning a closed compost that vermin cannot get into. These are available for purchase at your local do-it-yourself store. Don't set it up just under the kitchen window; otherwise you might get flies in the warmer season.

2. If you are composting a lot of garden waste, you need to create an open garden compost consisting of two to three simple pens made of oil- or tar-protected wooden planks, preferably 1 meter square, or 3 feet square, each. It sometimes takes more than a year for the organic matter that you throw in to convert to earth—this, of course, depends on how much and what you are throwing in. So, more than one compost pen is a good idea.

3. Variety in your compost is important, although there are certain materials that should not end up in your compost, such as oak leaves, thorny rose stems, and weeds that you are trying to get rid of. You can learn more about this from the many resources on composting available on the Internet and in widely available books. (See Resources.)

4. Achieving well-composted soil depends mostly on three factors: the balance of carbon versus nitrogen in the substances that

you throw in (again, you can learn about this through Resources); the maintenance of a balance between moisture and dryness (some say good compost should feel like a wrung-out washcloth); sufficient air circulation so that the microorganisms can breathe, get to work, and multiply.

5. A good compost should not be a smelly, fly-ridden affair. If yours becomes like this, you likely need to throw in some sawdust or mulch and circulate. Be sure that you are putting all of your animal waste (chicken, etc.) into the closed, warm compost. Alternatively, if your compost becomes too dry, it is either in too sunny a location or you need to throw in some fruit leftovers.

6. If the waste material is not breaking down fast enough you can solve this yourself without spending a cent. Do as the Swedish playwright August Strindberg did: Use a little urine.

With your compost now in place, you will notice that nettle begins to grow somewhere near it, perhaps around it. Nettles cherish rich soil. In April the food pages of the newspapers in Scandinavia fill with information about how to use nettle to make soup, pies, and other delicacies of the season. This is the time when the first nettles sprout up around the compost. Here's a good recipe.

NETTLE SOUP

The best bet for a good nettle soup, says Inni-Carine, is to gather the plants very young, not more than 5½ inches or 14 cm high. Pluck the leaves off the stems (use gloves), put them in a pan with hardly any water, and bring to a boil. Let boil for only a minute or two until you see the leaves wilting. Put in a colander. Press all excess humidity out of the nettles. Roll them into a ball, press even more water out of it, hold around it, and cut in fine strips by hand (or you could use a food processor). For every amount of fresh nettles that you use, you need half the amount of *buljong*, or broth (for 1 quart or 1 liter of fresh nettles you need ½ quart or ½ liter of *buljong*). Add the cooked, pressed nettles to the *buljong* and gently warm, mixing together. Add whatever: a couple of tablespoons of butter, cream, or crème fraîche. Season with salt and pepper. You can also stir in an egg yolk or two. Serve with either a dash of sour cream, or finely chopped hard-boiled eggs, or even an egg yolk in each soup plate. There are so many ways.

Simplicity

Writing from the most northern outpost of the Roman Empire in the first century A.D., Tacitus noted the following: "Their food is simple—wild fruits, wild meat, and sour milk." The cover of a 2001 cookbook I have entitled *New Scandinavian Cooking*[5] has on it the picture of an ordinary young man digging into a plate of salmon with a little lemon squeezed on top, a plain slice of whole-grain bread, and a glass of milk. Things haven't changed much. Scandinavians treasure simplicity.

When we harvested our first beetroots here on the island, I wondered what to do with them. Steam them and then what? Nothing much, is the correct answer, if you are making good Scandinavian "pure energy" food. How about melting a little butter with some snippets of parsley from your windowsill herbarium on the peeled, steaming beetroot and eating it, just like that, out of a bowl? That was a suggestion made by a friend who kept coming with buckets of them from her mother.

This simplicity of preparation allows the rich textures, flavors, and colors of nature to be revealed on your plate and to touch your palate. From a health point of view, it is also a helpful approach, since, more often than not, the goodness of the food gets delivered to you more intact than through complicated preparation. One way that Norwegians typically prepare cod suddenly comes to mind. It is my favorite fish dish, full of juiciness and texture. Fantastic.

NORWEGIAN-STYLE COD

Two large, thick fresh cold fillets (over 1 foot, or 30 cm)
3 quarts (1 liter) water
¼ cup (½ dl) salt

Bring to a gentle simmer enough salted water to cover the cod fillets when eventually you put them in. Immerse the cod fillets in the boiling salted water for 4 minutes. Transfer quickly onto a plate and serve with a few boiled potatoes. Eat immediately and wash down with one fine glass of red wine.

This economically valuable fish is being overfished in many places. Do not buy cod that has likely not had the chance to mate (a whole fish under 1½ feet, or 45 cm, or fillets smaller than 1 foot, or 30 cm). If you can find out how the cod was fished, so much the better; bottom trawling destroys marine environments. In the United States, Pacific cod seems to be the most ethical choice among cod types available on the market at present.

Unpretentiousness

According to the *Hávámal*, a series of Norse poems, the Vikings believed that being generous in offering others food was to ensure a good obituary. I have thought of this when I have asked for someone to pass me the butter, and then got a wooden butter knife with a lump of butter on it ready for spreading. Handing over that butter knife is as though to say, "Since I know that you won't take enough butter yourself, I am going to anticipate your thoughts and give you a proper helping." This kind of undisguised generosity results in a feeling of unpretentiousness about Scandinavian food and dining.

In his travel journal entry for June 2, 1732, Carl Linnaeus meets a frightful-looking peasant woman during his journey in the north of Sweden. Her face "was the darkest brown from the effect of smoke" and her neck "resembled the skin of a frog." He is very hungry and asks whether she can provide any food. She offers him a fish that is perhaps not so fresh, since its mouth is full of maggots. Linnaeus starts to lose his appetite and then asks whether there is anything else around. She replies that there is cheese made of reindeer's milk, but that it is about a mile away. When Linnaeus asks whether he can buy some, indicating that he would like her to get some for him, she answers, "I have no desire that thou shouldst die in my country for want of food."[6]

The unpleasantries of this story aside, this kind of straightforward generosity inhabits almost everything that I can think of in real Scandinavian dining today. It comes partly from a rural peasant tradition that dominated life in Scandinavia until the twentieth century. In modern times, it also comes perhaps partly from the social democratic movement in Scandinavia, which promoted the idea that all people should be entitled to the same basic privileges. The highly awarded Swedish national culinary team at least believes that this unpretentiousness, expressed in the lack of a strong hierarchy in their kitchen, is a recipe for success.

A couple Claes and I once visited to buy a boat put out some very welcome lunch for us on one cold and rainy day. I was seven months pregnant with twins and grateful for the offer. We looked out at the magnificent view over the sea for a few minutes and then turned around to find a beautiful, old rustic wooden table lit up by one simple gas lamp. There was one steaming hot loaf of rye bread ready to be sliced up, a pot of butter with the usual wooden knife in it, a pot of honey, an enormous pie-shaped chunk of grevé cheese (hard, with holes in it like Swiss cheese, but creamier and with a stronger flavor) with a cheese knife and one big pot of strong, hot coffee. I sat down, expecting a plate and some utensils to be placed before me. Nothing arrived, and the hostess began to dig in, taking care not to make a ski slope out of the grevé. Silly me; no other utensils or plates were required. Everything that was needed was there with the generous and totally unpretentious chunks of delicious, fresh food on the table. Our hosts suggested that we take a little extra for the road, and I was happy to accept that offer. This unpretentiousness around food unblocks our social reservations about food and eating. It is another important factor in ensuring that the pure energy of the food gets to us.

Tradition

The good food traditions of Scandinavia are based on two factors: the food of the common man since Viking times, and the seasons. In 1555, Olaus Magnus Gothus lamented in his *History of the Nordic Peoples* that "foreign sausage makers and grill masters" had encouraged the people of the north—who once had a "light wonderful simplicity in their food and drink," which made them "healthy, powerful, strong, wise, and enduring"—to extreme excesses.[7]

Perhaps he was commenting on the awful excesses of the court, where dignitaries sometimes ate and drank themselves to death, or perhaps he was just nostalgic for the Scandinavia of the past as he sat writing in exile in Italy. Recent archaeological research into the cooking pots and ovens of the Vikings shows that he had a point when it came to the healthfulness of the common man's food during Viking times. These people seem not to have been the pork-devouring battle machines that they were portrayed as in the Norse sagas. Fish, seafood, cabbage (especially kale), root vegetables, nuts, peas, beans, and porridge were staples. Garlic, spring onions, and leeks were used. Bread made of rye, oat, barley, and wheat, sometimes mixed with peas and flaxseeds and usually unleavened, was common. During a sailing visit to Birka, one of the four main Viking settlements in Scandinavia, I watched two people demonstrating the preparation of a common Viking meal on a reproduction of a cooker that would have been used during those times. A simple vegetable stew simmered in a heavy iron pot hung over a fire from a metal stand. Viking food? Absolutely.

In general, these elements of diet during Viking times continued to be the diet of the common man through the centuries and up to the present day. Of course, one should not idealize the life of Scandinavian peasants in centuries past. There was usually not enough food to go around, and people were often hungry and malnourished. Still, the essential elements that the common person hoped to have on his or her plate were very similar to those that many people still have on their plates today. Most nutritionists today would say that it is good stuff. Very, very good.

Fish
Low domesticated-animal consumption, occasional consumption of wild animals
Whole-grain bread with an emphasis on rye, barley, and oats
Beans, peas, onions, root vegetables
Cabbage
Soured milk with low-fat content
Wild apples, lingonberries, rose hips, blueberries, cloudberries

The emergent Scandinavian spa industry of the eighteenth century was good at picking up on the healthfulness of this common man's food. In essence, it saw as one of its missions to bring the more affluent in society back to basics. Urban Hiärne, the father of the Scandinavian spa industry, came up with a set of dietary rules for his guests, many elements of which came from this common man's diet. The excessive domesticated meat consumption of the affluent was shunned, and the first propagandists for vegetarian diets found voice for their beliefs. Our only year-round neighbor consumes hot oat porridge when he comes home from work in the evenings. Evening porridge is an old prescription of the eighteenth-century spa industry, which is based on common man's food. It is filling, warming and calming to the stomach. Since our neighbor is out crossing the lake to get to work in his motorboat at a quarter to six in the morning on most days of the year—just as long as the water is not frozen—I can understand his need for consuming an evening meal that ensures sound sleep.

To eat commonly is one aspect of tradition in Scandinavia. To eat seasonally is another. Eating seasonally is about much more than getting food that is fresh, which is healthful in itself. To eat food that is in season is to express your natural rhythm, to tune yourself in, so to speak. In this very act of choosing to eat seasonally, you are plugging yourself into the gigantic source of inspiration and power that nature provides. In Scandinavia, eating seasonally during the colder months also means eating foods that have been prepared for that season during a previous one. Otherwise, a seasonal menu from the north of Scandinavia might become rather spartan: dried reindeer meat, lichen, and snow would be the seasonal menu for several months!

Living and harvesting here on our busy island, I have devised a pure-energy food calendar. This calendar is an annual reminder of what seasonal foods I can combine with our other standard fare. It creates an excitement about food that has gone amiss in today's jet-flown food industry. Everyone should have one. Even if you don't have the possibility of harvesting that much yourself, you can choose to buy local ingredients in season and base your food calendar around this. The ingredients of the different seasons become something to look forward to using and eating. Suddenly your whole year is energized with the new possibilities that each season will present in your kitchen and on your plate. There is also a valuable element of respect for food that this kind of seasonal eating brings into life. It is easy to gobble down a hamburger and not think about it twice. You could pick a hamburger up at any one of a number of fast-food outlets and have one every day of the year, if you really wanted to. It is not particularly good for you and you will probably not feel that satisfied after you have eaten it. My local lamb steak is available for purchase once a year from the local lamb producers association, who are concerned with providing their animals a good life. I prepare and eat it with care. I savor each bite. I don't eat too much of it and, in this quantity, it is good for me.

MY PURE-ENERGY FOOD CALENDAR

SPRING	SUMMER
Nettles	Wild and cultivated strawberries
Rhubarb	Red and black currants
Sweet water fish	Wild raspberries
Radishes	Gooseberries
	Cherries
	Elderberries
	Herbs
	Lettuces, tomato, cucumber
	Spinach

AUTUMN	WINTER
Plums	Kale
Pears	Lamb and wild meat (frozen)
Apples	Frozen berries
Rowanberries	Stored root vegetables from the
Crayfish	autumn
Lingonberries	Dried mushrooms
Rose hips	
Root vegetables	
Wild mushrooms	
Sweet water fish	
Lamb and wild meat	

Sensuality

From my opening story, you might be able to tell that my experience of Scandinavian food is filled with sensuality and romance. Part of falling in love with my husband was falling in love with his adoration of great food, Scandinavian style. If food can create a feeling of love, then it is taking us a long way toward feeling well: it is giving us the purest of energies.

The best of Scandinavian cuisine is sensuous because of all the features I have named above. Simplicity, freshness, cleanliness, unpretentiousness, and tradition are all features that appeal to our basic instincts. Many contemporary Scandinavian chefs are furthering this romance by abandoning the emphasis on being technically correct, a legacy of the French kitchen, some say, for an emphasis on flavor. The flavors and textures of nature have become their focus. This is a hopelessly romantic development that is taking them from strength to strength, particularly as they venture to combine traditional Nordic ingredients with food preparation ideas from other countries.

Dale Brown refers to the fact that the Vikings adored oysters and mussels, and other romantic foods. Vikings are not usually portrayed as besotted lovers who craved the food of love, so Dale Brown was unusually perceptive!

Nutritious Ingredients of
the Scandinavians

Since Dale Brown, the wellness-promoting aspect of Scandinavian food seems to have been a little subdued. Scandinavian chefs have been winning international competitions and acclaim internationally, including in the United States—Sweden is the only country to have won the Food Olympics twice in a row—yet the best and most healthful aspects of Scandinavian food have not entered global household practice in the way that pasta and sushi have. On the other hand, these chefs readily admit they do not always have health first in mind. In addition, having met one of the stars of Sweden's international culinary team, I am convinced that it is, in fact, total and utter modesty that has been winning Scandinavians competitions: Their capacity to surprise is very great. This may be another reason that Scandinavia's wellness food has remained rather anonymous.

Typical Scandinavian ingredients are extremely good for you, and are given the thumbs-up by most nutritionists. For this reason, I believe that Scandinavian food can be held up with the more famous wellness-promoting cuisines of Japan and the Mediterranean. Eating fish on a regular basis seems to promote longer life. Ingredients such as cabbage, apples, and certain types of berries can help to prevent and fight serious diseases such as cancer, heart disease, and degenerative brain diseases. The consumption of whole grains such as rye, barley, and oats keeps the digestive system in order, as do soured milk products. Root vegetables and wild meats, prepared in the right manner are a great source of low-fat carbohydrate and protein. All of these are quintessentially Scandinavian ingredients.

Fish

Norway's first feature film was made in 1907. Unsurprisingly, it was called *The Perils of the Fisherman*. Fishing has long been an essential feature of Norwegian culture. When we arrived in Norway, the first dish that our young three-year-olds were presented with was fish dumplings in white sauce, which is standard fare for young Norwegians. Norway, along with Iceland, continues to top the per capita consumption of fish in the world. The average Icelander eats more than 90 kilograms, or 198 pounds, of fish per person annually, thereby consuming nearly four times as much fish as the average Westerner. Fish consumption has for some time been linked to health and longevity, and Icelanders are indeed up there among the longest-living people in the world. This seems to be nothing new. Olaus Magnus wrote in 1555 that Icelanders were known for becoming very old (over one hundred years), using fish spread rather than butter on their bread.[8]

So, why is it that fish, in general, is so good for us? There are many reasons. In particular, I want to highlight Scandinavians' love of fatty fish with its high content of omega-3 fatty acids. The benefit of this wonder substance is explained in the table below.

FISH: NUTRITION POINTS

- An excellent source of protein (15–20 percent)
- A good source of vitamins A and B (particularly B_1 and B_6) and many essential minerals.
- Our most important source of selenium, an antioxidant thought to be active in preventing cancer and strengthening the immune system.
- Several favorite Scandinavian species, such as cod and pike, are very low in fat.
- Some beloved Scandinavian fatty fish, including salmon and herring, contain omega-3 fatty acids important for:
  - Countering the "bad" omega-6 fats common in Western diets.
  - Reducing the risk of heart disease and stroke by decreasing amounts of "bad" cholesterol (LDL) and increasing amounts of "good" cholesterol (HDL).
  - Reducing the risk of cancer by reducing the level of prostaglandins.
  - Reducing the risk of rheumatic trouble through an anti-inflammatory effect.
  - Possibly stimulating our mental capacity, making us learn faster and strengthening our concentration, also possibly reducing the risk of degenerative brain diseases such as Alzheimer's.
  - Possibly making us less aggressive, less stressed, and generally hap-

SALMON SAFETY

Salmon was once the staple diet of household servants in Sweden. A day with something other than salmon on one's plate was a special one. At that time salmon was harvested wild from waters that were less contaminated than they are today and were thus a healthy staple diet. This is true for all of the sources from which our food today comes. Unfortunately, for all the foods we consume today, it is true to say that what we eat may be harvested from sources more contaminated, certainly by industrial pollutants, than in the past. We can minimize industrial contamination getting into our bodies by increasing the awareness of where the food we eat comes from. Here are a few pointers for salmon, which is a good food that has been particularly highlighted in the media.

1. *If you can get wild salmon (or other wild fish) rather than farmed, that may be better. However, again check the source: Wild salmon are overfished in areas and also subject to industrial pollution. In the United States, wild Alaskan salmon is your best bet.*

2. *The health of farmed salmon varies, depending on where the salmon farm is located. If the farm is in a large, well-maintained body of water with a good natural current (and thus with a greater capacity to deal with the waste from salmon pens), the fish are likely to be better for consumption. Overall, salmon farming has been criticized for the damage it can do to the environment.*

3. *Most contaminants are found in the skin of the fish or in the fat just beneath it. Do not consume the skin. Most of the fat is lost in the cooking process. Make sure you drain it off.*

4. *Watch out for improvements in the fish-farming industry, which is working on ways to reduce levels of PCBs (polychlorinated biphenyls) and dioxins in the fish by finding a substitute for some of the fish oil in feed. These contaminants accumulate in farmed fish through their consumption of matter from other fish in which these substances have already accumulated.*

For more on what and how to choose your fish, check www.blueoceaninstitute. org/seafood/ or www.worldwildlife.org/windows/marine/you.

pier through an impact on levels of a feel-well substance called serotonin in our bodies.

More recently, there have been concerns about the effects of environmental pollution and fish-farming techniques on the fish that we eat. Industrial dioxins have been found to accumulate in the tissue of fatty fish, and farmed fish have often been fed antibiotics to avoid diseases developing in the highly overcrowded environments in which they are cultivated. In the jungle of information and advice about fish that one encounters today, my suggestion is to know the source of the fish that you eat. At the end of the day, this is a good rule of thumb for almost any food that you consume, since similar questions crop up with all the foods that we eat.

Many people in Scandinavia have a "fish" story behind them. One of my neighbors works in a day-care center looking after three-to-five-year-olds all week. On weekends during the colder months, she metamorphoses into the toughest of fisherpersons. Her enthusiasm for fishing adds new meaning to getting involved with food. Her partner and his son are both hardy people who also enjoy fishing, but when the cold rain arrives, the fishing rods get reeled in and they head for the car. She and her female friends from the day care, on the other hand, sling their rain gear on and continue while the males look on from the car. An act of Scandinavian feminist defiance? No, they actually like it. Her female friends from the day care had zero experience of fishing prior to her inviting them out about a year ago. Now they are all "hooked" and have standing weekends when they all come out and fish together. Once the tough work is over, everyone hops into the wood-fired waterfront hot tub, from which they can continue to enjoy the bad weather and the cold rain. The men prepare the fish in the sensible warmth of the kitchen. I don't know how they prepare it. Probably without too much fuss. This is my no-fuss salmon recipe.

NO-FUSS BROILED SALMON
WITH LEMON BALM

2.2 pounds (1 kg) fresh salmon fillet
Salt and pepper

4 tablespoons olive oil

Fistful of fresh lemon balm, crushed

2 cloves garlic, crushed

Preheat the broiler in your oven. Rinse the fish, pat it dry, and lay on a baking sheet lined with a piece of parchment paper. Season the fish with salt and pepper. Prepare the topping by mixing together the olive oil, lemon balm, and garlic. Spread evenly over the salmon. When the broiler is hot, put the salmon in for about 15–20 minutes, or until well cooked on the outside and a darker pink on the inside. Serve with steamed new potatoes and a salad.

Shellfish

Scandinavians are great lovers of shellfish, which is similar in nutritional value to fish (see the nutrition points for fish, above). It is really great stuff unless you are allergic to shellfish, in which case you should make sure to stay well clear of any food substance containing shellfish, particularly when disguised in the form of shellfish stocks, which restaurants sometimes use as a base for sauces and soups. It is well known that shellfish are often affected by water pollution to a higher extent than fish, so it is important to know where they come from when you buy them. In Scandinavia there are very strict controls on the farming and sale of shellfish, so the danger of being seriously affected by water pollution through shellfish tends to be low.

August in parts of Scandinavia is crayfish season. They are prepared in a distinctive style: cooked in salt water with dill. This is the way that common people during the nineteenth century adapted the crayfish eating habit of the court, which tended to consume this shellfish with exotic spices. There is a whole culture of celebration that has developed around these crayfish—the last hurrah of summer and the celebration of impending change. Just as the summer offers us its last warmish evenings, our glass-enclosed gazebo is lit up with candles and a large bowl of crayfish with stalks of dill placed in the middle. For such a ceremonious dinner, with songs and speech-giving, crayfish is a very hands-on meal, with a lot of slurping and sucking going on to get all the good flavor out of the crayfish. Swedish crayfish are making a gradual comeback after having been almost entirely wiped out by disease. The second Thursday in August is the official premiere for putting the cages down in the water. Cooked with a little less salt and minus large quantities of aquavit, it can be considered a good, nutritious "pure energy" food.

My own preference is for seafood soup with mussels, shrimp, and fish, served with yogurt aioli. My children lap up the soup itself, and, of course, the mussels and unshelled shrimp provide a lot of entertainment. There is no way to be pretentious while consuming this soup, since a lot of finger-work is involved. Have ready a bowl for the shells and another bowl with water and segments of lemon for rinsing your fingers. We tend to enjoy this soup most on stormy nights, when we can imagine the perils of the fisherman out on the high seas.

SEAFOOD SOUP WITH YOGURT AIOLI
FOR A STORMY NIGHT

SOUP:

2 shallots, chopped

2 cloves garlic, chopped

1 small onion, finely chopped

4 tablespoons extra-virgin olive oil

1¼ cups (3 dl) crushed tomatoes

2 tablespoons tomato paste

2 cups (5 dl) fish stock

¾ cup (2 dl) dry sherry

1 large fresh cod fillet or other firm-fleshed white fish fillet, completely deboned

2 pounds (900 g) blue mussels in their shells, scrubbed

14 ounces (400 g) shelled raw shrimp

Pinch of salt and pepper

Dash of Tabasco sauce
Handful of parsley, chopped

YOGURT AIOLI:
1 cup (2.5 dl) yogurt with at least 3 percent fat
2 cloves garlic, crushed

Sauté the shallots, garlic, and onion in the olive oil in a large, deep, thick-bottomed cooking pot for about 2 minutes over medium heat. Mix in the crushed tomatoes, tomato paste, stock, and sherry. Bring to boil and turn down the heat so that the mixture just simmers. Add the cod fillet, the mussels, and the raw shrimp and mix gently into the soup. Cover and simmer gently until most of the mussels have opened (5 minutes). Remove cover and discard mussels that have not opened (do not attempt to pry open and consume). Add salt, pepper, Tabasco sauce, and parsley. Serve with yogurt aioli and a slice of steaming cumin bread (see recipe under Bread and Grains). A note on your choice of fish: If you choose cod, remember to select a fillet that is more than 1 foot (30 cm) in length.

Wild Meat

Scandinavians prize wild meat of deer, moose, reindeer, rabbit, hare, and various types of wild birds. This is partly because it is safely available in Europe's last wilderness, and also partly because people believe that the quality and healthfulness of the meat is better than that which comes from domesticated animals. To a great extent, this is correct.

WILD MEAT: NUTRITION POINTS
- Contains only a few percent fat, much lower than meat from domesticated animals, which is in the order of 25–30 percent.
- Contains omega-3 fatty acids, around 2.5 percent, not found in domesticated animals.

There may be some people who are wondering how I can possibly write about the consumption of wild animals as part of an approach to well-being. After all, the consumption of wild meat is pretty exclusive in most parts of the world (if it is available at all), and killing beautiful, wild creatures seems distasteful. Isn't meat bad for us full stop? Shouldn't we be saving wild animals from extinction?

In Scandinavia I have encountered a culture of hunting that is unique in the world, and which I believe can fit in with an approach to well-being. I have spoken with a number of hunters who are friends of mine, trying to figure out what their views are. I am not a hunter myself, but I have been invited along on hunting expeditions.

Hunting in Scandinavia is still a part of life. It tends not to be a trophy sport. The animals are hunted for consumption. Particularly in the case of moose, the most important game for hunting, it is necessary to control numbers, since there are no other predators. Hunting is not glamorized, rather it is something that many people do. Like fishing and all of the other forms of food gathering that are common to this part of the world, people come very close to nature, they enjoy it, they take from it, and they respect the fact that nature needs time to regenerate itself.

Wild meat is eaten sparingly and with tremendous delight. Those who enjoy a good moose steak will find that a regular steak from domesticated cattle is really quite mediocre. One of the hunters I know grimaces when his wife makes food with "bought meat," by which he means meat from domesticated animals. Wild meat in Scandinavia was my reintroduction to meat after not eating it for many years. Since wild meat is low in fat, it does not leave you with the same feeling of heaviness that red meat from domesticated animals does. We all know eating a lot of red meat is not good for us. The occasional steak of wild meat is probably the best that we can do for ourselves, if we enjoy having meat in our diets.

Something that I have noticed when I see hunters in Scandinavia in the outdoors is how observant they are of their environment. Indeed, getting a hunting license in Sweden requires considerable learning about the behavior of wild animals. One of my friends who is a hunter has taken me down the river where he hunts duck. He explained to me, in very precise terms, the living pattern of these birds, their interaction with other animals and with their surroundings, and what a fair moment to shoot them would be. He had gone to great lengths to keep their stocks up on his property. He described how gut-churning it felt to injure an animal, and how one *had* to find the animal if it managed to get away. I have got the impression from him and from others, that no good hunter should romanticize hunting. At the same time, it is a powerful stimulant to natural rhythm. A good hunter relates very closely to his environment.

Claes's aunt Karin came to us on my second Christmas in Sweden with a wild deer steak from an animal her husband had shot during the autumn hunting season. It was accompanied by an old and trusted meat thermometer, a few juniper berries, and a letter with a recipe in it. I followed the directions. Light and superb for anyone who is a red-meat eater.

DEER STEAK ROASTED WITH JUNIPER

1 tablespoon olive oil
1 tablespoon butter
3.3–4.4 pounds (1.5–2 kg) fine cut of deer steak for roasting
6 whole cloves garlic
Salt and white pepper
8 juniper berries, crushed
Beef stock for basting

Preheat the oven to 320°F (160°C). Melt together the oil and butter in the skillet pan. Brown the deer steak in it. Place the deer steak in a roasting pan. Make some small cuts in the meat at different spots and tuck in the garlic. Season with salt, pepper, and the crushed juniper. Insert a meat thermometer and roast in the oven. For rare meat, remove the steak when the thermometer has reached 140°F (60°C). Add a few minutes more if you like it more cooked. During roasting, avoid letting the steak become too dry by basting with beef stock. Enjoy with a wild mushroom sauce. See the recipe under Wild Mushrooms.

In America there have been concerns about consuming wild meat or game raised on farms, since there have been incidences of prion's disease, or chronic wasting disease (CWD) among deer and elk. The first thing to stress is that these incidences are still limited. Where the disease spreads, increasingly strict controls have been put in place by state and federal authorities to stop its spread. Since you cannot today buy wild meat in the United States—you need to hunt it yourself—the issue for most consumers who want to try game is how good the controls are at domesticated game farms. I have been told by the Wisconsin Department of Natural Resources that if captive game producers want to sell their meat products in retail stores or in restaurants, these animals have to be inspected at either a state or federally inspected facility. They additionally told me that where results of testing for CWD had been positive, whole farms had to be depopulated of their game herds.

Dairy Products

My husband's grandfather—the same person who built our stone terraces at the age of seventy—used to eat a bowl of *filmjölk*, a smooth and refreshing-tasting soured milk product, with a sprinkling of ginger on top and a slice of Swedish hard bread for lunch. He was not alone. Scandinavians love dairy products of all kinds. Some of them, like the well-known Scandinavian hard cheeses, should only be eaten in very small quantities; thus the cheese slicer, a Norwegian invention that is a clever graterlike knife for achieving very thin slices of this rich food. Other Nordic dairy products have some good health benefits if eaten in moderation, as long as you are not lactose intolerant.

Filmjölk comes from the very old Scandinavian preservation strategy for milk by souring it. The modern version of this soured milk is something like lowfat buttermilk. *Filmjölk* with live cultures like acidophilus in them are known for keeping the digestive system in good form. The same effects can be had from low-fat yogurt with live cultures. Whenever I have been on antibiotics, I have tried to eat more *filmjölk* with live cultures, to replace the needed good bacteria in my system. There are lots of sugary fruit-flavored versions, which are best avoided. The real thing, smooth and wonderful to the taste, perhaps with a little muesli or fruit thrown in for texture and a great flavor combination, say, with a little ginger, is best.

FILMJÖLK (LOWFAT BUTTERMILK WITH LIVE CULTURES): NUTRITION POINTS

- Helps to restore and/or maintain the balance of needed bacteria in the stomach.
- Also has antibacterial effects similar to antibiotics and therefore might be useful in preventing dangerous diseases such as dysentery and salmonella.
- Strengthens the immune system.
- Possible cancer prevention food, particularly for breast and colon cancer.

Another dairy product that can work little miracles, which I have run into in Scandinavia, is called *messmör* in Swedish. It is a thick spreadable substance that looks something like peanut butter and has an appealing taste of mild, slightly salty caramel. It is made by boiling down the water, or whey, that is left over when cheese is made.

Messmör is a boon to good health that many good Scandinavian mothers know about. Due to its high iron content and its beneficial digestive effects, *messmör* can be a great plus for women during pregnancy. A tablespoon or two of *messmör* gives a terrific caramel flavor to gravy for wild meats. Norwegians like *mesost,* or the cheese that is distilled from the whey that *messmör* is made from. Icelanders consume something called *skyr*, which is also made of whey, but with quite different results as far as flavor and texture are concerned. It is extremely low in fat, only 0.2 percent. It is spreadable, a bit like a soft cheese, and can also be eaten like yogurt. There are many fruity flavored types of *skyr* out on the market today. Fun, but the best, nutrition-wise, is still the original.

- Relatively low in fat
- High iron content
- High calcium content
- Great aid to the digestion when things get a little clogged

To date, *messmör* is not widely available on the American market, although there are a few specialty stores that sell it. Low-fat German quark cheese closely resembles *skyr* and is widely available in food stores.

Bread and Grains

One thing I noticed pretty quickly when I first came to Scandinavia was that the amount of supermarket shelf space taken up by squishy, white bread made of highly refined wheat—the stuff my German mother used to call harmonica bread—is fairly small. The bread sections tend to be large and are filled with all manner of breads made of rye, barley, and oats. These types of grain are great health boosters, and Scandinavians love them.

There is a great deal of tradition and concern for practicality that influences what you can find in the bread section of Scandinavian supermarkets today. *Tunnbröd,* or thin bread, for example, is a northern Scandinavian tradition, since it was a great way of making use of barley, the only grain that could be grown in that region. Barley lacks gluten and is therefore not suitable for making leavened bread.

BARLEY: NUTRITION POINTS

- Contains many essential minerals such as potassium, calcium, magnesium, and zinc.
- An excellent source of different types of B vitamins.
- Believed to prevent high cholesterol levels by reducing the human body's own production of cholesterol. People with a high consumption of barley tend to have a lower prevalence of heart disease than those who do not consume much barley.

- Has a high level of water-soluble fibers, which are good for keeping the digestion in order.
- Possibly a preventive measure against cancer of the colon.
- Considered to have a calming effect and prevents ulcers.

Rye also grows well in Scandinavia's cold climate, and the people of this region eat large amounts of rye bread by world standards. Rye is the basis for the bread part of the Danish *smørrebrød,* a dark bread made of sour rye dough and topped with all sorts of innovative delights. Finns have strong food traditions with rye, including bread and other dishes such as *kalakukko* (small fish baked in rye dough) and *mämmi* (a baked Easter-time dessert). Icelanders get my medal for innovative ways of making bread: *Hverabraud* is a rye bread made by putting a simple rye dough into a covered pot and placing it into a hot spring. Depending on the temperature, the bread is left there for six to twenty-four hours.

Rye is usually the basic ingredient in one of Scandinavia's most renowned exported food products: hard bread. This type of bread originated from a clever approach to preserving rye wheat during the summer and winter, when water-driven mills were not operational. These hard, flat breads usually had a hole in the middle and were stored through the winter on a pole hung horizontally from the kitchen ceiling so that children and mice could not get at them. The saying goes that hard bread baked at the birth of a child could last without getting moldy until the engagement of that person, if it was properly stored.

RYE: NUTRITION POINTS

- High in insoluble fiber, which assists digestion.
- High in soluble fibers, which reduce blood fat levels, preventing heart problems and strokes.
- Believed to reduce the risk of cancer in the prostate, breast, and colon due to the presence of lignans, a phytoestrogen, or growth regulating hormone.
- A *slow food* with a low glycemic index, and good for avoiding rapidly shifting blood sugar levels.

Here is a tasty recipe of rye bread with cumin, which I created to eat with soup. The emphasis is on medium-ground rye flour rather than on the usual villainous refined white flour.

RYE BREAD WITH CUMIN

3¼ cups (8 dl) medium-ground rye flour

2½ cups (6 dl) fine-ground wheat flour (white flour)

1.8 ounces (50 g) fresh or powdered yeast

2 cups (0.5 liter) lukewarm water (97°F, or 37°C)

2 tablespoons honey

3.4 ounces (1 dl) canola or olive oil

1 tablespoon salt

3 tablespoons whole cumin seeds

Extra white flour for kneading

By hand: Mix together all of the dry ingredients in a bowl. If using powdered yeast, mix this in too. Then add water. If using fresh yeast, dissolve yeast into the warm water prior to adding to the other ingredients. Add honey and oil. Knead the dough by hand on a floured board for 10 minutes. If the dough is too sticky, add some wheat flour. Add salt and cumin during the last 3 minutes or so of kneading. Place the dough in a lightly oiled bowl in a warm place in the kitchen, and cover with a dry kitchen towel. Allow to rise for half an hour or so until the dough has doubled in size. Knead once again for the same time as before. Split the dough in half and form into loaves on a greased baking tray. Preheat the oven to 475°F (250°C). Allow the dough to rise again for half an hour. Lower the oven temperature to 425°F (225°C). Spray the loaves with water and bake for 25 minutes. Enjoy with seafood or other soup.

In a dough processor: Put all the ingredients, except the salt and cumin, into the processor. Process on Low for 2 minutes and on Medium for 5 minutes. Add in the seasoning in the last minute of mixing. Proceed as for preparing the bread by hand.

For the second round of kneading, run the food processor on Medium for 5 minutes.

When the north wind starts blowing cold air onto our little island, it is time for a bowl of hot oatmeal with milk, honey, and raisins. This little dish is unbelievably delicious and warming, and is packed with loads of pure energy.

OATMEAL FOR A NORTH WIND

1¾ cups (4 dl) oatmeal

3 cups (8 dl) low-fat milk

3–4 tablespoons honey

⅓ cup (1 dl) raisins

Warm all of the ingredients in a pot, stirring slowly over medium heat. Once thickened, and just beginning to simmer, remove from heat. Lap up and enjoy the warmth surging through your body! You can use water as an alternative to milk, if you prefer it.

Oats are another cold-resistant grain that Scandinavians have historically savored. They are the classic ingredient for porridge, which was eaten in less prosperous times for breakfast, lunch, and dinner in many different forms, such as fried, with or without milk. Today in Scandinavia, people consume oats more in the form of bread, particularly hard bread, into which oats have been mixed with other grains.

OATS: NUTRITION POINTS

- Reduce blood fat levels, thus reducing the risk of heart and coronary diseases.
- One of the richest sources of silicon, which might assist in preventing Alzheimer's disease.
- Contain essential minerals such as calcium, iron, potassium, and magnesium.

- One of the best sources of vitamin B_1, an antioxidant.
- A slow food and therefore good for regulating blood sugar and in-sulin levels.
- Calming to the nerves and stomach.

Scandinavians remain super keen on porridge for their young children, particularly drinking porridge for infants and toddlers. There are different types. The most common tends to consist of a mixture of oat, rye, wheat meal, and skimmed milk powder and has a pleasant malted flavor. There are nonmilk versions for lactose-intolerant children. By the time my twins were six months old, I had forgotten what a night's sleep was like. My ever-practical Swedish child minder suggested that I start giving them a bottle of *välling*, or drinking porridge, just before bed to fill them up. This worked wonders. I could sleep, they were more satisfied, and life slowly started to transform itself. Thank you, *välling*.

Wild Mushrooms

The joy of discovering a bed of golden chanterelle is enough to last any Nordic person through the long, cold winter. Having been out on many autumn mushroom-picking expeditions by now, I have come to understand this joy. It is a great thrill to find a non-worm-infested bed of first-class edible wild mushrooms.

I find it hard to believe that the consumption of wild mushrooms was not a Scandinavian idea. It wasn't, apparently. King Karl XIV Johan, a

IF YOU ARE WORRIED ABOUT PICKING YOUR OWN . . .

An expanding range of wild and cultivated mushrooms can be bought in supermarkets today. These include shiitake, portabello, cremini, oyster, enoki, chanterelles, and porcini. They can be purchased either at local supermarkets or gourmet shops, depending upon the season. Portabello, shiitake, and cremini are the most common in ordinary supermarkets. You can often get dried porcini as well.

Frenchman imported from the ranks of Napoleon's generals to become king of Sweden and Norway in 1814, and from whom the present Swedish royal family is descended, is credited with bringing with him and popularizing this good idea. Today, few other countries can compete with Nordic fervor for mushroom picking. I should know. One of our summertime neighbors has the best chanterelle spots on our island mapped. She has bagged them before I can even get a start. In revenge, our dog, Lucy, once stole a bagful from her terrace. Later on, I was forced sheepishly to admit to her that Lucy had stolen her bag of chanterelles.

Learning to pick the right mushrooms is an art unto itself. The learning process starts early. There are autumn radio programs teaching kids about mushrooms. They even sing about mushrooms. One refrain goes: "Have you seen Mr. Chantarelle, Mr. Chantarelle, Mr. Chantarelle?" By local standards, I was ancient when I started mushroom picking at the age of twenty-nine. A few years on, I thought I was pretty savvy, with eight edible sorts under my belt. Then I met someone living in my area who had written mushroom lexicons. It is extremely important to know what you are picking. A mistake can be very dangerous. So perhaps it is not such a bad idea that I stick to the eight that I know.

WILD MUSHROOMS: NUTRITION POINTS

- Consist of 90–95 percent water and therefore low in fat and calories.
- Rich in fiber.
- Contain essential minerals such as zinc, manganese, iron, and selenium.
- Chantarelles are rich in vitamin D.

WARNING: Be sure of what you are picking, so read up. A few varieties can be deadly! Warnings have been given about mushrooms picking up radioactivity. Cooking them removes most of this.

Once you have eaten wild mushrooms, the commonly cultivated button mushrooms that you can buy in most supermarkets pale in taste. Tore

Wretman, a legend in Swedish culinary history, said that this is the best way to prepare wild mushrooms.

After cleaning the mushrooms, without using water, cut the mushrooms in pieces. Let the mushroom melt in a pot in its own water. Drain. Let some butter melt in a frying pan and add the drained mushrooms. Fry on low heat, slowly, slowly. . . .

We have tried frying the mushrooms in olive oil with a bit of crushed garlic, as a healthful alternative, and this seems to work just fine. I have in the past saved some of these autumn mushrooms, particularly when I have a few different types to mix together, for Christmas dinner gravy. After letting the mushrooms "melt" in their own water and draining them, I chop them fine in the blender and then freeze this mushroom purée in small sealed plastic containers. The gravy is heavenly over root vegetables and wild meat, and you don't have to worry about that red light for calories going off the minute you look at the gravy jug. This gravy is not a high-fat version.

WILD MUSHROOM GRAVY

¾ cup (2 dl) mushroom purée (as above)
A few tablespoons of the pan juices from meat, if you are eat-
    ing the gravy with roasted meat
1¾ cups (4 dl) beef or vegetable stock
1 tablespoon corn flour
¼ cup (0.5 dl) reduced fat crème fraîche
Pepper

Melt the mushroom purée over gentle heat. As it is melting, stir in the pan juices and stock. Cover and simmer for 5 minutes. Blend flour to a smooth liquid with a few tablespoons of cold water and stir into the pot. Simmer gently for another five min-utes, stirring constantly. Remove from heat. With a handheld beater, mix in the crème fraîche. Season with pepper. Serve immediately and enjoy in moderation.

Cabbages

Cabbage, anyone? Usually there aren't many takers on that offer. Wonder why? In Scandinavia it is usually because so many adults have bad memories of overcooked, foul-smelling leaves from school lunches. Cabbage has been done a great injustice over time, both here and elsewhere. It has usually been overcooked, causing foul-smelling sulphide to be released into the air. Treated properly, cabbage is a fantastic food, bursting with flavor and goodness. One great added bonus of cabbage is that many types keep for a long time (for weeks) if kept cool. When we have run out of fresh vegetables here on our island, I can usually find a cabbage that is still in good shape after some time of storage in our cold cellar.

Scandinavians have been eating cabbage for a long time. The Vikings ate it, and in medieval times it became a staple. Vegetable gardens were often called cabbage gardens. The King's Garden in Stockholm, now a popular place to catch a caffe latte, was once the royal cabbage garden. The first cookbook printed in Sweden, in 1650, contains many recipes using cabbage: white cabbage soup, sour cabbage, and numerous recipes for kale, cauliflower, and savoy cabbage.

All types of cabbages, eaten raw, or gently cooked, are supremely good for you. Here's why.

CABBAGES: NUTRITION POINTS

- Rich in fiber and therefore good for the digestion.
- Rich in minerals and vitamins.
- Low in calories.
- Strengthens the immune system.
- Considered a natural cancer shield. Lowers the risk of cancer of the lung, stomach, and colon and recommended in treating cancer that has already developed.
- White cabbage: the most potent cabbage variety as far as fighting cancer is concerned. Red cabbage is similarly effective.

- Kale: one of the best sources of vitamin C. Super high in carotene, potassium, calcium, and iron.
- Broccoli: High in antioxidants, with an abundance of vitamins A, B, and C, minerals, beta-carotene, and folic acid. Works against respiratory infections. Strengthens the liver.

Red cabbage is my favorite. Rather than create more bad memories for Claes, who, it seems, had many bad overcooked cabbage days at school, I often prepare red cabbage without cooking it at all. Here is a recipe for which guests keep asking for more. Yes, cabbage salad.

DELIGHTFUL MEMORIES
RED CABBAGE SALAD

¼ medium-sized head red cabbage, chopped into bite-sized chunks
½ red onion, finely chopped
2 cloves garlic, crushed
1 red pepper, chopped into bite-sized chunks
2–3 apples, washed, cored, and chopped into bite-sized chunks
1 cup (2.5 dl) half-fat crème fraîche
1 tablespoon mayonnaise
1 tablespoon honey
¼ cup (0.5 dl) canola or olive oil
Salt and pepper

Combine the raw ingredients in a bowl and toss. Mix together dressing ingredients in a food processor or with a handheld egg-beater. Pour over raw ingredients and toss again. Season with salt and pepper. Serve as a starter or side salad to just about anything.

Root Vegetables

Finland's prime minister, Tarja Halonen, burns for vegetables, particularly root vegetables. She has seven greenhouses at her summer home, where she grows and harvests the vegetables herself. Her summer and autumn harvests are so large that they last her and the family all winter. She allegedly shed about forty pounds on a diet of root vegetables from her own harvest.

Root vegetables hold an exalted place in the Scandinavian garden. Some county laws from medieval times stipulated that every peasant was obliged to maintain a turnip garden, even if he had no other fields. Before the introduction of potatoes during the eighteenth century, these were a staple food. Once potatoes were introduced from South America, it took some time before they became accepted as a staple food. People were suspicious and believed they were the food of the devil! By the end of the nineteenth century, Swedes alone were consuming on average 267 pounds (121 kg) of potatoes per person annually. This has reduced in modern times due to concerns that potatoes are fattening (which, of course, they are if you consume them in the form of french fries, chips, and the like) and that they have a high Glycemic Index (GI), meaning that they send blood sugar levels up quickly and are thus dangerous in societies where diabetes has become a serious problem.

The good news for Scandinavians is that their most treasured root vegetable, the new potato, which has a revered status in the midsummer celebrations, emerges as having only a moderate GI. Consumed with generous amounts of chopped dill, new potatoes are a divine accompaniment to my midsummer salmon.

Yet root vegetables include a wide variety of foods with an excellent nutrition value. I value them for the long time that they keep in our outdoor stone cold cellar. And the humble potato, which has taken such a battering of late—well, if you are worried about what it means for your health, just remember that there are many types and that, prepared in the right way and eaten as part of a balanced diet, even potatoes can offer you many valuable nutrients.

SELECTED ROOT VEGETABLES: NUTRITION POINTS
- Potatoes: Very low in fat and relatively high in carbohydrates. A good source of vitamin C. Contain several of the B vitamins and important

minerals such as potassium and magnesium. May have a certain preventive effect against viruses, and even cancer, due to the presence of antioxidants.

- Swedish turnips (Rutabagas): High vitamin C content.
- Red beets: Contain silicon, which is important for hair, skin, and blood vessels. Good for the digestion.
- Horseradish: High vitamin C content.
- Carrots: The richest source of beta-carotene, which is beneficial in the prevention and treatment of cancer. Also beneficial for the heart, circulation, eyesight, skin, and lungs.

In Sweden, pickled red beets are a favorite side dish to the famous Swedish meatballs and many other dishes. Here I offer an alternative. One of my favorite ways to prepare beets is to combine them with two other Scandinavian favorites: hazelnuts and dill.

STEAMED BEETROOT WITH HAZELNUTS AND CREAMY DILL SAUCE

6 medium-sized beetroots
4 tablespoons canola or olive oil
1 cup (2.5 dl) crème fraîche
Large sprig fresh dill, finely chopped, or 1 tablespoon dried dill
⅓ cup (1 dl) hazelnuts, roughly chopped
Ground black pepper

Cut off the leaves of the beetroot, leaving enough stem so that the beetroots don't bleed while cooking. Simmer the beetroots in lightly salted water for about 1 hour. Drain off the water and let the beetroots cool before slipping off the thick outer skin. While you are waiting, prepare the dill sauce. Combine oil, crème fraîche, and dill in a food processor or mix together manually with an eggbeater. Chop the beetroots into quarters or smaller, if you wish, and arrange in a bowl. Lightly brown the hazelnuts in a pan. Scatter the hazelnuts over the beetroot. Serve as a salad starter on a bed of lettuce or as a side dish with the dill sauce and ground black pepper on top.

Apples, Pears, Plums, and Cherries

Idun was married to Brage, the Viking god of knowledge, language, and poetry. Idun was the goddess of spring and eternal youth. She kept the apples in a box which the gods would eat when they grew old. Then they all would be young again, and would be so until Ragnarök, the end of the world. . . .

There is definitely something in this story, as told by Snorre Sturlasson, the Icelandic poet of the thirteenth century.[9] There is probably no way of achieving eternal youth, but at least an apple a day, washed and dried, will keep you in good form and help you to age gracefully.

APPLES: NUTRITION POINTS

- The pectin and fibers in apples have a colon-cleansing effect, reducing the risk of colon cancer.
- Apples have an antibacterial effect, protecting against viruses, and generally strengthening the immune system.
- Apple eaters have a lower risk of developing respiratory disease than people who do not consume the fruit.
- Apple cider might be effective in preventing rheumatism.

Apples are indigenous to the Nordic region, and Scandinavians have been eating them for as long as humans could survive in the North. The Vikings considered apples to be a must for their long voyages across the Atlantic, as well as their last journeys: Traces of apples have been found in Viking burial sites. The apples that they ate were wild and sour. Scandinavians have the cloisters and monasteries to thank for developing the many sweet and wonderful varieties of apples that can be found in this part of the world today. They were so successful in this pioneering project that the largest numbers of varieties of apples today are allegedly to be found in Scandinavia.

September in many parts of Scandinavia is apple season. People in the countryside are grateful for passersby and friends who are interested in picking their apples. There are so many of them. Our builder, Lars, who lives nearby, has left us an open invitation to remove as many apples as possible from his property in the autumn. My hairdresser tries to pawn off her tasty apples in bowls in the waiting room of her salon. An orchard not far from where we live is the only farm I know that manages to make use of all of their apples, since one of the owners inherited a gigantic cider press. It is relatively easy to grow high-quality apples in Scandinavia. The long summer nights give the apples plenty of taste and sweetness, and the cold winters keep the insects in check.

One September, we tried to assist our friends Tage and Eva to get rid of their many apples. They own a picturesque eighteenth-century estate in central Sweden passed down through six generations. Their apple orchard is a sight to behold. There are so many different varieties. Claes and I loaded up two industrial-sized plastic garbage bags with apples, while Tage pruned his trees and talked about his views on ecology. The children had already made off with as many apples as they could hold. Upon arriving home, we took the apples directly to my mother-in-law, who, with slightly furled eyebrows and a deep sigh, realized that she was in for several days of preparing her famous, deceptively simple and delicious apple mousse. Marianne made the same mousse without a recipe for seventy-five years. I managed to squeeze this simple recipe out of her.

MARIANNE'S APPLE MOUSSE

Best-quality tart apples
Water
Sugar

Fill a large cooking pot two-thirds full with tart apples. Pour in enough water so that it covers about half the height of the apples. Cook on medium heat until the apples are soft enough to pass through a sieve. Cool. Press the apples through a sieve with a wooden spoon into a clean cooking pot. Heat the apple mousse gently and add sugar to taste. Choosing high-quality local apples, if you can, will reduce the amount of sugar that you need to add to make this recipe taste good. Cool and serve with yogurt or a little milk. Children adore this.

During August and September, we reroute the path to our sauna house. This is because a pear tree that grows just outside the sauna house becomes so heavy with pears that it starts drooping over the usual path. Before we came to the enlightened conclusion that it would be wise to reroute the path, we hit our heads on hard, maturing pears each time we were on our way to the sauna. Starting a sauna with a headache is not such a good idea. Once the pears are picked, we have them in a large basket on our terrace, so that anyone who is feeling as if they need a little snack en route can grab a pear. We do the same with our plums and cherries. This little snack has become so popular among our family members that if I want to make anything with these fruits, I have to reserve a portion early.

POACHED PEARS WITH
VANILLA AND CINNAMON

4 medium-sized ripe, but not soft, pears
Lemon juice
4 tablespoons water
1 tablespoon vanilla sugar
1 teaspoon ground ginger or cinnamon

Peel, core, and quarter the pears. Place them in a heavy-bottomed cooking pot and sprinkle with a little lemon juice to avoid discoloration. Just a few drops will do. Add water. Sprinkle pears with vanilla sugar and ginger or cinnamon. Simmer

gently covered until the pears are soft but not mushy. Serve with
a dollop of berry jam, and some plain yogurt or whipped cream.

Berries

Wild berries are a treasured feature of Scandinavian cuisine. Lingonberries and rowanberries are commonly eaten in the form of a jam or jelly with meats and potatoes. Scandinavian summer is just not the same without the beloved strawberry. Cloudberries are a northern specialty, with a delicious caramel flavor that adds a special festive air to any meal.

I have counted at least fourteen types of wild berries that Scandinavians pick and use in their kitchen. Berry picking has become a favorite twentieth-century Scandinavian pastime for three reasons. First, the ancient laws of the land allow for widespread access to nature and the forests. Second is the advent of the freezer, which allows for the preservation of berries. Third is the availability of sugar, which is another means of preserving the berries. Lingonberries and cloudberries were the only berries that were picked and stored to any wide extent before the twentieth century, since they contain their own natural preservative.

A lot of the things that we do with berries mean that we have to add sugar to them. For the more sour varieties, this can be quite a lot. Using raw honey, which has no refined sugar added to it and which has not been heated to more than 117°F (47°C), is a good idea, particularly as honey does not upset blood sugar levels as much as refined sugar does. Eating the sweeter berries just after picking, as our children do, is, of course, the most healthful way to benefit from their goodness.

SELECTED BERRIES: NUTRITION POINTS

- High vitamin C content, particularly in rose hips, black currants, and rowanberries.
- Excellent antioxidant capacity, particularly in blueberries, blackberries, cranberries, strawberries, and raspberries. Antioxidants protect us against serious diseases such as cancer, heart disease, diabetes, Alzheimer's, and Parkinson's.

- Lingonberries contain essential minerals, vitamin B_1 and B_2, as well as benzoic acid, which is claimed to be helpful in treating rheumatism.
- Blueberries are a household cure for the treatment of diarrhea, are antiviral, high in antioxidants, and may improve eyesight and protect against degenerative eye diseases.
- Raspberries, because of their high content of phytochemicals, might be effective in preventing and curing certain types of cancers.

Fruit and berry soups and creams are popular in Scandinavia. Some of them have excellent medicinal value. Rose hip soup is standard fare for fighting a cold, since it is so rich in vitamin C. Blueberry soup or cream is standard for drying up a loose tummy. Cranberry soup is useful in getting rid of urinary infections. The great thing about these soups is that you don't have to argue with your children to get them to eat them.

CURRANT SOUP

1 quart (1 liter) red and/or black currants, rinsed and stalks removed
Water
Sugar or honey
2 tablespoons cornstarch

Place the currants in a pot and add enough water so that it covers about two thirds of the berries. Cook over medium heat, until the berries soften, stirring occasionally. Add sugar or honey to taste. Mix cornstarch with a little cold water until mixture is smooth. Slowly pour this liquid into the pot, and stir over medium heat. The berry mixture should thicken into a cream, which is like a thick soup, within a short period of time. If it doesn't, make a little more of the cornstarch mixture and add to the pot. Serve with yogurt or a dollop of whipped cream.

When I think of picking berries here on our island, I think of family and togetherness. I think of the beautiful love and peace that exist in this simple act. I think of how well I feel once we have returned home with buckets full.

And so, I find myself ending this chapter where I started it: with my cherished wild strawberries, which have come to symbolize for me the purest energy of all.

SEVEN

Achieving Meaning Beyond
and for Ourselves

E ARLY in this book, I told you that on this island in Scandinavia there were four things that I had learned well-being is about: nature, creativity, personal space, and intimacy. When I reflect on the totality of what I have experienced, on all of my travels and on the dramatic life change that coming to the island brought about, I realize that there is a fifth. I reserve it for this last chapter because it is a big idea. I take you through the famous story of young Nils Holgersson in order to introduce it.

In *The Wonderful Adventures of Nils*, by the Nobel Prize–winning Swedish author Selma Lagerlöf (1858–1940), young Nils Holgersson learns what gives his life meaning through an amazing adventure in nature. A bad-tempered and uninterested boy to start with, Nils suddenly finds himself transformed into an elf and whisked off on the back of the barnyard goose that follows along with a flock of wild geese as they migrate across the country. Out in the wild as an elf, the size of nature is magnified many times over. There are numerous dangers and many moments of great beauty. Nils is humbled at the same time as he develops closeness to those creatures in nature, who become his friends and with whom he forges a bond of survival. On returning, Nils sees his home and those who inhabit it in a new perspective. In fact, the way that he sees the whole world has become quite different. It is his world, his home, and his family—and to each he understands that he has a special responsibility. The farm cow, Mayrose, usually wary of the ill-tempered young man, notices a difference in him when he returns.

> "He was just as little now as when he went away, and wore the same clothes; yet he was completely changed. The Nils Holgersson that went away in the spring had a heavy, slow gait, a drawling speech, and sleepy eyes. The one that had come back was lithe and alert, ready of speech, and had eyes that sparkled and danced. He had a confident bearing that commanded respect, little as he was. Although he himself did not look happy, he inspired happiness in others."[1]

In the spirit of Nils, this chapter is about the way this Nordic approach to well-being can bring meaning into your life. It is about the way this personal approach is as much a new beginning for you as it is for your nearest, your community, and planet Earth. It is about why meaning, whether you are religious or not, is essential to you. And it is about the way *this* global nomad learned about the linkage between meaning beyond oneself and well-being on a small island in Scandinavia.

My Own Search for Meaning

During the seven years that I worked with the really serious threats to our planet and race—poverty, environmental degradation, war—I didn't take them very seriously. That does not mean that I didn't care about them. Rather it means that I found a way of keeping a sanity-preserving distance between myself and these monstrous problems, while at the same time working with issues that I could say were meaningful. But in the end, what could I, little spot on this planet, really do to change anything? It was an unconscious strategy of self-preservation that worked for a while but also kept one critical thing to my well-being at bay: my sense of meaning.

I remember sitting on the ground in a circle of impoverished local chieftains in a place that few people visit but which several foreign mining companies had irresponsibly visited and destroyed. I had lived for a week among people whose lives, and whose children's lives, had been maimed by industrial contamination. The chieftains were interested in what I had to say about accessing finance for cleaning up their environment from various foreign aid institutions. If I had allowed myself to experience their grief, I would have delivered what I had to say in tears. I don't know whether that would have been particularly useful to the chieftains. Instead, I formed a little psychological cocoon around myself within the circle and delivered the information in a businesslike manner. What other options did I have?

Retreating to the island was, in some ways, an expression of my desire to escape from the big, bad world that I had seen during those seven years. Here life would be perfect, beautiful, peaceful. It would be an island of light, inaccessible to the dark forces of this world. I would find meaning in the perfection, I thought. But the first year of life on the island brought with it many so-called imperfections. Nature humbled us just before Christmas with a flood. Although our sturdy, hundred-year-old miner's cottages sheltered us well, many things broke down. When the flood ended with the freezing of the water, our water pipes froze and we had a tremendous time unfreezing them in surrounding temperatures of minus 25°C (−13°F). We were at the mercy of nature and entirely in one another's hands.

Then, one day during the first summer, I noticed that the grass had disappeared from the top of an area where the effluent water from my laundry room ran out. There were instead big circles of bare ground. I also noticed that in the gigantic underground container that my kitchen drainage ran into, nothing was breaking down. I began to look at the contents of the stuff that I was throwing down the drain—mostly detergents. They might as well have been written in ancient hieroglyphics, as they were totally incomprehensible, at least to this nonchemist. So I started an investigation and ended up tossing almost all of my cleaning agents and replacing them with environment- and human-friendly ones—most of them common things that one keeps in the kitchen cupboard (e.g., *såpa,* or pine oil–based detergent; vinegar; baking soda; lemon juice).

Nature on the island had taught me two vital Nilsian things during that very first year: who mattered and what mattered. It had humbled me and taught me to love back the people who loved me. It had at the same time shown me the power that I had over my own environment. The dark forces that I had tried to escape were not out there somewhere, but right there inside of me, alongside the light. It was up to me as to which forces I would unleash. And there was the core of my meaning: What choices would I make?

Beyond this, I began to feel that by doing things right in my own home and environment that I could do a tremendous amount for those people less fortunate than me in faraway places. Love begets love. Equal treatment begets equal treatment. Clean water, soil, and air in one place beget clean water, soil, and air in another. Things are deeply intertwined on this intricate planet. What was most amazing to me was that I could do this by making positive life choices that were also good for my own personal life. Most of all, I felt that each of us who lived a relatively privileged life could make the greatest difference to all of those much less privileged if we stopped preaching and got busy in our own literal and figurative backyards. I thought of the watchwords of development aid: encourage people to take ownership of their lives, participate, and act locally. Shouldn't I be doing the same thing?

Developing Consciousness, Meaning, and Well-being

All of us need to find ways of dealing with the same dilemma as the one that I have and continue to do. That is, if we want to be whole and well. Seeing the world as mean, dangerous, and unsafe can have extremely negative effects on our minds, emotions, and bodies. Some health experts have even suggested news fasts, in which people turn off their radios and televisions and avoid surfing to news sites, in order to reduce these feelings. I am not so sure that I believe in this escape from reality, although this depends on just how much media you take in each day. But I am quite sure that once you switch on the box again, you will be back at square one.

To me, a large part of the answer is to adopt an approach to personal well-being that raises your consciousness about your world and what it is possible to do in the microcosm of your own life in order to contribute to its betterment. This results in your getting, or at least augmenting, one vital thing that is indispensable to how you see your life and thus your well-being: your sense of meaning.

Life meaning is an idea that people everywhere have always struggled with. Today, the struggle seems to have become more intense, with the modern theory of evolution telling us that everything happens by accident, and modern science posing great challenges to religious scripture and belief. PCs and the technological age challenge tangible human contact and family life. Yet people gain meaning from the same things that they always have: being engaged with their families, friends, homes, and communities.

There are some people who choose to take the struggle against the wrongs and injustices of this world further by acting in a public way, sometimes on the international stage. We should applaud and support people who fight genuinely for human rights and saving our planet's resources. We need each and every one of them. And we can help them by getting it right in our own lives.

Getting It Right in Your Own Backyard: A Scandinavian Story

One Scandinavian has done more than most to help people like us to get it right in our own backyard, at least environmentally. I tell you his story to illustrate how connection to nature can motivate a life view and what it can lead to. The organization he created provides information that might also be useful to you in implementing the environmental side of your new lifestyle, although, not being a scientist myself, I cannot guarantee the validity of all the research.

Karl-Henrik Robért began with a love of the outdoors "preferably in

THE NATURAL STEP...

was established in the United States in 1996, having been established in Sweden during the 1980s. Its main activity is to help industries reduce their impact on the environment. Companies such as McDonald's and Monsanto have been partners in the Natural Step process. Its Web site, www.naturalstep.com, provides valuable information for anyone from its Publications Library, including simple steps that individuals can take in their daily lives to increase the sustainability of our planet.

that marginal area between town and open country where human creations coexist with nature."[2] Today he is better known as the founder of The Natural Step (TNS), which is established in nine countries as a force helping mainly businesses to identify and adopt ecologically sustainable practices.

During the 1980s, this doctor specializing in cancer research looked through his microscope at different kinds of living cells and concluded that:

> from a biological standpoint, we are not the masters of nature or even its caretakers. The basic structures and functions of our bodies are nearly identical to those of eagles and seals, all the way down to the molecular level. We are a part of nature.[3]

This was not only a scientific observation, but also a very Scandinavian one. Scientists can look at the same thing and still see different things through the microscope. This man saw the oneness of nature and man's equal place in it. From this and other observations came a booklet and audiocassette that in 1989 went to every Swedish household and explained the way the world's ecosystem works, based on the knowledge of fifty top Swedish scientists. Within a short period of time big business became interested. The Scandic Hotels, for example, created recyclable hotel rooms through which one thousand rooms reduced their plastic waste by 70 percent, and their metal waste by 50 percent. They saved 40 tons of soap in one year by changing to liquid soap dispensers, reduced fuel and water consumption by using more efficient washing machines, and increased their market share due to a positive public response to these initiatives. What could happen if you started to get outside more often? You never know.

The Little Big Steps

While inspirational, it is not necessary for you to quit your job and get the head of state (in this case, the Swedish king) onboard for your arguments, in order to do something for your world and thus to gain some life meaning. There are the small steps that, if each of us could take, would amount to a very big one. These steps are about how we live our lives: how we recreate, how we relax, what we eat, how we design and maintain our homes. Pursuing some of the ideas that I have outlined in this book can result (in some cases, automatically) in your making choices that are good, not only for yourself but for your environment and for others. Below, I discuss some of them just to give you a taste of the sort of meaning that this approach to well-being can provide you.

Outdoor Life and the Greenery

Once the creators of the Swedish Skogsmulleskolan (Forest Troll School— see Chapter 2) inspired children to participate in the outdoors by creating mythical figures of the forest, the sea, and the mountains, they finally found it necessary to create Nova and the planet Tella. Nova was born on this amazingly beautiful and clean planet, which she invites the children to visit in order to show them how to look after their own planet. Once you begin to get involved in the outdoors, you will likely go down the same path as the creators of Tella.

I have myself become a Tella fan, recreating outdoors on this island. During the warmer season we sometimes have irresponsible visitors who leave their garbage behind. I stuff empty plastic bottles and bags left behind into my pockets to dispose of them after my walk. One of our neighbors does the rounds with a garbage pick and a bag. I repeat in my head this lovely saying, although I do sometimes take with me a few mushrooms or berries in addition to the memories:

Take nothing but memories,
Leave nothing but footprints,
Kill nothing but time,
Above all, have fun.

During my morning swims, I wonder whether there is anything I could stop using in our household that might possibly contaminate this pristine bay. I sort out all the many bottles of cleaning agent that have built up in my closet over time. I get onto the Internet and check out some savvy Web sites that can help me to learn what to use and what not to use (see Web sites in Resources section). I dispose of the stuff that will eventually ruin my morning swim. I try to use less of everything that I have left to reduce concentrations of my household waste building up in the environment.

I water my plants in the evenings in the light of the dim midnight sun, rather than during the warm, sunny days when the water evaporates almost as soon as it leaves the hose. I stand and water most of my garden with a hose rather than with a sprinkler, which I could forget about and leave running for longer than necessary. I get the chance to meditate on the beauty of the moment. I think of what I would like to plant in the bare patches that will easily grow in this sandy, stony place without too much care. I think of some of the beautiful wildflowers that I have seen in an area nearby, requiring nothing but some warm sand to grow in. My spot can happily provide that. No special treatment, water, fertilizer, or extra soil required.

When the trees have lost all their leaves and I am out raking just before the snow covers the outdoors, our big metal recycling pile reveals itself. Since we have no garbage collectors, we take our scrap metal to the recycling station every now and then. This means dragging it all into a boat and then into the trunk of a car. Perhaps it is a plus that this activity is such a hassle. One thinks twice about buying things and about whether that old stereo couldn't just be given one more chance.

Ask yourself how you want your outdoors to be when you are out recreating in it. Do you want clean air? Good, clean soil? Green, leafy trees? Water safe to swim in? Think about what you can do in your own personal life to achieve these goals. It will make a difference, particularly to how you feel about yourself.

Of course, there are many preferable environmental choices that we could make in experiencing this particular dimension of well-being. For instance, choose to visit a spa that takes ecology into account. What does this mean? It means raising such questions as: How do they generate their electricity? What do they do with the many waste products generated by the spa, particularly waste water? Are the products used environmentally friendly? A spa that I visited in southern Gotland (see Resources) had gone to great lengths: Most of its electricity was generated through a seventeenth-century windmill; it used a specialized ecologically conscious system for maintaining the pool water and had installed an ecologically friendly drainage system purchased in Finland. I toured this environment-friendly infrastructure set high on a hill overlooking a stunning small fishing village and the long, stony Baltic coastline. I imagined that any guest at this place would feel particularly happy about being there.

What I have been describing is a choice that you make in order to have the experience of relaxation that also gives you an added feeling of personal security. But where can the results lead? I have found that they lead into thinking about how one interacts with other human beings, and the importance that one attaches to quality in human interaction. Sauna, water therapy, massage, and herbalism are often about the promotion of human intimacy, of being open to the touch of another person, and of sensuousness. Despite the bare-all style of much of today's media, an increasing number of people feel alone and left out in the cold. In some parts of the world, they literally are, in gigantic numbers.

What you learn about the importance of intimacy from the approach to relaxation and healing that I lay out in this book could take you in different directions. It helped one man massage young children and criminals by using intimacy as a tool to prevent and to deal with some of today's most pressing social problems (see Chapter 4). My young daughter climbs up on the couch behind me and massages my shoulders spontaneously, partly as a result of this man's initiatives in the day-care system, where children learn about massage. For most of us, learning about the value of intimacy through relaxation techniques will result in our greeting a smile from the stranger who crosses our path with a smile, and better listening to the person speaking. A little smile and an open ear can go a very long way.

Design

The ideas for essential design that I lay out in Chapter 5 take you down the path of creating homes and workplaces that increase your security and the security of planet Earth. These days, people tend to see threats everywhere, but least of all in the design and construction of their own homes, which perhaps pose the greatest long-term threats to human security.

When I visit the anthroposophic center not far from me here in Sweden, I feel secure. This is not because I belong to their movement (which I do not), but because I see around me designs that work with their environment and not against them. I find a deep sense of peace in knowing that the man-made structures around me are not at war with nature. On first visiting, my attention was mostly arrested by a beautiful, gentle series of waterfalls: their liquid drainage and cleaning system. The water runs peacefully from one ceramic bowl to another and in this way gets cleaned. By the time it reaches its end destination it is ready to be let out into the sea and is swimming-quality water.

In our own home on the island, we have found that designing ecologically, in so far as possible in this nineteenth-century house, is also good for our bank account. For instance, in an effort to increase the long view from the front of our house, we rebuilt our living room with eight large windows. It crossed our minds that the long view could cost us a whopping heating bill and a bad conscience, the many windows exposing us to the autumn and winter storms. Two design features saved us. One was that the living room is facing south, so that the heat of the sun's warmth is maximized inside the house. Even more importantly, each window is triple-glazed in order to avoid a draft and provide insulation. If you live in a warm location, the same principles will be true, but in reverse. Build facing north, and insulate well.

Maximizing the heat while keeping the heating bills down is certainly a Scandinavian specialty. Prior to arriving in Scandinavia, I had lived in different locations in the UK, where, despite my love of England and its magnificent people, I must admit to always feeling cold in the cooler seasons, and this without trying to conserve on the heating bills. Aside from investment in good technology, the Scandinavian penchant for achieving the long view humanely contributes to keeping the temperature up and the bills down.

Some technological solutions that make efficient use out of resources are also old in Scandinavia. When we made the decision to undertake that one-year "experiment" and live on the island, we felt reassured that we had two heavy, cast-iron stoves and two tall tiled ovens to warm us if ever the electricity was cut in the cooler months. Visiting some castles in Sweden, I noticed that these tiled stoves were often found next to large French-style fireplaces, which were the fashion of the day. The large, open fireplaces served absolutely no practical purpose, as far as heating the rooms of these large palaces was concerned. All of the heat just went right up the chimney. It was the closed, tiled energy-efficient stoves with channels for conducting the heat back down into the room that gave people warmth. There are different versions of these stoves in the other Scandinavian countries. A friend of ours who is a scientist once told us that no heating technology has yet been invented that is as effective and resource efficient as the *kakelugn* (tiled oven), which was invented in 1767. So, when you are thinking of installing your own home fireplace, make sure you check into models that are energy-efficient—more warmth in a cold winter using less wood equals a cozier you and a happier planet.

Inspiration from your own outdoors will provide you with the best choice of natural materials for furnishing your home. Choosing as local as possible saves on the energy expended in transport. You will also be able to get a better idea of whether the natural material you are after is harvested in a sustainable way. If the materials are local—for instance, locally grown wood—you will want to make sure that it is a sustainable resource, so that your outdoor experience is not ruined. Homes in Scandinavia commonly include a lot of sustainably homegrown wood. Mahogany from far-flung places that will effectively be destroyed by the unsustainable harvesting of the earth's last mahogany forests will drop right off your list.

Playing with the natural light in a skillful way can shift until a little later the time that you have to start switching on the lights. Maintaining the principle that you should be able to see the clear lines of objects and furnishings inside your home may also lead you down the path of being much more restrictive about what you buy and thus eventually have to dispose of. Clearly, there is a tremendous amount that you can do to make your home a place of meaning beyond yourself.

Food

Getting involved with food harvesting and preparation, even if only occasionally, will turn your attention to a number of important questions. You will ask yourself what the fish on your plate ate and swam in, and what was in the soil that the potatoes were pulled out of. You will wonder whether the berries and other fruits have been sprayed with harmful chemicals.

These are extremely relevant questions, as demonstrated by a blood test taken by a Swedish politician in 2003 to test for seventy-seven different types of potentially harmful chemicals, in order to demonstrate the need for a new regulatory framework for chemicals. Those chemicals do not break down quickly in the environment and are accumulating in animals and humans. They are known for interfering with our hormone and reproductive systems, as well as affecting our unborn children. The blood test detected twenty-eight of these chemicals in the Swede's blood, and Sweden already has very strict rules about what can be "dumped" on the environment.

Where will your well-justified suspicions lead you? In my case, to growing some of my own stuff organically and to voting with my wallet. But it is not only suspicions that will be aroused. You will also experience a greater desire for the taste of the ingredients themselves and, with this, freshness. Fulfilling this desire is also good for the environment, since it means that you will be encouraged to buy locally and seasonally, and thus save on the energy costs of transporting the goods. My local farmer has initiated a local effort to gather used egg cartons for selling newly laid eggs in. All of us in the community contribute and thus save on the packaging.

Children

The well-being of children is something that is always on my mind. Of course, you might say that this is natural to me, since I am a mother. However, I do think that whether you have children or not, there is something about the well-being of children in your community that will be compelling to you. All of us have been children at one time and so know how important the quality of childhood is to shaping the rest of one's life. We know that the children are our future.

There is something very basic about getting in touch with nature that brings out the child in each of us. We are equal in the face of it (no one is more grown up), and we feel a special freedom and creativity that can often be lacking in routine adult lives. The wonderful story of *De Badande Vännerna,* or *The Society of Bathing Friends,* brings out how a nature-based approach to well-being can become an expression of concern for children.

One summer afternoon in 1814 ten young men from town—some of them public servants and some of them businessmen—gathered to bathe in the sea just in front of the medieval wall of Visby in Gotland, as they were in the habit of doing. On this particular meeting, they decided to form a society that eventually adopted some higher aims. The society created a host of social services and places that made a big difference to the children of Visby, particularly the poorer children: a school; the town's first savings bank, which provided some of the children with their first savings books and a four-kronor (50-cent) deposit; a foster home and the botanical gardens behind the place where they swam. The gardens, which I had the pleasure of walking through behind the high medieval walls, provided a workshop for young gardening trainees. Everything that the Bathing Friends did was somehow connected to their feeling that all children too should have the chance to experience the freedom and possibility that they did when they swam in the sea.

You could think of some equally important but perhaps slightly less ambitious ways to include your children or children you are close to in a life of well-being. Take your children on walks with you sometimes; get them to help you plant the tulip bulbs for the spring; rub their backs; let them build a little *koja,* or hideout; include them in the gathering and preparation of food. In each of the lifestyle areas that I have taken you through, there are many ways for you to include the children, if you just put your creativity to work.

Finding *Your* Island

Whether this new life leads you to make small changes in your own life or to take up certain causes that you find worthwhile, I do not know. What I can tell you with confidence is that whatever approach you take, it will bring an immeasurable sense of security and gratification to your life as well as to the lives of others. The most important thing is not to let this life pass you by and to venture to live it.

Today, when I look out through the windows of my home on the island during the dark winter nights, the scene is illuminated by more than just the constellations. Our friends Willy and Vendela, with their son, Victor, have built a house and moved in on the island directly facing us. They live there all year, not despite the challenges but because of a vision. During their first summer here, we helped them to transport eight goats over to their island by boat. None of them has a background in tending goats or working the land. No. They have something much more powerful: the vision of a life of nature, creativity, inner sanctum, intimacy, and meaning. A decade ago it would have been impossible for me to understand them. But today it is the dream of a life that I have felt compelled to try to bring to you wherever you are. You see, you don't have to seek out a Swedish island in order to live this good life. It resides in the richness of your natural world and inside of yourself. All that you have to do, dear reader, is dare to discover it.

Resources

by Julie Catterson Lindahl
and Rachel Stenback

WELCOME to an experience of well-being. This section includes references in this book, as well as listings of companies, organizations, and books that can take you further on this nature-based approach to good living. The listings focus on Nordic and Nordic-related companies, organizations, and destinations. At the same time an effort has been made, wherever possible, to highlight resources that are available in the United States which can help you to move your life in a nature-oriented direction. Each resource includes a brief description and contact details, including Web address, wherever possible. Official sources of information on Scandinavia have been provided as cultural resources on the Nordic countries. Neither these organizations nor any of the others listed are responsible for any of the views expressed in this book.

You are also welcome to visit www.wellnessofscandinavia.com for more information. Here you can communicate directly with Julie on the island.

U.S. Resources

Here is a list of resources that can be useful if you would like to pursue the ideas about well-being expressed in this book. Please remember that this is a relatively short and eclectic selection, and makes no attempt to be comprehensive. If you begin to look around in your area, you are sure to find many more resources that are more relevant to you.

Also note that many resources listed in the next section, Scandinavian Resources, are often accessible in the United States as well, for example, through online ordering of products, so make sure to check those resources, even if you are not planning on traveling to Scandinavia.

TWO: OUTDOOR LIFE AND OVERCOMING
THE FITNESS DILEMMA

Informational Sites and Journals

Country Skier, L.L.C.
P.O. Box 550
Cable, WI 54821
Tel: 715-798-5500
E-mail: info@crosscountryskier.com
Web: www.crosscountryskier.com

Cross-Country Skier, the journal of Nordic skiing, provides a wealth of information on cross-country skiing, including technique and training, health and fitness, the environment, destinations, and general interest features. Articles and information are posted on the Web page, where you can also subscribe to the magazine.

MountainZone.com
Web: www.mountainzone.com

MountainZone.com is an excellent resource if you are looking for information on things you can do in the mountains. Among other things, the Web site covers skiing, biking, hiking, climbing, and paddling and canoeing. The site features loads of interesting reading, great pictures, and links.

Nature of the Northwest
800 N.E. Oregon Street, Suite 177
Portland, OR 97232
Tel: 503-872-2750
TDD: 503-872-2752
Email: info@naturenw.org
Web: www.naturenw.org

Nature of the Northwest is a very good source of information on outdoor activities in the northwestern part of the United States. Among other things, it provides information and regulations on hiking, fishing, camping, mushroom gathering, and berry picking, and includes information on forests and wilderness areas. Learn more on its Web page.

National and International Organizations

The International Nordic Walking Association
Web: http://inwa.nordicwalking.com

If you are interested in learning more about Nordic Walking, the International Nordic Walking Association, and the high-quality sporting company Exel, are good places to find out more. (See Scandinavian Resources.) The goal of INWA is to promote people's overall well-being and physical condition in this activity, which is rapidly growing in popularity, and which most anyone can easily learn to do.

National Park Service Headquarters
Director
National Park Service
1849 C Street, N.W.
Washington, DC 20240
Tel: 202-208-6843
Web: www.nps.gov

National parks can be an excellent place to experience different outdoor activities in a beautiful, natural setting. Almost all national parks offer children's activities, including a Junior Ranger program. The address for the national headquarters is listed here; however, there are several regional offices as well. Visit the Web page for lots of valuable information on all of the parks, and for detailed information as to which activities each park offers.

National Wildlife Federation
11100 Wildlife Center Drive
Reston, VA 20190-5362
Tel: 703-438-6000
Web: www.nwf.org

Founded in 1936, the National Wildlife Federation is the largest private, nonprofit conservation education and advocacy organization in the country. Through a number of educational programs, conservation efforts, and educational wildlife and outdoor experiences (many of which focus on the family), the NWF works toward its goal of raising awareness and involving people of all ages in its drive to conserve and protect the environment. A visit to the Web page is enjoyable, interesting, and educational, and also features a "Kidzone" for children and teens.

QAJAQ USA
P.O. Box 5851
Traverse City, MI 49696
E-mail: info@qajaqusa.org
Web: www.qajaqusa.org

A member of the Greenland Kayaking Association, *Qaannat Kattuffiat,* the Qajaq USA strives to maintain valuable kayaking traditions, while working to promote and develop Greenland kayaking in the U.S. If you are interested in Greenland kayaking or finding interesting events or sources of information, visit their Web page to learn more about Greenland kayaking, to subscribe to the newsletter, or to become a member.

Sierra Club

National Headquarters
85 Second Street, 2nd Floor
San Francisco, CA 94105
Tel: 415-977-5500
Fax: 415-977-5799
E-mail: information@sierraclub.org
Web: www.sierraclub.org

With more than 700,000 members, the Sierra Club is America's oldest, largest, and most influential grassroots environmental organization. Keeping nature in focus, the Sierra Club works to protect communities and the planet. Among other things, along with working to protect the environment, it also offers members a wide variety of exciting outdoor activities, in beautiful natural areas. The Web page contains a wealth of information on environmental issues. Visit the site to learn more, and/or to join this dedicated organization.

Tours

Borton Overseas

5412 Lyndale Avenue South
Minneapolis, MN 55419
Tel: 612-822-4640
Toll-free: 800-843-0602
Fax: 612-822-4755
Web: www.bortonoverseas.com

If you are interested in taking a unique vacation to Scandinavia, Borton Overseas organizes several different tours. Hiking in the mountains, skiing, fishing in northern Norway, and biking in Denmark are some of the tempting outdoor-oriented excursions. Borton Overseas will even tailor a program to meet your own specifications and desires.

Nordic Saga Tours

303 5th Avenue S., Suite 109
Edmonds, WA 98020
Tel: 425-673-4800
Toll-free: 800-848-6449
Fax: 425-673-2600
E-mail: NSTours@nordicsaga.com
Web: www.nordicsaga.com

Nordic Saga Tours offers several interesting tours to Scandinavia, many of which focus on outdoor life experiences; can arrange travel and accommodations for you to participate in different ski events, such as Finland Border to Border, Vasaloppet in Sweden, and the Birke-beinerrennet Ski Race in Norway; and offers activity and adventure tours in Lappland, Sweden, and Finland. Visit the Web page to learn more.

Northern Lights Expeditions
P.O. Box 4289
Bellingham, WA 98227
Tel: 360-734-6334
Toll-free: 800-754-7402
Fax: 360-734-6150
E-mail: info@seakayaking.com
Web: www.seakayaking.com

Northern Lights Expeditions is a Washington-state-based company that offers guided sea-kayaking adventures. The expeditions focus on experiences in nature and viewing wildlife. Learn more, and see many kayak-inspiring photos, on the Web page, or contact them for more information.

Events

American Birkebeiner Ski Foundation
P.O. Box 911
Hayward, WI 54843
Tel: 715-634-5025
Toll-free: 800-872-2753
Fax: 715-634-5663
E-mail: birkie@birkie.com
Web: www.birkie.com

Taking place each February in Wisconsin, the American Birkebeiner is North America's largest ski marathon. Covering 35 miles from Cable to Hayward, the Birkie comes from the Norwegian Birkebeiner, which is held each year in Norway to commemorate the feat of Birkebeiner skiers in Norway, in 1206. Thousands participate each year. Visit the Web page to learn more—or to be inspired to participate yourself.

Mora Vasaloppet
P.O. Box 22
Mora, MN 55051
Toll-free: 800-368-6672
Fax: 320-679-4840
E-mail: information@vasaloppet.org
Web: www.vasaloppet.org

A Minnesota version of the Swedish Vasaloppet takes place each year in February in Mora, Minnesota. There are many different races, including various long-distance races, and there is also a *Miniloppet*, which is a special event for children under the age of thirteen. Learn more, and find out how you can participate, on the Web page.

Active Clothing for Active Kids

Hanna Andersson
Web: www.hannaandersson.com

Hanna Andersson is a clothing company specializing in children's attire. The clothing is of high quality, is soft, and allows for freedom of movement for active children. It has expanded to include an adult line. You can request a free catalog on the Web page.

THREE: THE IMPORTANCE OF BEING GREEN

National and State Organizations/Projects

U.S. Composting Council
4250 Veterans Memorial Highway, Suite 275
Holbrook, NY 11741
Tel: 631-737-4931
Fax: 631-737-4939
E-mail: admin@compostingcouncil.org
Web: www.compostingcouncil.org

The U.S. Composting Council provides tips on building your own compost. The Web page also contains links to other sources of information on the subject.

Plant Conservation Alliance
Bureau of Land Management
1849 C Street, N.W., LSB-204
Washington, DC 20240
Tel: 202-452-0392
E-mail: plant@plantconservatory.org
Web: http://www.nps.gov/plants

The Plant Conservation Alliance works to solve problems of native plant extinction, as it encourages people to "think globally, act locally." The Web page, loaded with interesting information, is an inspirational place to learn how you can become involved in preserving native plants in your area. A wealth of links will also certainly inspire you to learn more about what you can do, whatever your geographical location.

**Asheville Parks and Recreation Department and the Bountiful City Project,
Implementing Edible Forest Ecosystems in City Parks**
Dr. George Washington Carver Edible Park
Stephens-Lee Recreation Center

30 George Washington Carver Street
Asheville, NC 28801

The Dr. George Washington Carver Edible Park is the first edible public park system in America. Designed around permaculture forest gardening principles, which mimic natural forest ecosystems, all vegetation within the park is edible and perennial. Asheville Parks and Recreation, the organization behind the creation of the edible gardens, and the Bountiful Cities Project, formerly called the City Seeds Project, work together to maintain the edible park. Community involvement is also critical to caring for the gardens, where the goal is to create model projects that will educate the public on environmental issues and solutions.

Herbal Recipes

ABKIT, INC./NatureWorks
207 E. 94th Street
New York, NY 10128
Toll-free: 800-226-6227, ext. 119 or 121
Fax: 212-860-8323
E-mail: info@abkit.com
Web: www.natureworks.com

NatureWorks sells the famous Swedish Bitters, an excellent recipe for aiding digestion. On the Web page you can read more about Swedish Bitters and other products, and order online.

FOUR: SENSITIZATION AND THE RIGHT TO RELAX

Sauna

The Sauna Stop
Web: www.saunastop.com

If you are interested in adding a sauna to your home, you might want to consider some of the products from this company, which imports and sells saunas and sauna equipment from Finland. It has a wide range of products, from sauna kits to sauna soaps and scents of various kinds.

YMCA
Web: www.ymca.net

Try your local YMCA to see if it has saunas available for use. Unfortunately, we cannot guarantee the quality of each sauna, but the YMCA could be a good place to start sauna bathing if you do not have the luxury of bathing in your own sauna.

Massage

Swedish Institute
College of Health Sciences

School of Acupuncture and Oriental Studies
School of Massage Therapy
226 W. 26th Street
New York, NY 10001
Tel: 212-924-5900
Fax: 212-924-7600
E-mail: admissions@swedishinstitute.org
Web: www.swedishinstitute.org

Since 1916, the Swedish Institute has trained students to become massage therapists, and since 1996, to become classically trained acupuncturists. If you are interested in attending the school, you can request information on the Web page. In any event, the Web page is an excellent source of information on the subject of massage. There you can read the newsletter, *Si*news, and find many interesting links.

Personal Care Products for Relaxation

Midani Erbe
Web: www.midanierbe.it

Based out of Italy, Midani Erbe produces Scandinavian Salt Cream, based on an old recipe originally from Finland. The company's products are available in stores in the United States, as well as from retailers who sell the products online.

Smallflower
E-mail: info@smallflower.com
Web: www.smallflower.com

Retail store:
Merz Apothecary
4716 N. Lincoln Avenue
Chicago, IL 60625

Founded in 1875, Merz Apothecary carries an extensive line of products from around the world, all related to health and well-being. Since 1998 it has expanded to offer online shopping. The company sells everything from essential oils to specific items mentioned in this book, such as natural products containing birch for the hair. To learn more about Merz Apothecary's interesting history and shop for products, visit the Web site.

FIVE: ESSENTIAL DESIGN AND THE CREATION OF HOME

Recommended Reading

The Not So Big House
By Sarah Susanka
Published by Taunton Press
Web: www.notsobighouse.com

The Not So Big House brings to light a new way of thinking about what makes a place feel like home. U.S.-based architect Sarah Susanka's inspiration for this book stems from a growing awareness that new houses were growing in size but lacked comfort. Susanka advocates tailoring our houses to fit the way we really live, in proportion and scale of our human form. The book, which has been hailed widely as a success, is available in bookstores and through the above-listed Web page.

Interior Design

25 FinnStyle
115 Washington Avenue N.
Minneapolis, MN 55401-1619
Tel: 612-341-4075
Toll-free: 866-FINNISH
E-mail: info@finnstyle.com
Web: www.finnstyle.com

If you are interested in purchasing Finnish design products, this store is a good place to visit, either in person or online. It carries a broad range of products, from furniture (including from Alvar Aalto and Artek) to lighting, glassware, cookware, and gifts. It also showcases the works of young Finnish designers. Online shopping is available.

White on White
888 Lexington Avenue
New York, NY 10021
Tel: 212-288-0909
Fax: 212-288-9218
E-mail: whiteonw@aol.com
Web: www.whiteonwhiteny.com

A kind of Nordic oasis in Manhattan, this shop has a Swedish feel. Its product line comprises a whole lifestyle concept, where quiet beauty, high quality, and natural simplicity are leading ideas. White on White is a beautiful store, and definitely worth a visit. See the Web page for a glimpse into the product line.

SIX: PURE ENERGY AND A
NORDIC TASTE OF WELL-BEING

Mushrooms

MykoWeb
Web: http://www.mykoweb.com

MykoWeb is a Web site devoted to mushrooms—both the science of mycology (study of fungi) and to mushroom picking as a hobby. If you are interested in learning more about the pastime, or about mushrooms in general, this is a good place to start. Visit the site to find lots of related information, including everything from recipes to photos, and more than two hundred links to other mushroom-related sites.

Wild Meat

Department of Natural Resources (DNR)
Web: http://www.dnr.state.wi.us

For issues and questions on food safety, for example in the case of wild meats, try your local DNR. This is the Web page for the Wisconsin division, which provided excellent information on hunting and wild meat in the United States.

Getting Kids to Eat Well

Bon Appétit! Musical Food Fun
Web: http://bonappetit.cathymarcy.com

Cathy Fink and Marcy Marxer have created a fun, educational, Grammy-winning CD for children, entitled *Bon Appétit! Musical Food Fun*. The CD encourages good, nutritional eating for children, through lively music and text, and is available for purchase on the Web page, where you can also learn more about the idea, and find children's activities and informative links on the subject of children and nutrition.

Nordic Food Stores

Ingebretsens Scandinavian Gifts & Food
1601 E. Lake Street
Minneapolis, MN 55407
Tel: 612-729-9333
Toll-free: 800-279-9333
Fax: 612-729-1243
E-mail: info@ingebretsens.com
Web: www.ingebretsens.com

Ingebretsens is a Scandinavian import store in the Twin Cities that has books, food products, and Scandinavian gift items. Several food products that are mentioned in this book can be found there. For those who cannot visit the store in person, online shopping is available.

Nordic Delicacies, Inc.
6909 Third Avenue
Brooklyn, NY 11209
Tel: 718-748-1874
Toll-free: 800-34-NORDIC or 800-346-6734
Fax: 718-833-7519
E-mail: NORDICDELI@aol.com
Web: www.nordicdeli.com

Nordic Delicacies, Inc., is a Scandinavian food and gift shop, which has several products of interest and offers online shopping. Here you can purchase *såpa*, the green soap described in this book, and also several food products, such as Wasa breads and herring.

Restaurants

There are several excellent Scandinavian restaurants in the United States. Although we cannot guarantee that all of the fare served by the restaurants below is good for your waistline, they provide a taste of Scandinavian fare that is often healthy and delicious.

Restaurant Alta
363 Greenwich Avenue
Greenwich, CT 06830
Tel: 203-622-5138

Christer Larsson believes in serving fish. This is part of his heritage from his home country, Sweden, where fish, particularly salmon, has formed a staple part of diet for centuries. Christer set up Restaurant Alta in Greenwich after years of running top restaurants in New York City. Alta's fare is first-rate, according to some of our fussier sources.

Restaurant Aquavit of New York
13 W. 54th Street
New York, NY 10019
Tel: 212-307-7311
E-mail: info@aquavit.org
Web: www.aquavit.org

Aquavit, considered to be one of New York's top restaurants, features new Scandinavian cuisine by award-winning chef Marcus Samuelsson. Alongside the restaurant, there is an informal café that serves traditional Swedish fare. If you'd like to get an idea of what you can experience at Aquavit, you may now order *Aquavit: And the New Scandinavian Cuisine,* a beautiful coffee table book about Samuelsson's fare, at www.amazon.com. Visit Aquavit's Web page to view a tempting sample menu.

Ulrika's
115 E. 60th Street
New York, NY 10022
Tel: 212-355-7069
Fax: 212-355-7046
E-mail: ulrikas@att.net
Web: www.ulrikas.com

Chef Ulrika Bengtsson presents traditional Swedish cuisine at her restaurant and through catering. A sample menu showing the classic Swedish dishes can be viewed online. The Web page also features recipes for you to try at home.

Recommended Reading

The Newman's Own Organics Guide to a Good Life
By Nell Newman, with Joseph D'Agnese
Published by Villard Books, a division of Random House, Inc.
Web: www.newmansownorganics.com

This inspirational book by Nell Newman contains practical tips on how to live "the good life," a life where environmentally sound choices not only help the world around you, but also directly benefit you personally. Among other things, she discusses food, transportation, energy and water use, and gardening, The approach is fresh and personable.

Environmentally Friendly Design

BuildingGreen, Inc.
122 Birge Street, Suite 30
Brattleboro, VT 05301
Tel: 802-257-7300
Fax: 802-257-7304
E-mail: info@buildinggreen.com
Web: www.buildinggreen.com

BuildingGreen is a company that works to provide information to help building-industry professionals and policy makers improve the environmental performance and reduce the negative impacts of buildings on the environment. Through a variety of resources, the company can help architects, designers, and owners create projects that reduce ecological impact, while still maximizing economic performance.

Environmental Design + Construction
2401 W. Big Beaver, Suite 700
Troy, MI 48084
Tel: 248-362-3700
Web: www.edcmag.com

The first magazine dedicated to the growing green building industry is available through subscriptions and with a wealth of information available on the Internet. The magazine covers many topics related to ecology and building green, such as resource and energy efficiency, alternative and renewable energy sources, indoor air quality, and life-cycle assessment. For more information, or to subscribe, visit the Web page.

Organizations for Environmental Improvement & Conservation

National Audubon Society
700 Broadway

New York, NY 10003
Tel: 212-979-3000
Fax: 212-979-3188
Web: www.audubon.org

For a century the Audubon Society has been striving to teach people to appreciate nature, while working to conserve wildlife and wildlife habitats. Through a national network of community-based nature centers and chapters, members can get involved in their local environments. The Society runs fun events for the education of children (and parents). Joining is inexpensive, although donations beyond this are encouraged.

Environmental Media Services
1320 18th Street, N.W., 5th Floor
Washington, DC 20036
Tel: 202-463-6670
E-mail: ems@ems.org
Web: http://www.ems.org/household_cleaners/alternatives.html

Environmental Media Services is a nonprofit organization that works to expand media coverage of critical environmental and public health issues. The Web site is a useful tool, especially the link listed above, which focuses solely on recommending eco-friendly alternatives to commercial cleaners and other household products. Their site also includes a long list of articles and links to more information on eco-friendly household cleaners.

The Natural Step
116 New Montgomery Street, Suite 800
San Francisco, CA 94105
Tel: 415-318-8170
Fax: 415-974-0474
Service Inquiries: services@naturalstep.org
Web: www.naturalstep.org

Founded in Sweden in 1989, the Natural Step is an international advisory and research organization that works with some of the largest resource users on the planet (companies and governments) to create solutions and tools designed to accelerate economic, social, and environmental sustainability. Contact services @naturalstep.org if your company is interested in these advisory service offerings.

Scandinavian Resources

The following is a listing of wellness resources in Scandinavia. Once again, this is not to be regarded as a comprehensive list, rather as a list of places that we have encountered and like for a lifestyle of well-being. Many of the companies also offer services in the United States, for example, products or general information online.

Tours and Getaways

Byaliv
Box 128
980 63 Kangos
Tel: 46-978-322-44
Fax: 46-73-033-033-4
E-mail: tornedalen@byaliv.com
Web: http://www.byaliv.com

Byaliv consists of a group of enthusiastic people in the far north of Sweden who have formed an organization around their local village life, and what it has to offer. Of the many activities it provides, several focus on health and wellness. These include summer and winter outdoor activities, along with sauna experiences combined with herbs in beautiful natural settings. During your time with Byaliv you will be treated to healthful, mostly local foods. At Byaliv you can learn how the local Sami culture lives with the eight seasons of the year. They are happy to tailor-make health and wellness experiences to suit your needs.

Lomarengas Finnish Country Holidays
Web: www.lomarengas.fi

This Finnish company arranges country farmhouse or country cottage vacations, where you can stay at a Finnish farm, for a unique and close-to-nature vacation. Many of the cottages and farms are located in beautiful natural areas, often close to ski trails and lakes. Lomarengas can also help to arrange other vacations, such as cyling and fishing in Finland. Convenient online booking is available on the Web page, which also includes detailed information and pictures on the farms and cottages.

Nature's Best
E-mail: info@ekoturism.org
Web: www.naturesbest.nu

Nature's Best is a quality label for Swedish Ecotourism, which has been created to guarantee high-quality tour products, in combination with contributions to nature conservation, environmentally friendlier ways of traveling, and caring for the cultural heritage of the destination. See a list of quality-approved tourism operators in Sweden that provide exciting outdoor experience, and learn more about ecotourism on the Web page.

Snöå Bruk
780 51 Dala-Järna
Sweden
Tel: 46-281-240-18
Fax: 46-281-240-45
Web: www.snoabruk.se

Located in Dalarna, Sweden, Snöå Bruk is a peaceful place to visit. Here you stay in a hostel where the accommodations are affordable, simple yet clean, and with access to a kitchen. However, much time will probably not be spent indoors, since the surroundings are beautiful and the cuisine, in the Manor House, is delicious. Many outdoor activities are possible here, including hiking, biking, swimming, canoeing, fishing, and golfing, and in the winter, cross-country skiing.

Biking

Bike Denmark
Olaf Poulsens Allé 1A
DK-3480 Fredensborg
Denmark
Tel: 45-48-48-58-00
Fax: 45-48-48-59-00
Web: www.bikedenmark.com

If you are interested in taking a bike tour of Denmark, this company can arrange it. It organizes tours, provides routes and maps, and will even transport your luggage for you, all to make for a worry-free and enjoyable bike trip across the Danish countryside.

The Danish Cyclists Federation
Dansk Cyklist Forbund
Rømersgade 7
DK-1362 Copenhagen
Denmark
Tel: 45-33-32-31-21
Fax: 45-33-32-76-83
Web: www.dcf.dk

The Danish Cyclists Federation supplies general information on biking vacations and biking in Denmark.

Hiking

The Norwegian Mountain Touring Association (DNT)
Mailing address:
Postboks 7 Sentrum
0101 Oslo
Norway
Visiting address: Storgata 3 Oslo, Norway
E-mail: info@turistforeningen.no
Web: www.turistforeningen.no

For the past 135 years, this organization has facilitated breathtaking experiences in Norway, by providing marked routes and hiking trails, and opportunities for hikers to stay cheaply in mountain cabins all over the country. Norway's largest outdoor leisure organization, it also offers guided hiking tours, and in the winter, 3,728 miles of mountain trails for cross-country skiing in national parks. Guided "ski hut to hut" tours are offered in the winter. The DNT also promotes well-being in the mountains, through guided trips that combine mountain hiking with different aspects of life in nature, such as good food.

Sailing

Scandinavian Charter Yachts
Gamle Drammensv. 30
1369 Stabekk
Norway
Tel./Fax: 47-6710-88-55
Mobile Tel: 47-9008-0875
E-mail: pj@sailingyachts.com
Web: www.sailingyachts.com

If you are interested in chartering a yacht in Scandinavia or are planning to take your own vessel there, this company can assist you. With broad local knowledge it will help connect you with a suitable charter vessel or offer expert advice for your own cruising plans. It also offers onboard pilotage and shore-activity planning. See the Web page for more information, or contact the company directly.

Tammsvik Konferens & Herrgård
Tel: 46-8-584-719-99
Fax: 46-8-582-425-29
E-mail: info@tammsvik.se
Web: www.tammsvik.se

If you are interested in sailing in Sweden, Tammsvik Konferens & Herrgård (Conference and Manor House) rents out its sailboat, *Sway af Tammsvik,* complete with a captain, chef, and crew, for up to eight people to stay on board, or for twelve people on a day trip. You can sail where you prefer, for instance in Stockholm's archipelago, around the coast of Sweden, or to the islands of Öland or Gotland. The Manor House is also a nice place to stay or to have a conference. Visit the Web page for more information and lots of appealing photos.

Cross-country Skiing

Birkebeinerrennet
P.O. Box 94
N-2451 Rena
Norway
Tel: 47-6244-29-00
FAX: 47-6244-29-01
E-mail: renn@birkebeiner.no
Web: www.birkebeiner.no

Taking place each year in March in Norway, the Birkebeinerrennet commemorates *birke-beiner* (birch leg) skiers, who used their skill and speed to save two-year-old Prince Håkan from pursuers in 1206. Today it has become a popular skiing event. Visit the Web page for more detailed information.

Rajalta Rajalle-hiihto
Aapiskuja 6 B, 97700 Ranua
Finland
Tel: 358-16-3559-298
Fax: 358-16-3559-200
E-mail: anitta.jaakola@ranua.fi
Web: www.ranua.fi

The Rajalta Rajalle-hiihto, "From Border to Border," is a seven-day, 258-mile cross-country skiing event. Definitely a challenge but not a race, participants ski across Finland, from the Russian to the Swedish border. Various travel agents arrange trips to Finland to participants in the event (see listing for Nordic Saga Tours, page 252), and you can also learn more by visiting the Web site listed below.

Vasaloppet Mora
Vasaloppets Hus
SE-792 32 Mora
Sweden
Tel: 46-250-392-00
Fax: 46-250-392-50
E-mail: info@vasaloppet.se
Web: www.vasaloppet.se

Vasaloppet in Dalarna, Sweden, is the oldest, longest, and biggest cross-country race in the world. Thousands take part every year, most not to win but simply to enjoy the skiing. Anyone is welcome to participate.

Long Skating

Stockholms Skridskoseglarklubb
c/o Orla Öhrn
Näsby Allé 45
183 55 Täby
Sweden
Tel and fax: 46-8-768-23-78
E-mail: kansli@sssk.se
Web: www.sssk.se

Founded in 1901, the Stockholm Ice Skate Sailing and Touring Club is the largest and oldest skating association in Scandinavia. The most popular activity within the club is the popular sport long skating. The club is dedicated to providing information on the best and safest skating, and in order to join you may have to take a skating course. There are about two hundred similar clubs all over Sweden, and they all do long-distance skating in archipelagos and on lakes. www.skridsko.net has links to several clubs.

Fishing and Hunting

Angling Club LAX-Á
Vatnesendablettur 181
203 Kopavogur
Iceland
Tel: 354-557-6100
Fax: 354-557-6108
E-mail: info@lax-a.is
Web: www.lax-a.is

Angling Club Lax-á is a company specializing in angling and hunting. They offer fishing on the top salmon, trout, and char rivers in Iceland, and each tour is tailor-made by the Lax-á team. Lax-á also sells and plans fishing in thirty salmon and trout rivers in Iceland, Argentina, Greenland, Russia, Scotland, and Ireland.

Namsen Adventure
7800 Namsos
Norway
Web: www.namsen.no

Namsen Adventure offers salmon fishing in one of Norway's best rivers for this activity, the Namsen. Located in a very beautiful area of Norway, it offers accommodations in traditional Norwegian-style cabins, and can assist with travel arrangements. Along with fishing, the company also arranges hunting expeditions.

Fishing in Finland
www.fishingfinland.com

This is the private Web page of an enthusiastic fisherman, which contains lots of tips and practical information on fishing in Finland, along with a guide for planning a fishing vacation in Finland.

Outdoor Gear

Exel Oyj
P.O. Box 29
FIN-52701 Mäntyharju
Finland
E-mail: sport@exel.fi
Web: www.exelsports.net
Web (site on Nordic Walking): www.nordicwalking.com

The Finnish sporting-goods company Exel sells high-quality equipment for many different activities, including Nordic Walking poles. They also have an informative Web site dedicated to Nordic Walking, where you can learn more about the sport, including practical information and tips on how to get started.

Fjällräven AB
E-mail: info@fjallraven.se
Web: www.fjallraven.se/en

Helly Hansen
Web: www.hellyhansen.no

Hestra
Web: www.hestragloves.com

Haglöfs
E-mail: haglofs@haglofs.se
Web: www.haglofs.se

There is no bad weather, only bad clothing; that is why there is high-quality clothing and equipment from companies such as Fjällräven, Helly Hensen, and Haglöfs, to permit outdoor activities in almost any kind of weather and conditions.

THREE: THE IMPORTANCE OF BEING GREEN

Nordic Gardens

Botaniska Trädgården
Villavägen 8
752 36 Uppsala
Sweden
Tel: 46-18-471-28-38
Fax: 46-18-471-28-31
E-mail: botanical.garden@botan.uu.se
Web: www.botan.uu.se

Linnéträdgården
Svartbäcksgatan 27
753 32 Uppsala
Sweden
Tel and fax: 46-18-10-94-90
Web: www.linnecus.uu.se

Linnés Hammarby
Web: www.hammarby.uu.se

Excellent general-information site on Linné
Web: www.linnaeus.uu.se/online/

All of these gardens are associated with the work of Carl Linnaeus. Uppsala University Botanical Garden is the oldest botanical garden in Sweden. The garden itself is located in a historical part of Uppsala, right next to the castle and the cathedral. Two other gardens include Linnaeus's own garden, Linnéträdgården, and his peaceful country home just outside of the city, Linné's Hammarby. For visiting information, see the first three Web pages listed above.

Rosendals Trädgård
Rosendalsterrassen 12
115 21 Stockholm
Sweden
Tel: 46-8-545-812-70
Fax: 46-8-545-812-79
Web: www.rosendalstradgard.com

These gardens are a great place to visit while on a trip to Stockholm. Located in the middle of the city, they offer visitors a chance to get close to nature. They have a schedule of events for each season and also have an appealing café and shop.

Wij Trädgårdar
816 26 Ockelbo
Sweden
Tel: 46-297-554-20
Fax: 46-297-554-35
E-mail: info@wij.se
Web: www.wij.se

Featuring flowers, vegetables, and other plants native to Scandinavia, Wij Gardens in Ockelbo also includes buildings for more exotic plants, a garden library, an agricultural park, art exhibitions, a huge wetland, a forestry park, a rosarium, and restaurants. This Nordic center for plants and garden has also taken upon itself the task of becoming a workshop for rehabilitation through the greenery. Inspired by Lars Krantz, a charismatic creator of outdoor spaces for living.

Örtagården i Dals Rostock
Brunnsparken
464 50 Dals Rostock
Sweden
E-mail: kerstin@rostock.se
Web: www.rostock.se

This is an herbal garden with approximately 350 plants of historical interest, all of which are labeled with plant information. The garden itself was created in memory of Johannes Henriksson (1853–1935), who was one of Sweden's foremost experts on medicinal plants. Now the herb garden, run by Kerstin Ljungqvist, who originally designed the garden, is open to the public twenty-four hours a day, every day, during the growing season. Together with the herb garden, there is a geological area, along with a museum and summer café, which are open between noon and evening, from midsummer to mid-August. Admission is free of charge, although donations are appreciated. Guided tours can be arranged, when booked in advance. Plants and various herb products are also available for purchase.

Nordic Herbals

Tær Icelandic
10 John Street
London
WC1N 2EB, United Kingdom
Tel: 44-1753-759-720
E-mail: info@taer.com

Tær means *pure* in Icelandic. In 1985, Thury Gudmundsdottir and her husband, Gunnar Astvaldsson, bought the farm Hvammur II, one half of what had been for centuries one of Iceland's great estates. They were keen to continue a generations-old family tradition of producing herbal creams. All the herbs contained in the products are grown on an organic farm in the northwest of Iceland. The key herbal ingredient, yarrow, is renowned for its nourishing, healing properties. Start with a visit to the Web site, which is an experience of relaxation in itself. The products are launching in the United States. You can additionally request a Braille book of ingredients, directions, and descriptions.

FOUR: SENSITIZATION AND THE RIGHT TO RELAX

Sauna

The Finnish Sauna Society
Vaskiniementie 10
FIN-00200 Helsinki
Finland
Tel: 358-9-6860-560
Fax: 358-9-679-180
Web: www.sauna.fi

Founded in 1937, the Finnish Sauna Society functions to preserve the traditional sauna culture of Finland, and also to inform about sauna today.

The Sauna Site
Web: www.saunasite.com

This site is a great information source on sauna: everything from the history of sauna to how to build one yourself.

Svenska Bastuakademien/Kansli
Kukkolaforsen 184
953 91 Haparanda
Sweden
Tel: 46-922-310-00
Fax: 46-922-310-30
E-mail: bastuakademien@kukkolaforsen.se
Web: www.kukkolaforsen.se/bastu/bastuakademien/sv_
bastuakademien.htm

The Swedish Sauna Academy is an organization dedicated to preserving the culture and information on sauna in Sweden. The Web page provides a wealth of links to information on the subject of sauna, many of which are in English.

Tylö
Web: www.tylo.com

A specialist in sauna equipment, heaters, and steam baths, Tylö AB is a Swedish company that exports its products to more than eighty countries worldwide. If you are interested in adding a sauna to your home, the company carries a line of prefabricated standard sauna rooms and will even build saunas to meet individual specifications. Tylö's products are available in the United States

Nordic Spas

The Blue Lagoon
Blue Lagoon Ltd.
Box 22
240 Grindavik
Iceland
Web: www.bluelagoon.is

The renowned Blue Lagoon Geothermal Spa in Iceland is a unique and interesting place to visit if you are in Iceland. It also offers online shopping for its spa products based on the lagoon's unique active ingredients: mineral salts, silica, and blue green algae.

Naantali Spa Hotel
Matkailijantie 2
21100 Naantali
Finland
Tel: 358-2-44-550
Fax: 358-2-44-55-101
E-mail: info@naantalispa.fi
Web: www.naantalispa.fi

Naantali Spa is located right on the beautiful Finnish archipelago, and offers a wide range of spa and beauty treatments, including various sauna baths and treatments utilizing extracts from Arctic plants. See the Web page for a listing of spa and beauty services offered, along with hotel information, description, and photos. Naantali Spa is classified as a Royal Spa of Europe.

Sturebadet AB
Sturegallerian 36
114 46 Stockholm
Sweden
Tel: 46-8-54501500
Fax: 46-8-54501510
E-mail: info@sturebadet.se
Web: www.sturebadet.se

Founded in 1885, Sturebadet is an interesting historical spa to visit if you are in the Stockholm area. It offers spa treatments, and guests can relax in the pleasant surroundings of the restaurant, which features many delicious items.

Varbergs Kurort Hotell & Spa
Nils Kreugers Väg 5
Box 152
432 24 Varberg
Sweden
Tel: 46-340-629800
Fax: 46-340-629850
E-mail: info@varbergskurort.se
Web: www.varbergskurort.se

Named finalists in March 2003 for "Europe's Best Spa" by *Professional Spa* magazine, Varbergs Kurort & Spa is located right on the sea, on Sweden's beautiful west coast. A wide range of packages is available, along with a number of treatments, including a seaweed massage, which is one of this spa's specialties. Other highlights include the 32°C (90°F) saltwater swimming pool, sauna, fully equipped gym, and the Spa Restaurant.

Storhogna Högfjällshotell & Spa
Box 43
840 92 Vemdalen
Sweden
Tel: 46-682-413030
Fax: 46-682-413042
E-mail: info@storhogna.com
Web: www.storhogna.com

Located in beautiful Vemdalen in the Swedish mountains, Storhogna Högfjällshotell & Spa provides comfortable living (either in the hotel or in cabins) and spa experiences in a natural area where many different outdoor activities can be enjoyed. In the winter, skiing is the main attraction, but there are summer activities as well, such as hiking, fishing, and mountain biking. Their main building is an experience of design for well-being.

Riksgränsen Alpina Spa
Tel: 46-980-400-80
E-mail: info@riksgransen.nu
Web: www.riksgransen.nu

Located in the far north of Sweden, along the Norwegian border, Riksgränsen is known for its first-rate skiing, and is a beautiful place to visit, winter or summer. The spa offers sauna, pool, Jacuzzi, exercise, and several spa treatments. One new treatment, Same-zen by Kerstin Florian (www.kerstinflorian.com), is inspired by the native people and nature around Lappland. This treatment includes cleansing, bath, and a massage with birch oil and hot stones, done in front of a fire in a tepee, set to Sami music.

Rondane Spa høyfjellshotell og hytter
Mysuseter 2675 Otta
Norway
Tel: 47-61-23-39-33
Fax: 47-61-23-39-52
E-mail: hotel@rondane.no
Web: www.rondane.no

Offering spa services in the breathtaking Norwegian mountains, Rondane Spa combines wellness with wilderness. Spa treatments are coupled with wilderness experiences, such as snowshoe and rafting tours, and Rondane can also customize arrangements.

Suderhälsan Spa
Suders Hamra
620 10 Burgsvik
Sweden
Tel: 46-498-49-90-90
Fax: 46-498-49-90-10
E-mail: info@suderhalsan.com
Web: www.suderhalsan.com

Suderhälsan overlooks a small fishing village on the dramatic and stony southern coast of magical Gotland. After an international life, the Hammarskjölds retreated to this beautiful place and revived the old spa culture of this community (where the locals once went to take the waters) by establishing their own small and very remarkable spa. Suderhälsan is an ecological spa, generating most of its energy from a seventeenth-century windmill.

Historical Spas

Loka Brunn
Stiftelsen Kungliga Gyttjebad och
Brunnsanstalten Loka
71294 Grythyttan
Sweden

Tel: 46-591-63100
E-mail: kurortsmuseum@lokabrunn.se
Web: www.lokabrunn.se

Loka Brunn is a natural spring that has been a source of vital energy for more than 250 years. Today it is a charming village, with many different buildings, including Scandinavia's only museum on spa history. Now it is once again an active spa, which is a center of leisure and conference activities.

Medevi Brunn
59197 Motala
Sweden
Tel: 46-141-911-00
Fax: 46-141-915-32
E-mail: medevibrunn@swipnet.se
Web: http://home.swipnet.se/~w-50413/english.htm

The oldest spa in Scandinavia, Medevi Brunn's history dates back to the late 1600s, when it was recognized for the healthful properties of the natural well upon which it rests. People still visit Medevi today, largely due to its attractive location, but also for its historical value.

FIVE: ESSENTIAL DESIGN AND THE CREATION OF HOME

Retailers and Commercial Organizations

Artek
Helsinki Head Office:
Eteläesplanadi 18
00130 Helsinki
Finland
Tel: 358-9-613-250
Fax: 358-9-6132-5260
E-mail: info@artek.fi
Web: www.artek.fi

Artek, the internationally recognized design brand, has a long tradition as a manufacturer of outstanding articles for daily use. Based in Finland and founded by Alvar Aalto, Artek stands for timeless design created by motivated and progressive thinkers. The company is still active today, with products being sold and exhibited in many different countries, including the United States. Artek has three showrooms in Finland and one in Stockholm.

BoConcept
Club 8 Company A/S
Mørupvej 16
7400 Herning

Denmark
Tel: 45-70-13-13-66
Fax: 45-96-26-72-16
E-mail: boconcept@boconcept.com
Web: www.boconcept.com

The Danish company BoConcept offers a line of attractive, functional modern design furniture. BoConcept aims to give people a sense of feeling at home, and they do this by creating simple, high-quality, and affordable furnishings. There are 131 different stores in twenty-four countries (including the United States), along with studios and dealers in thirty other countries. Find the retailer nearest you, and/or order a catalog, on the Web page.

Designtorget
Box 16414
103 27 Stockholm
Sweden
Tel: 46-8-508-315-20
Fax: 46-8-24-65-23
E-mail: kulturhuset@designtorget.se
Web: www.designtorget.se_default.asp

Functioning as a marketplace where both established designers and up-and-coming new talent can share space to sell their work, DesignTorget is an interesting place to visit. There are several stores in Stockholm.

Ergonomidesign AB
Box 140 04
Missionsvägen 24
167 14 Bromma
Sweden
Tel: 46-8-506-672-00
Web: http://www.ergonomidesign.com

Ergonomidesign specializes in products made to fit and serve the human body. The award-winning group has designed several clever items that can be purchased in various retail stores. Find out more, and see some of their clever ideas, on the Web page.

G.A.D.
Södra Kyrkogatan 16
621 56 Visby
Sweden
Tel: 46-498-24-82-30
Fax: 46-498-29-06-45
E-mail: info@gad.se
Web: www.gad.se

G.A.D. Stockholm:
Tomtebogatan 5
113 59 Stockholm
Sweden
Tel: 46-8-545-480-08
Fax: 46-8-545-480-09
E-mail: gadstockholm@gad.se
Web: www.gad.se

This clean, simple, skimp-on-nothing furniture design company produces items that exude a feeling for nature, translated for modern interiors. It is the brainchild of Kristian Eriksson, a former IT executive, who left the bright lights of the big city to become a carpenter on the charming island of Gotland. Eriksson is unflinching in his commitment to deliver pieces of substance and meaning in a world where, he says, "everything is surface."

Georg Jensen Flagship Store
Amagertorv 4
DK-1160 Copenhagen
Tel: 45-33-11-40-80
Fax: 45-38-14-99-43
E-mail: gj@georgjensen.com
Web: www.georgjensen.com

Founded in 1904, Georg Jensen has over 120 stores in thirteen countries. Beginning as a workshop creating unique and exclusive silver jewelry, the company now offers a wide range of gold and silver jewelry, watches, cutlery, and design items for the home. Its pure, elegant Scandinavian design idea is reflected on the Web site.

IKEA
Web: www.ikea.com

This is the Web page for the immensely popular Swedish interior-design store IKEA. Here you can order a catalog and find the store closest to you, or just be inspired by the images on the Web page.

Iittala oy ab
Hämeentie 135
P.O. Box 130
00561 Helsinki
Finland
Tel: 358-204-3910
Fax: 358-204-39-5180
Web: www.iittala.com

This Web page has links to the Iittala's and Arabia's Web pages—two famous examples of Finnish design products for the home.

Klässbols Linneväveri
Damastvägen 5
S-671 95 Klässbol
Sweden
Tel: 46-570-460185
Fax: 46-570-460408
E-mail: info@klassbols-linne.se
Web: www.klassbols.se

Klässbols is one of the foremost producers of linen goods in Sweden today supplying the table-cloths and napkins for the Nobel dinner in Stockholm each year. Visit the Web page to order a catalog.

Mariebergs Kakelugnsmakeri
Stångjärnsgatan 13
753 23 Uppsala
Tel: 46-18-128511
Fax: 46-18-128515
E-mail: info@mariebergskakelugnsmakeri.se
Web: www.mariebergskakelugnsmakeri.se

Mariebergs saved many antique Swedish tiled stoves from the destruction of old homes that took place in Sweden during the 1960s and 1970s. Today the company has a large assortment of restored antique tiled stoves, you can also order newer versions as well. Mariebergs has several offices around Stockholm.

Nedholm Design AB
Bror Nilssons Gata 6
SE-417 55 Göteborg
Sweden
Tel: 46-31-744-07-80
Fax: 46-31-23-33-52
Web: http://www.nedholm.se

This Swedish company creates practical design products for the home, crafted from light Nordic birch. It sells a modern version of a Swedish classic for increasing the effects of candlelight: a wall-attached candleholder backed by a mirror.

Stockholms Kakelugnsmakeri
Stora Knapersta
Långholmen
SE-117 33 Stockholm
Tel: 46-8-669-6020
Fax: 46-8-668-5880
E-mail: info@sk-ab.com
Web: www.sk-ab.com

A family business with a long history of making, renovating, and selling antique Swedish tiled stoves, it is also engaged in projects to create newer-style stoves. Here on the attractive island of Långholmen in central Stockholm, you can visit the workshop where there is a small museum displaying various types of *kakelugnar*. There is no English on the Web site, but you can reach them this way in any case.

Växbo Lin
Box 3583
SE-82195 Bollnäs
Sweden
Tel: 46-278-666-200
Fax: 46-278-666-090
E-mail: info@vaxbolin.se
Web: www.vaxbolin.se

Combining age-old traditions for linen preparation with modern, award-winning design, Växbo Lin is an interesting and scenic place to visit. Located in Hälsningland, Växbo Lin has renovated the old linen production village to a museum where you can see the entire process, from preparation of raw materials to award-winning, finished products, including table runners, napkins, towels, and pillows. The highly absorbent, compostable linen dishcloths make an innovative, inexpensive gift. The products are also available throughout Sweden, and in select locations in the United States.

White Sense
Web: www.mezzoshowroom.com

Here you can find beautifully designed products for the home, by designer Martine Colliander, who takes light and simplicity as the inspiration for her high-quality home products.

Yllet
S:t Hansgatan 19
621 56 Visby
Sweden
Tel: 46-498-21-40-44
Fax: 46-498-21-40-17
Web: www.yllet.com

Also at:
Drottninggatan 106
111 60 Stockholm
Tel: 46-8-796-76-40
Web: www.yllet.com

Based out of Visby on the island of Gotland, Sweden, Yllet is a store where natural materials, timeless design, and Swedish production combine to create beautiful clothing. While the focus is on clothing made from wool from Gotland, Yllet also produces items from linen, cotton, and silk. Although small, Yllet's shops are well worth a visit for the rich variety offered.

Östergötlands Ullspinneri AB
Storeryd
599 92 Ödeshög
Sweden
Tel: 46-144-230-88
Fax: 46-144-230-89
E-mail: ullspinneriet@telia.com
Web: www.ullspinneriet.com

Four-time recipient of Utmärkt Svensk Form (Excellent Swedish Design Award), Östergötlands Ullspinneri is a Swedish company that produces high-quality wool products in appealing modern designs. While the manufacturing of the products is based on tradition, the designs are frequently renewed. This combination of old and new is what makes this company's wool products so appealing. A range of special services is also available, including prototype development of their own designs.

Places of Interest & Museums

The Alvar Aalto Museum
P.O. Box 461
Alvar Aallon katu 7
40101 Jyväskylä
Finland
Tel: 358-14-62-48-09
Fax: 358-14-61-90-09
E-mail: museum@alvaraalto.fi
Web: http://www.alvaraalto.fi

Founded in 1966, the Alvar Aalto Museum is housed in a building designed by the famous Finnish architect. The museum functions as an Aalto information center, organizes exhibitions in Finland and abroad, works to preserve Alvar Aalto's buildings, and produces publications.

Archtours
Linnankoskenkatu 1 a 2
00250 Helsinki
Finland
Tel: 358-9-454-3044
Fax: 358-9-445-742
E-mail: archtours@archtours.fi
Web: http://www.archtours.fi/en

Experts on architecture and design, Archtours offers many interesting and varying architectural tours of Finland and the Baltic States. Archtours will also tailor-make programs and itineraries to meet customers' needs.

Arkitekturmuseet
Skeppsholmen
11149 Stockholm
Sweden
Tel: 46-8-587-270-00 or 46-8-587-270-02
Fax: 46-8-587-270-70
E-mail: info@arkitekturmuseet.se
Web: www.arkitekturmuseet.se

The Museum of Architecture in Stockholm features ongoing exhibitions, along with temporary and touring exhibitions. On the Web page you can search the archives and photo library, and learn more about the museum. If you are in the Stockholm area, this museum is worth a stop. Admission is now free.

Arne Jacobsen
Web: www.arne-jacobsen.com

This Web page contains historical information on the famous Danish designer, from quotes by the artist to photos of his designs. Here you can find a list of manufacturers of his products.

Capellagården
Vickleby
386 93 Färjestaden
Sweden
Tel: 46-485-36132
Fax: 46-485-36171
E-mail: capellagarden@cg.hik.se
Web: www.capellagarden.se

Capellagården is a school of craft and design founded in 1960 by famous designer Carl Malmsten. Today it is a private school and a special place either to attend or to visit. Classes are open to all, and some of the classes offered include Cabinet Making and Furniture Design; Ceramics; Textiles; and Ecological Gardening. Call in order to book a visit or a class.

Ellen Keys Stiftelse Strand
Ellen Key's Strand Museum
Alvastra
Ödeshög
Sweden
Tel: 46-8-644-22-40
Fax: 46-8-644-75-85
Web: www.ellenkey.se

Located close to Vadstena, Sweden, activist and author Ellen Key's home is now a museum. Key became well known, among other things, for her essay *Skönhet för alla,* or "Beauty for

All," first published in 1897 and translated into English by Frank Lloyd Wright's second wife, Mamah Borthwick. Key emphasized, among other things, the need for simplicity and light in the home.

Gripsholms Slottsförvaltning
Gripsholms Slott
647 31 Mariefred
Sweden
Tel: 46-159-101-94
Fax: 46-159-108-07
Web: www.royalcourt.se

This Royal Castle is a breathtaking sight in the harbor of Mariefred in Sweden. The interior provides an excellent example of Gustavian design.

Icehotel AB
981 91 Jukkasjärvi
Sweden
Tel: 46-980-66-800
Fax: 46-980-668-90
E-mail: info@icehotel.com
Web: www.icehotel.com

Each year the Icehotel is built anew out of ice. Beautiful sculptures, chandeliers, and even the beds that guests sleep on are formed out of ice and snow. Together with the famous Ice Bar, where even the glasses are made from ice, and the beautiful Ice Chapel, guests can view sculptures made from ice and snow. In the spring the Icehotel melts again, leaving behind only memories. A second ice hotel was built in Canada in 2001.

Kulturhuset i Ytterjärna
PL 1800
153 91 Järna
Sweden
Tel: 46-8-554-302-00
Fax: 46-8-551-506-44
E-mail: info@kulturhuset.nu
Web: www.kulturhuset.nu

Well-known for the belief that good design promotes a process of healing, Kulturhuset is the home of the Anthrophosophic Center. A fascinating place to visit, the center is made up of several buildings, including a clinic and a concert hall in luminous color, which "metamorphose into one another." Their water-cleaning system and other ecologically designed outdoor areas are well worth a visit.

Norsk Folkemuseum
Museumsveien 10, Bygdøy
N-0287 Oslo
Norway
Tel: 47-22-12-37-00
Fax: 47-22-12-37-77
E-mail: nf@norskfolkemuseum.no
Web: www.norskfolkemuseum.no

Conveniently located close to Oslo, the Norwegian Museum of Cultural History (Norsk Folkemuseum) boasts an expansive open-air museum that features 150 buildings from different regions in Norway. Here you can also try traditional foods, view folk dancing performances, and see traditional arts and crafts, including many examples of rosemaling. The Web page includes a calendar of events.

Radisson SAS Royal Hotel
Hammerichgade 1
Copenhagen DK-1611
Denmark
Reservations Tel: 45-38-15-65-00
Fax: 45-38-15-65-01
Hotel Tel: 45-33-42-61-00
Toll-free reservations from U.S.: 800-333-3333
E-mail: Reservations.Royal.Copenhagen@Radissonsas.com
Web: www.radissonsas.com

The Radisson SAS Royal Hotel in Copenhagen was designed entirely by Arne Jacobsen, interior and exterior. The preceding Web page on Arne Jacobsen has more information on the hotel.

Skansen
Post Box 27807
S-11593 Stockholm
Sweden
Tel: 46-8-442-80-00
Fax: 46-8-442-82-80
E-mail: info@skansen.se
Web: www.skansen.se

Skansen is the world's oldest open-air museum. An appealing place to view traditional design, Skansen shows a unique collection of historical buildings from many parts of Sweden that have been transported to this special hill overlooking Stockholm harbor. Skansen also features a program of traditional festivities.

Sundborn, Carl Larsson Gården
790 15 Sundborn

Sweden
Tel: 46-23-60053
Fax: 46-23-60653
Web: www.clg.se

Carl Larsson Gården in Sundborn is the home of the famous Swedish artist Carl Larsson and his family. The home was made famous through Larsson's paintings and, for many, represents aspects of home design that are quintessentially Swedish.

Villa Mairea
29 600 Noormarkku
Finland
Tel: 358-10-888-44-60
Web: www.alvaraalto.fi

Villa Mairea, designed by Alvar Aalto in the 1930s, is a masterpiece of nature near design. Villa Mairea can be toured by the public; booking an appointment in advance is necessary.

Design Centers

Danish Design Center (DDC)
H C Andersens Boulevard 27
1553 København V
Denmark
Tel: 45-33-69-33-69
Fax: 45-33-69-33-00
E-mail: design@ddc.dk
Web: http://www.ddc.dk

Established in 1978 for the purpose of increasing design awareness, the DDC works to promote design in society and industry, and to promote Danish design both in Denmark and abroad. At the same time, they work to strengthen designer-business ties. Their center is worth a visit for the ongoing thematic exhibits.

Design Forum Finland
Exhibition:
Mannerheiminaukio 3
00100 Helsinki
Finland
Tel: 358-9-629-290
Fax: 358-9-611-918
Office:
Erottajankatu 15–17 A
00130 Helsinki
Finland

Tel: 358-9-6220-810
Fax: 358-9-629-489
E-mail: info@designforum.fi
Web: www.designforum.fi

Maintained by the Finnish Society for Crafts and Design, Design Forum Finland is Finland's leading expert body in arranging exhibitions of contemporary design. Design Forum organizes exhibitions both in Finland and abroad, and also focuses on various projects that promote design. Design Forum is perhaps Finland's leading information center on Finnish design. Publications and electronic information are also available, including the publication *Form Function Finland*.

Designforum Svensk Form
Holmamiralens väg 2 (Skeppsholmen)
SE-111 49 Stockholm
Sweden
Tel: 468-463-3130
E-mail: info@svenskform.se
Web: www.svenskform.se

Designforum Svensk Form, a meeting place in Stockholm for everyone interested in design, is a design center with exhibitions, a library, periodicals room, picture archives, and a shop. It also offers a program of seminars and lectures. On the Web page you can find current exhibitions and events, and you can also become a member, which will entitle you to a subscription to their periodical, *Form*, provided in English and Swedish languages.

International Academy for Design and Health
Research Center Design and Health
Uthagsv. 18A
136 49 Haninge
Sweden
Tel: 46-70-453-90-70
Fax: 46-8-745-00-02
E-mail: academy@designandhealth.com
Internet: www.designandhealth.com

Based in Sweden, the International Academy for Design and Health is a nonprofit organization that works at an international level to encourage and develop research on the relationship between culture, design, health, and economic impact. This academy is active on many levels, including a number of international events.

Norsk Form
Kongens gate 4
N0153 Oslo
Norway
Tel: 47-22-47-74-00

Fax: 47-22-47-74-19
E-mail: norskform@norskform.no
Web: http://www.norskform.no/

Norsk Form believes that good physical surroundings are important for a high quality of life, and works to actively encourage this, through knowledge and education. Norsk Form's activities include hosting events, publishing books and a regular bulletin, arranging seminars and conferences, and presenting awards for excellent design and architecture.

SIX: PURE ENERGY AND A
NORDIC TASTE OF WELL-BEING

The number of excellent food experiences to be enjoyed in the various Scandinavian countries is endless and growing with an extremely innovative pool of inspired chefs and other creators of food experiences. Below is the smallest taste of what is available, mostly in Sweden.

Food Markets

Several of the Nordic capital cities have food markets where you can view, smell, and taste all kinds of superb fresh local ingredients. Some of them offer indoor options if the weather doesn't oblige. We have also provided a marketplace reference for northern Sweden, so that you can get a taste for that region of Scandinavia.

Jokkmokk's Winter Market (January 29–February 6 annually)
www.jokkmokksmarknad.com

Much more than a winter food marketplace, Jokkmokk Winter Market celebrates its 400th year in 2005. Here you can experience the reindeer-dominated food world of the Sami of northern Scandinavia. A superb cultural introduction to the far North. It is well arranged for foreign visitors with an English language Web site.

Kauppatori (Central Market Square)
South Harbor
Helsinki

There are three other open-air markets in peninsular Helsinki, but this is the most accessible to visitors on a limited stay. There is also an indoor market building.

Rådhuset Harbor Area
Oslo

Here you can buy and enjoy seafood, much of which has come right off the fishing boats.

Östermalmshallen
Östermalmstorg
Stockholm

Östermalmshallen in central Stockholm provides a mouthwatering display of specialties and also houses a number of restaurants where you can enjoy the excellent ingredients. Indoors.

Food Centers

Fuglebjerggaard
Hemmingstrupvej 8
3200 Helsinge, Denmark
Tel: 45-48-39-39-43
Fax: 45-48-39-39-44
E-mail: kontor@fuglebjerggaard.dk
Web: www.fuglebjerggaard.dk

This is the workshop and ecological farm of the well-known Danish food activist and author of cookbooks Camilla Plum and her husband, Per Kølster. Camilla and Per run cooking and team-building courses, as well as run excursions. Booking in advance is essential. Otherwise, a visit to their café and to the area, right at the Danish coast not far from Copenhagen, is a relaxing half-day outing.

Måltidens Hus i Norden
Grythyttan
Sweden
Tel: 46-591-340-60
Fax: 46-591-340-88
E-mail: info@maltidenshus.com
Web: www.maltidenshus.com

In 1993 the Swedish Pavilion created for the 1992 World Exhibition in Seville on the basis of the theme "The Light of Inspiration" was moved to Grythyttan just near the Swedish city of Örebro. Entrepreneur Carl-Jan Granqvist turned the Pavilion into the Nordic House of Culinary Art that it is today. Måltidens Hus is now a center for educational programs, exhibitions, seminars, conferences, and research projects. The Web site describes some unusual experiences in their magnificent modern Gastronomy Theater and the largest cookbook museum in the North, which you can enjoy with the help of students there if you book in advance. You can also enjoy guided tours. The nearby restaurant and hotel in Grythyttan offers an excellent menu and a charming environment.

Restaurants

While there are many excellent healthful food experiences to be had in the Nordic countries, we cannot guarantee that all the dishes listed on the menus of the following are good for your waistline. Rather, these listings provide a first-rate experience of the many great ingredients mentioned in this book. Most of the options below are pricey, although well worth it for a special occasion. Almost all of the listings are in Sweden, but there are many good restaurants in the other Nordic countries as well.

Grythyttans Gästgivaregård
Prästgatan 2
712 81 Grythyttan
Sweden
Tel: 46-591-147-00
Fax: 46-591-141-24
E-mail: info@grythyttan.com
Web: www.grythyttan.com

The restaurant and hotel are located near Måltidens Hus i Norden, where you can enjoy some excellent Swedish fare. The inn first opened its doors in 1640.

Kalf-Hansens Matatelje AB
Backstugan i Gamla Filmstaden
Råsundavägen 150
SE-169 36 Solna
Tel: 46-8-83-05-15
Fax: 46-8-83-81-30
E-mail: rune@kalf-hansen.com
Web: www.kalf-hansen.com

In the historic cultural environment provided by Stockholm's Old Film City, once the workplace of Greta Garbo, Ingrid Bergman, and other familiar names, Rune Kalf-Hansen and his wife, Carina, have set up a food workshop focused on making the most out of seasonal ingredients. At Matatelje you won't find a tomato dish available in January. Through his cooperation with Simon Irvine, master gardener at Läckö Palace, Kalf-Hansen is expanding Matatelje's capacity to be self-sustaining in many vegetables and herbs throughout the growing season. By phoning ahead you can find out what the possibilities might be for you to dine there. It doesn't function as a usual restaurant, and booking is necessary. Lunch is served for anyone who would like to come once a week.

Hotel Borgholm
Trädgårdsgatan 15-19
387 31 Borgholm
Tel: 46-485-770-60
Fax: 46-485-124-66
E-mail: info@hotellborgholm.com
Web: www.hotellborgholm.com

On the charming island of Öland, Chef Karin Fransson prepares what is regarded as some of the best restaurant food in Sweden with the help of her herb garden. She is a known radio personality in Sweden, sharing recipes with the public, which she also does on this Web site. A visit to Hotel Borgholm at the time of Öland's well-known Harvest Festival is the best way to get the most out of this food experience, although it is a popular place all year round.

Noma
Strandgade 93
Copenhagen
Tel. 45-3296-3297
E-mail: noma@noma.dk
Web: www.noma.dk

The creators of Noma traveled north rather than south for a couple of months in order to research Nordic food traditions and ingredients. They came up with this first-rate restaurant overlooking the harbor of Nyhavn in Copenhagen, where simplicity, first-rate Nordic ingredients, and healthful thinking in preparation play important roles. Although the food can sound challenging, foreign visitors report longing to return once they have left.

Oaxen Skärgårdskrog
Oaxen
153 93 Hölö
Tel: 46-551-531-05
Fax: 46-551-531-70
E-mail: info@oaxenkrog.se
Web: www.oaxen.se

Located in Stockholm's southern archipelago on the eastern side of the island of Oaxen, this restaurant was voted Sweden's best restaurant in 2002–3, and its chef, Magnus Ek, competes in the Swedish international culinary team. Here you can enjoy many of the specialties of the local environment, including sea buckthorn berries. Their kitchen garden makes them self-sufficient in salads and herbs for most of April to September. Open for Christmas with a fantastic Christmas smorgasbord as well.

Petri Pumpa
Kronovalls Vinslott
SE-273 95 Tomelilla
Tel: 46-417-197-10
Tel (booking): 46-417-197-10
Fax: 46-417-232-16
E-mail: kronovall@petripumpa.se
E-mail (booking): bokningen.kronovall@petripumpa.se
Web: www.petripumpa.se

With eighteenth- and nineteenth-century furnishings in the different rooms of this palace near Lund in southern Sweden, Petri Pumpa has a special setting to serve up its renowned cuisine. Thomas Drejing, considered by some as the Ingmar Bergman of the culinary world in Sweden for his commitment to showing up great ingredients as they are, elevated this restaurant to the level of a food idea during the past twenty years. Local, seasonal ingredients from the region are the focus.

Other Food Resources

Laila Spik
Sirkasgatan 10a
SE-96 231 Jokkmokk
Sweden
Tel. 46-70-35-90-941
E-mail: laila.spik@same.net

Laila Spiik has served food gathered from her native Lappland in northernmost Sweden to some very remarkable guests, including the king and queen of Sweden. Today she spends her time spreading knowledge about how to use ingredients from the wild that most wouldn't think of using in the kitchen, both at home in Sweden and abroad. Contact Laila directly to arrange a unique experience of gathering, preparing, and enjoying food from the wild.

New Scandinavian Cooking with Andreas Viestad
Web: www.scandcook.com/intro.html

Viestad's charismatic presentation of Norwegian cuisine has made *New Scandinavian Cooking with Andreas Viestad,* a popular television program and book in the United States. Visit the Web site above to learn more.

The Northerner Scandinavia AB
Hantverksvägen 15
43633 Askim
Sweden
Tel: 46-31-68-19-91
Fax: 46-31-68-19-93
E-mail: info@northerner.com
Web: www.northerner.com

The Northerner is a large Internet shopping site with a wide variety of Nordic food products, including several items that have been mentioned in this book, such as rose hip soup, herring, messmör, and välling. The Northerner also sells a variety of other Scandinavian products, including wooden butter knives, clothing, and gift items, and will soon be expanding their line to include books.

GENERAL INFORMATION ON THE NORDIC COUNTRIES, IN SCANDINAVIA AND IN THE UNITED STATES

Scandinavian Tourist Board
P.O. Box 4649
Grand Central Station
New York, NY 10163-4649

Tel: 212-885-9700
Fax: 212-885-9710
E-mail: info@goscandinavia.com
Web: www.goscandinavia.com

The Scandinavian Tourist Board is the joint tourist board for Denmark, Finland, Iceland, Norway, and Sweden. Their Web page has a wealth of information on these countries.

The American-Scandinavian Foundation
The American-Scandinavian Foundation at Scandinavia House
58 Park Avenue
New York, NY 10016
Tel: 212-879-9779
E-mail: info@amscan.org
Web: www.amscan.org

Founded in 1910, the ASF is a publicly supported, nonprofit organization that serves as a link between the United States and the five Nordic countries. They have an extensive program of fellowships, grants, trainee placement, publishing, membership offerings, and cultural activities. Scandinavia House, which houses the ASF, offers a wide range of programs that illuminate the contemporary vitality of the Nordic countries, such as concerts, readings, lectures, language courses, and children's programs. Visit the Web page to learn more.

Denmark

An official tourism site to Denmark
Web: www.visitdenmark.com

This site provides travel and tourist information that is both informative and interesting. Here you can find lots of good tips if you are planning a trip to Denmark, view pictures, and order information.

DANHOSTEL
Vesterbrogade 39
1620 Copenhagen V
Tel: 45-3331-3612
E-mail: ldv@danhostel.dk
Web: www.danhostel.dk

There are 100 DANHOSTEL youth and family hostels in Denmark, and each differs in facilities, activities, prices, and locations. However, all have one thing in common: a relaxed, informal, stress-free environment, where the main goal of guests is to stay in a place and initiate positive experiences with family, friends, colleagues, or other guests. A visit to the Web page will provide a good idea of what to expect from DANHOSTEL, including prices and facilities, along with specific details and contact information.

Finland

Finnish Tourist Board—MEK
Head Office:
P.O. Box 625, Töölönkatu 11
00101 Helsinki, Finland
Tel: 358-(0)9-4176-911
Fax: 358-(0)9-4176-9399
E-mail: mek@mek.fi
Web: www.finland-tourism.com

Established in 1973 to promote tourism, the Finnish Tourist Board, MEK, works in close co-operation with the Finnish tourist and travel industry to promote and develop enticing products for tourists. Its appealing Web page is a good source to search for information on Finland, as well as a place from which to order informative brochures on the country.

Kulttuuri.net is "A Gateway to Finnish Culture on the Net"
Web: www.kulttuuri.net/english

Kulttuuri.net is a Web page specializing in links related to Finnish culture: artists, associations, media, organizations, and specialist services.

The Finnish Youth Hostel Association – SRM
Yrjonkatu 38 B 15 (2nd floor)
00100 Helsinki
Customer service: info@srm.inet.fi
Tel: 358-(0)9-565-7150
Fax: 358-(0)9-565-71510
Web: www.srmnet.org/

This is a good source of information on staying in youth hostels in Finland, which are simple and affordable.

Iceland

The official site of the Icelandic Foreign Service
Web: www.iceland.org

Iceland Naturally
Web: www.icelandnaturally.com

Iceland Naturally is a link to Iceland's products and services related to nature.

Icelandic Tourist Board
655 Third Avenue
New York, NY 10017

Tel: 212-885-9700
Fax: 212-885-9710
E-mail: usa@icetourist.is
Web: www.icelandtouristboard.com
Also: www.icetourist.is

Icelandtouristboard.com is the Web page for the Icelandic Tourist Board in North America. Icetourist.is is the official Web page of the Icelandic Tourist Board in Iceland. These two sites, together with icelandnaturally.com, are good, visually appealing sources of information on Iceland.

Norway

Site for the Norwegian Tourist Board
Web: www.visitnorway.com

Presented by the Norwegian Tourist Board, this site contains a wealth of information on Norway. Good information and beautiful photos, along with the ability to order brochures, make this a valuable site to visit if you are interested in traveling to Norway, or if you would just like to learn more about this destination.

Hostelling International Norway
Web: www.vandrerhjem.no

This site has good, concrete information for those who want to visit Norway and stay in hostels or mountain lodges. The accommodations are simple and affordable, as in the other Nordic countries.

The Norwegian-American Foundation
7301 Fifth Avenue, N.E., Suite A
Seattle, WA 98115
Tel: 206-526-8808
Fax: 206-284-2601
E-mail: info@nor-am.org
Web: www.nor-am.org

The Norwegian-American Foundation strives to further cooperation between all Norwegian American organizations, and to strengthen ties between Norway and North America. You can learn more on its Web page.

The Sons of Norway
Sons of Norway Headquarters
1455 W. Lake Street
Minneapolis, MN 55408-2666
Phone: 612-827-3611
Toll-free: 800-945-8851
Fax: 612-827-0658
Web: www.sofn.com

Sons of Norway, founded in 1895, is the largest Norwegian-American organization in the world. It strives to promote tradition and fellowship through cultural activities of many kinds. All (men, women, children, youth) are welcome to join. Visit the Web page for more information, along with a comprehensive list of links for more information on Norway.

Sweden

The official Web site of Sweden to the outside world

Web: www.sweden.se

Administered by the Swedish Institute, this Web page is the joint effort of Swedish Government Offices, the Swedish Trade Council, the Invest in Sweden Agency, the Swedish Travel & Tourism Council, and the Swedish Institute. Here you can find current issues, news, facts, and lots of other general and interesting information on Sweden, along with pictures and tourist information.

The official Swedish site for tourism

Web: www.visit-sweden.com

Visit-Sweden is the official Swedish Web site for tourism provided by the Swedish Travel & Tourism Council.

STF—Svenska Turistföreningen

Web: www.stfturist.se

This site has information for those who want to visit Sweden and stay in hostels or mountain lodges. The accommodations are simple and affordable.

The American Swedish Institute

2600 Park Avenue
Minneapolis, MN 55407
Tel: 612-871-4907
Web: www.americanswedishinst.org

Founded in 1929, ASI is an active cultural institute and museum that organizes Swedish cultural events for its members and visitors. It also has a bookstore, a gift shop, and a coffee shop. Check out the Web page for more information and for lots of links on Sweden and Scandinavia.

Consulates and Embassies in the United States

The following is a list of consulates and embassies in the United States for each of the Nordic countries. They often provide good Web pages with links to more information on their specific countries. Consulates can help with official travel needs, such as visas and passports, when needed. However, for more general travel information, visit their Web pages and our list of general information in the beginning of this section.

Denmark

Royal Danish Embassy
3200 Whitehaven Street NW
Washington, DC 20008
Tel: 202-234-4300
Fax: 202-328-1470
E-mail: wasamb@um.dk
Web: www.denmarkemb.org

Royal Danish Consulate General, New York
One Dag Hammerskjold Plaza
885 Second Avenue, 18th Floor
New York, NY 10017-2201
Tel: 212-223-4545
Fax: 212-754-1904
E-mail: information@denmark.org
Web site: www.denmark.org

Royal Danish Consulate General, Chicago
211 E. Ontario Street, Suite 1800
Chicago, IL 60611-3242
Tel: 312-787-8780
Fax: 312-787-8744
Web: www.consulatedk.org

Royal Danish Consulate, Los Angeles
12444 Ventura Boulevard, Suite 204
Studio City, CA 91604
Tel: 818-766-0003
Fax: 818-766-0302
E-mail: info@danishconsulate.org
Web: www.danishconsulate.org

Finland

Embassy of Finland
3301 Massachusetts Avenue NW
Washington, DC 20008
Tel: 202-298-5800
Fax: 202-298-6030
E-mail: info@finland.org
Web: www.finland.org

Consulate General of Finland
866 United Nations Plaza
New York, NY 10017
Tel: 212-750-4400
Fax: 212-750-4418
E-mail: finconny@ix.netcom.com
Web: www.finlandnyc.org

Consulate General of Finland, Los Angeles
1801 Century Park East, Suite 2100
Los Angeles, CA 90067
Tel: 310-203-9903
Fax: 310-203-9186
E-mail: info@finlandla.org
Web: www.finlandla.org/2.html

Iceland

Consulate General of Iceland
800 Third Avenue, 36th Floor
New York, NY 10022
Tel: 212-593-2700
Fax: 212-593-6269
E-mail: icecon.ny@utn.stjr.is
Web: www.iceland.org/us/nyc

Embassy of Iceland
1145 15th Street NW, Suite 1200
Washington, DC 20005-1704
Tel: 202-265-6653
Fax: 202-265-6656
E-mail: icemb.wash@utn.stjr.is
Web: www.iceland.org/us

Norway

The Royal Norwegian Consulate General, Minneapolis
800 Foshay Tower
821 Marquette Avenue
Minneapolis, MN 55402-2961
Tel: 612-332-3338
Fax: 612-332-1386
E-mail: cons.gen.minneapolis@mfa.no
Web: www.norway.org/embassy/embassy.cfm?location=Minneapolis

Royal Norwegian Embassy, Washington
2720 34th Street NW
Washington, DC 20008
Tel: 202-333-6000
Fax: 202-338-0515
Web: www.norway.org

Royal Norwegian Consulate General, Houston
2777 Allen Parkway, Suite 1185
Houston, TX 77019-2141
Tel: 713-521-2900
Fax: 713-521-9648
E-mail: cq.houston@mfa.no
Web: www.norway.org

Royal Norwegian Consulate General, San Francisco
20 California Street, 6th floor
San Francisco, CA 94111-4803
Tel: 415-986-0766
Fax: 415-986-3318
E-mail: cons.gen.sanfrancisco@mfa.no
Web: www.norway.org

Royal Norwegian Consulate General, New York
825 Third Avenue, 38th Floor
New York, NY 10022-7584
Tel: 212-421-7333
Fax: 212-754-0583
E-mail: cq.newyork@mfa.no
Web: www.norway.org

Sweden

Embassy of Sweden
1501 M Street NW, Suite 900
Washington, DC 20005
Tel: 202-467-2600
E-mail: ambassaden.washington@foreign.ministry.se
Web: wwww.swedenabroad.com/washington

Consulate General of Sweden
One Dag Hammrskjold Plaza
885 Second Avenue, 45th Floor
New York, NY 10017
Tel: 212-583-2550

E-mail: generalkonsulat.new-york@foreign.ministry.se
Web: www.swedennewyork.com

Consulate General of Sweden
1940 Wilshire Boulevard, Suite 700
Los Angeles, CA 90024
Tel: 310-445-4008
E-mail: la@consulateofsweden.org
Web: www.swedishoffices.org

Notes

1. Marceau, Marcel. *The Story of Bip.* New York: Harper & Row, 1976.

INTRODUCTION

1. See, for example: Prescott-Allen, Robert. *The Wellbeing of Nations: A Country-by-Country Index of Quality of Life and the Environment.* Washington, D.C.: IDRC/Island Press, 2001; Jeffrey D. Sachs, "The Best Countries in the World" in *Newsweek* (26 July 2004); the United Nations Development Program's annual *Development Index.*
2. *WHO Health Report 2003.*

ONE: A NORDIC-INSPIRED SCIENCE OF LIFE

1. Moberg, Kerstin Uvnäs. *Lugn och beröring: Oxytocinets läkande verkan i kroppen* (Relaxation & Touch: Oxytocin's Healing Effects in the Body). Borås: Natur och Kultur, 2001.
2. Bohlin, Jonas. *Liv* (Life). Färgfabriken, 1997, p. 22.
3. Hjálmarsson, Jóhann. *On Landscape,* translation by Sigurt-ur A. Magnússon in *Treasures of Icelandic Verse.* Rejkjavik: Mál og menning Publishers, 1996. Permission to reprint granted by the publishers.

4. For an outstanding account (written for a British audience but of great interest to a general audience), see: James, Oliver. *Britain on the Couch: Why We're Unhappier than We Were in the 1950s—Despite Being Richer, Treating a Low Serotonin Society*. London: Arrow Books Limited, 1998.

5. H.M. Queen Sonja of Norway. *Klangbunn: Vandringer i ord og bilder* (Klangbunn: Hikes in Words and Pictures). Labyrinth Press, 2002, pp. 16–17.

6. Skott, Carola. *Bota Blod och Läka Hjärta: Samer berättat om bot* (Cure the Blood and Heal the Heart: Samis Narrate Healing). Stockhom: Carlssons, 1997.

7. Lars Krantz quoted in *Sinnligt & Praktiskt* (Meaningful and Practical). Kooperativa Förbundet, 1998.

8. Swan, James A. "The Spirit of Place" in *Finnish Sauna, Japanese Furo, Indian Inipi: Bathing on Three Continents*. Helsinki: Building Information Ltd., 2000.

9. Moberg, *Lugan och beröring*, pp. 142–3.

TWO: OUTDOOR LIFE AND OVERCOMING THE
FITNESS DILEMMA

1. Børge Ousland quoted in a BBC World Service Interview just after completing his journey in 2001. Find out more about his many remarkable adventures and be inspired at www.ousland.no/eng/.

2. DrWeil.com (08/05/2003).

3. Sörlin, Sverker, and Klas Sandell, "Förändring och Kontinuitet" (Change and Continuity) in Sörlin and Sandell, *Friluftshistoria: Från 'Hårdande Friluftslif' till Ekoturism och Miljöpedagogik* (The History of Outdoor Life: From "Hardening Outdoor Life" to Ecotourism and Environmental Education). Stockholm: Carlsson, 2000, p. 261.

4. *Green Trees, Sunshine in Home, Linked to Longevity*. Reuters Health (26 November 2002).

5. McIntyre, Norman. "Internationella Tendenser" (International Tendencies) in Sörlin and Sandell, *Friluftshistoria* p. 239.

6. "Med känsla för ved" (A Feeling for Wood), *Allt Om Fritidshus* (All about Holiday Homes), Nr. 4 (August 2002).

7. H.M. Queen Sonja of Norway, *Klangbunn*, p. 147.

8. Graham-Campbell, James. *The Viking World*. New York: Ticknor & Fields, 1980.

9. Ritzen, Patrik. "Paddling när barnen får välja" (Paddling When Children Get to Choose), *Friluftsliv*, Friluftsfrämjandet (No. 3, 2003).

10. Fischer, Magnus. "På väg—en mental befrielse" (*On the Road—a Mental Freeing*), *Ute Magasinet*, Milvus Publishers (No. 6, 2002).

11. Thomasson, Björn. *Zen och Konsten att Paddla—En Filosofisk Fundering* (Zen & the Art of Paddling—A Philosophical Reflection). www.thomassondesign.com.

12. Gothus, Olaus Magnus. *Historia om de Nordiska Folken* (A History of the Nordic Peoples), first published in 1555, Chapter 4, Book 1.

13. *Friluftsliv*, Friluftsfrämjandet (3, 2003).

14. Lagerqvist, Lars O. *A History of Sweden*. The Swedish Institute, 2003.

15. Huntford, Roland. *Nansen*. London: Gerald Duckworth & Co., Ltd., 1997, p. 7.

THREE: THE IMPORTANCE OF BEING GREEN

1. Branston, Brian. *Gods & Heroes in Viking Mythology*. Glasgow: Collins, 1983, pp. 29–30.
2. My translation taken from the Swedish quoted in Bonekamp, Gunnevi, *Ut I Naturens Skafferi: Våra vilda bär och frukter med recept* (Out in Nature's Pantry: Our Wild Berries and Fruits with Recipes). Pedagogisk Information AB, 1998, pp. 14–15.
3. See: Beskow, Elsa. *Tomtebo barnen* (1919).
4. Harva, U. *Der Baum des Lebens* (*Annales Academiae Scientiarum Fennicae B 16:3*). Helsinki, 1922, in Tillhagen, Carl Herman, *Skogarna och Träden: Natursyn i Gångna Tider* (Forests and Trees: Views of Nature in Times Gone By). Stockholm: Carlssons, p. 59.
5. The Web site of the American Cancer Society says that proponents recommend infusing a teaspoon of birch bark (available for purchase in herbal medicine shops) in a cup of boiling water for fifteen minutes and drinking two to five cups of this tea a day and/or applying birch bark to the skin in the case of melanoma and other skin conditions.
6. Jernberg, Anita. *Natur och Trädgård inom vård och omsorg* (Nature and the Garden in Nursing and Care). Falun: Dalarnas Forskningsråd, Institutionen för Landskapsplanering SLU Alnarp, 2001.

FOUR: SENSITIZATION AND THE RIGHT TO RELAX

1. Kellner, Johnny, and Göran Ståhlbom. *Byggande och miljö: Om hälsa, välbefinnande och hållbar utveckling* (Building and Environment: On Health, Well-being and Sustainable Development). Stockholm: Byggförlaget, 2001, p. 76.
2. In Helamaa Erkki, "Sauna A.D. 2000" in *Finnish Sauna, Japanese Furo, Indian Inipi— Bathing on Three Continents*. Helsinki: Building Information Ltd., 2000.
3. Pentikkäinen, Juha. "The Spirit of *Löyly*" in *Finnish Sauna, Japanese Furo, Indian Inipi— Bathing on Three Continents*. Helsinki: Building Information Ltd., 2000.
4. Elias Lönnrot, the author of the *Kalevala*, was one of the first persons to emphasize the health benefits of sauna in medical circles.
5. Schildt, Göran, ed. "Finland Wonderland" in *Alvar Aalto in His Own Words*. Helsinki: Otava Publishing Company, p. 184.
6. Ogier, Charles (trans. Sigurd Hallberg, 1914). *Från Sveriges Storhetstid* (From Sweden's Great Power Period). Stockholm: Nordiska Museet och Liber Förlag, 1978, p. 100.
7. Prepared with reference to guidelines provided by Reijo Haajanen, an expert on smoke saunas and the art of binding birch whisks, to the daily Stockholm newspaper, *Dagens Nyheter*.
8. Saijonmaa, Arja. *Sauna: Myt och Livsstil* (Sauna: Myth and Lifestyle). Malmö: Richters, 1997, pp. 179–85
9. Saijonmaa, *Sauna*, p. 55.
10. From Olaus Magnus Gothus, Chapter 36, Book 5. My translation.
11. Tell, Johan. *Älskade Fritidshus: Fakta och Finurligheter om ett Svenskt Fenomen*. Stockholm: Bokförlaget Dagens Nyheter, p. 100.
12. Tillhagen, Carl-Hermann. *Vattnens Folklore: Sägen och folktro kring bäckar, älvar, sjöar och hav*. Stockholm: Carlsson, 1996, p. 45.

13. Tillhagen, *Vattnens Folklore*, p. 46.

14. Bergmark, Matts. *Bad och Bot: Om vattnet som läkemedel och njutningsmedel* (Bathing & Healing: About Water as Medicine and Enjoyment). Stockholm: Prisma Bokförlaget, 1985.

15. Hróarsson, Björn, and Sigurður Sveinn Jónsson. *Geysers and Hot Springs in Iceland*. Reykjavík: Mál og Menning, 1992, p. 29.

16. Moberg, Kerstin Uvnäs. *Lugn och beröring: Oxytocinets Läkande verkan i kroppen* (Calm & Touch: Oxytocin's Healing Effect in the Body). Borås: Natur och Kultur, 2000.

FIVE: ESSENTIAL DESIGN
AND THE CREATION OF HOME

1. Dilani, Alan, ed. "Psychosocially Supportive Design—Scandinavian Health Care Design" in *Design & Health—The Therapeutic Benefits of Design*. Stockholm: Svenskbyggtjänst, 2001.

2. Kellner and Ståhlbom, *Buggande och miljö*, p. 39.

3. Tranströmer, Tomas. "Memories watch me" quoted in Klas Tham, *Man in Architecture: On Man's Sensory and Emotional Needs in the Physical Environment* (June 1997, rev. April 1998), working paper.

4. Tham, *Man in Architecture*, p 9.

5. Kaplan, R., and S. Kaplan. *The Experience of Nature: A Psychological Perspective*. New York and Cambridge: Cambridge University Press.

6. Rybczynski, Witold. *The Most Beautiful House in the World*. New York: Penguin Books, 1989, p. 93.

7. Ladberg, Gunilla. *Mota Stressen: Hjärnergonomi på jobbet* (Prevent Stress: Brain Ergonomics at Work). Gunilla Ladberg Pedagogik & Språk, 2002.

8. Cargill, Katrin. *Swedish Style: Creating the Look*. London: Frances Lincoln Limited, 1996.

9. Quoting Niels Thorp, architect of many well-known large public and commercial buildings in Scandinavia. See www.ntorp.no.

10. See: Susanka, Sara. *The Not So Big House*. Connecticut: The Taunton Press, 1998, which became a best seller in the United States.

11. Forgey, Benjamin. *From Sweden,* "A Glass Box That Holds Real Promise—Design Unveiled for Embassy on the Potomac," *Washington Post* (13 February 2003).

12. Rybczynski, Witold. *Home: A Short History of an Idea*, New York: Penguin, 1986, p. 173.

13. Harwood, Barbara Bannon. *The Healing House: How Living in the Right House Can Heal You Spiritually, Emotionally, and Physically*. Carlsbad, Calif.: Hay House Inc., 1997.

14. For some ideas that you could try, see: Waddell, Sasha. *New Swedish Style*. London: Conran Octopus, 1996.

15. Swanberg, Lena Katarina. *Torpdrömmar* (Cottage Dreams). Stockholm: Forum, 2002, p.106.

16. Translated comment by Johan Huldt, former head of Svensk Form, Sweden's main design development and promotion organization in the magazine *Form* (Nr 06/2002).

17. Torekull, Bertil. *Historien om IKEA: Ingvar Kamprad Berättar* (The Story of IKEA: Ingvar Kamprad Tells). Wahlström & Widstrand, 1998, p. 184.

18. Aalto, Alvar. *The Architect's Dream of Paradise*. Lecture at the jubilee meeting of the

Southern Sweden Master Builders' Society in Malmö, 1957, in *Alvar Aalto in His Own Words*, ed. Göran Schilat, Keurru: Otava Printing Works, 1997.

19. Rybczynski. *Home*, pp. 44–49.
20. Swanberg, *Torpdrömmar*, p. 109.
21. Sturlasson, Snorre, *Edda, Skaldskaparmal.*
22. Elias Cornell quoted in Carl Christiansson's, *Bruno Mathsson: Dikten om Människan som Sitter* (Bruno Mathsson: Poem of the Sitting Person). Stockholm: Raster Förlag, 1992.

SIX: PURE ENERGY AND A
NORDIC TASTE OF WELL-BEING

1. Translated from Mats Ottosson's "Metafysik" in *Lantliv* (Country Life).
2. Holm, Inni-Carine. *Impulser fra mitt Kjøkken: Mat for glade mennesker*. Oslo: Gyldendal Norsk Forlag, 1975.
3. Brown, Dale. *The Cooking of Scandinavia*. New York: Time-Life, 1968.
4. From a polemical fairy tale entitled "Lovisa the Hen and Augusta the Pig" by Astrid Lindgren, published as a newspaper article in 1986.
5. Published by Mo' Media BV.
6. Linnaeus, Carl. *Travels*, ed. David Black. Twickenham: The Felix Gluck Press Ltd., 1979.
7. Gothus, Book 13, Chapter 36. My translation.
8. Gothus, Book 21, Chapter 4.
9. Translated from Sturlasson, *Edda*, Part 1, Chapter 25.

SEVEN: ACHIEVING MEANING
BEYOND AND FOR OURSELVES

1. Lagerlöf, Selma. *The Wonderful Adventures of Nils* and *The Further Adventures of Nils*. New York & London: Penguin Books (first published 1906, this edition in 1999), p. 234.
2. Robért, Karl-Henrik. *The Natural Step Story: Seeding a Quiet Revolution*. Canada: New Society Publishers, 2002, p. 6.
3. Robért, *Natural Step Story*, p. 13.

About the Author

Julie Catterson Lindahl is a writer on well-being in Scandinavia and the owner of Wellness of Scandinavia, a company devoted to raising the profile of Nordic well-being. She was raised in Asia and Oceania, Europe, and South America; received her university education in Germany, the United Kingdom and the United States; and has worked throughout the developing world. Her main interests in her writing include helping people to explore a vision of a better life and creating a meeting place for discussing values that people from different parts of the world can share. Ms. Lindahl previously worked as a consultant in organization and management for various international consulting firms, including Rambøll and KPMG Management Consulting. She holds a B.A. with a major in English literature from Wellesley College, and a master's of philosophy in International Relations from Oxford University. She was also a Fulbright Scholar on International Affairs in Frankfurt am Main. She lives with her husband and twins, a son and a daughter, on an inspirational island just off the coast of Stockholm. You can contact Ms. Lindahl and read more about her various activities at www.wellnessofscandinavia.com.